Murders in Mendocino

By Rosemary J. Palermo

Old Age Press
455 E. Ocean Blvd #303
Long Beach, CA 90802

Palermo, Rosemary J
Murders in Mendocino

Copyright 2016 by Rosemary J Palermo

All rights reserved. No part of this publication may be reproduced, distributed, or transmitted in any form or by any means, including photocopying, recording, or other electronic or mechanical methods, without the prior written permission of the publisher, except in the case of brief quotations embodied in critical reviews and certain other noncommercial uses permitted by copyright law.

ISBN: 978-0-9971618-1-6

To Tom and MaryAnn Thomson
I am so very grateful for our 40 years of friendship!

Thank you for introducing me to Mendocino, the magical place that started my writing career. Without you, none of this would have happened.

Table of Contents

Chapter 1 – Genocide 1

Mendocino Indian War 1
Kamdot Massacre – 1843 3
Andy Kelsey and Charley Stone – 1849 4
    Ben Kelsey 7
    Sam Kelsey 8
The Bloody Island Massacre - 1850 9
Chief Prieto – 1850 10
    Chief Suk Augustine and Upee......................................10
    Broken Promises 11
First Round Valley Massacre – 1854 12
    Pierce and Frank Asbill 12
    Nome Cult – Round Valley Reservation......................14
Round Valley Massacres – 1858-1859 16
    Eel River Rangers 17
John Bland – 1859 18
Eden Valley Massacre – 1859 19
Bloody Rock Mass Suicide – 1860......................................20
    Judge Serranus Clinton Hastings 21
    Henry Luther Hall...21
    Thomas J. Henley 22
    Captain Walter S. Jarboe 23
Bloody Run Creek – 1861 25
Nome Cult Reservation Massacre – 1862 26
George Bowers – 1863 27
Concow Death March – 1863 28
Johnson Heacock – 1866 31

Table of Contents

 Extermination 32
 Slaves and Concubines 33
 Genocide 33

Chapter 2 – Claim Jumpers 36

 William B. Poe - 1858 38
  George and Edwin Dutton 39
 Sol Harmon - 1891 40
  James Nathan Capell 40
  Julia (Poe) Harmon 41
 Rench and Catherine Angle 42
 Old Charlie - 1869 43
 William '*3 Finger Jack*' Atkinson - 1861 49
 Adams - 1865 50
  John B. Hargrave 51
  Susan Jane (Hargrave)(Davis)(Westerman)Brown 52

Chapter 3 - Money 54

 Jerry O'Cain - 1863 56
 Francis Holmes - 1865 57
  George W. Strong 58
 Israel Millett Millay – 1865 59
  Silas Gaskill 60
  William H. Bovey 63
  Joseph Jones Bell 63

Chapter 4 – Revenge 64

 Captain George W. Knight - 1867 66
 Henry Fairbanks – 1873 67

Table of Contents

Ella Snider 68

Chapter 5 – Family Feud 70

Coates Family 72
Frost Family 73

Coates – Frost Shootout - 1867 74
Samuel Bessee – 1872 76

Mary Coates 77

Elijah Frost III – 1879 78
Benjamin Franklin Frost – 1882 79
Martin Van Buren Frost – 1883 80
Jim Frost and Andreas Hamburg – 1885 81

George Gibson 82
Ed Jewell 82
Isom Frost 82

Chapter 6 - Impulse 84

John Rector - 1867 86
Irvin R. Wright – 1868 87

John Calvin Stewart 87

John Ketchapaw - 1868 89

Harrison Standley 90

Lazare Landecker – 1879 91

Elias Marks 93

James Harvey Carter – 1889 94

Franklin Pierce Lownes 95
Carter Children 96

Table of Contents

    Garrett Fitzgerald – 1889 97

        Andrew Clark 97

Chapter 7 - Kidnapping 100

    James Valentine Crowey - 1872 102

        William Riley Edington 103
        George William Cleveland 104
        John Gschwend Family 105
        Christine Gschwend 106

Chapter 8 - Jealousy 108

    John Benton Owens – 1873 110

        Owens Family 112
        James Huston Burke 112
        Bill Burke 113

Chapter 9 - Stealing Land 114

    Mrs. Katherine Strong - 1874 116

        David Henry Geiger 118
        E M Bailey 118
        James Alexander 119

    Southard and McCoy – 1880 120

        William Franklin Southard 121
        Welburn McCoy 121
        Marshall Howard 121

    Gardner and Fitch Boys – 1880 123

        John H. Gardner 124
        Juan B. Fitch 124

Table of Contents

Chapter 10 - Rejection 130

Mrs. Reynolds – 1877 132

Moore Family 133
Jerome Bonaparte Caneza 133

Andrew Jackson Shrum – 1878................................... 134

The Anthony Family 134
Suzanna Elizabeth (Helm) Shrum 135

David E. Shull – 1891 136

David E. Shull 137
Stonewall Jackson Roads...................................... 138
May Lillian Thurston 138

Mrs. Julia Scott – 1892 139

Chapter 11 - Outlaws 142

Mendocino Outlaws 144
Dollard and Wright – 1879 146
Henry De Haven – 1879 147

Al Courtwright 148

John Billings – 1879 150

George Gaunce 150
Hal E Brown 151

Doc John F. Wheeler – 1880 153

Chapter 12 - Framed 154

James Cox – 1884 156

Jim and Lizzie (Frost) Cox..................................... 156
Schemmerhorn Johnson....................................... 158

Table of Contents

Elizabeth Ann (Parks) Kell Cox Breedon 159

Chapter 13 - Vigilantes 160

Mr. and Mrs. Riche – 1890 162

    Fred Bennett 163
    White Caps 163
    Charles E. Blackburn 164
    Charles Walter Osgood 165
    Robert Cradwick 165
    B. F. Staley 165
    Evans, Bichard, Archer and Arcaro 165
    Martin and Lund 165

Chapter 14 - Stage Robberies 166

Buck Montgomery – 1892 168

    Charley Ruggles 169
    John D. Ruggles 169

Sheriff Doc Standley - 1896 171
John Riley Barnett – 1897 173

    Charles Meyers 174
    John Neely 175
    Frank Barrington 175
    P. Barrett 175
    Billy Rose 175

Chapter 15 – Fraud 176

Abner McNeill – 1875 178
Philip Gibney – 1881 178

    Robert Darr 179

Table of Contents

'Dutch' Fred Heldt – 1892 180
    Edgar A. Martin.. 182
    Nancy Heldt Darr 186
Armstrong McCabe – 1892.. 187
    Sabrina (Cafferty) McCabe 188
Chief Camilo Ynitia-1856.. 189
    Camilo's Strange Death 191
Henry Holden Bennet - 1856... 192
    Henry Harper Willard 193
The Willards 194
Joseph Willard – 1903... 194
Sheriff J. Henry Smith – 1905 194
    Henry Willard... 196
Joseph Knox 198
    John Knight.. 200

Chapter 16 – Gunslinger 202
    George W. Parker – 1893 204
        James D. Sherman... 205
    Mike Meagher - 1881... 206
        John Lambert Vallely... 207
    John D. Sherman - 1896 208

Chapter 17 – Round Valley Range War 210
    Round Valley Range War 212
    George E. White.. 212

Table of Contents

    Hannah Elizabeth Welling 214
    Elizabeth Alice Fetty 215
Owen Cunningham – 1869 217
    Elisha Cain 217
Augustus Daniel Packwood – 1877 218
Robert Grieves – 1878 219
Weck and Martha McPherson – 1879 220
    Frankie White 223
Staggs Poisoning - 1885 226
Newt Irwin – 1885 226
    William Nowlin 227
George Erickson – 1886 228
    George Orr 229
    John Norris 229
    Ben Arthur... 230
    Sheriff George Kunz 230
    Alexander Brick McPherson 231
Wylackie John Wathen – 1888 234
    Clarence White 235
    Jim Neafus... 236
    Sylvester 'Ves' Palmer... 240
Jack Littlefield – 1895 241
    Sheriff Bayliss Van Horn... 242
    John Lewis Crow 243
    Joseph F. Gregory 244
    Tom Hayden 245
    John Vinton 245

Table of Contents

Billy Williams – 1895 247
Tom Steele – 1897 248
    Louise Bogan White 249
    John Rohrbough 251
    Frankie White 252

Chapter 18 – Last Range War 254

    The Norgaard Family 256

Morris H Norgaard – 1910 257
    Tom Hayden 258
    Frank Hayden 259
    Elmer Norgard 260
    Little Chris Norgard 261
    Ethel (Norgaard) (Wathen) Beck 262
    The End 263

End Notes 264

Illustrations

1 -- Pomo Chief	10
2 - Pierce Asbill	12
3 - Judge Serranus Hastings	21
4 - Catherine Orender Angle Drew Christy	42
5 - Susan Hargrave Davis Westerman Brown	52
6 - Martin VB Frost	80
7 - Isom Frost	81
8 - Calvin Stewart	88
9 - Harrison Standley	90
10 - The Landeckers	91
11 - Frank Lownes	95
12 - John Gschwend	105
13 - James Huston Burke	112
14 - John 'Bill' Burke	113
15 - Juan B. Fitch	125
16 - Stoney Roads	137
17 - Buck Montgomery	168
18 - John D. Ruggles	170
19 – Sheriff Doc Standley	171
20 - Edgar A. Martin	183
21 - Mary Maxima and Maria Antonia Ynitia	192
22 - Frank Willard	194
23 - Joseph Knox	198
24 - Geoge E. White	213
25 - Hannah Welling White Lee	214
26 - Frankie White	223
27 - Wylackie John Wathen	234
28 - Jim Neafus	236
29 - Ellen and Ves Palmer	240
30 - Sheriff Van Horn	242
31 - Tom Hayden	258

Preface

Mendocino history belongs first to its Native American tribes, then to successive waves of settlers who 'claimed' it for Spain, Mexico, Russia and the United States. When Mexico ceded Alta California to the United States in 1848 after the Mexican American War, Land Grants issued by Spain and Mexico were guaranteed by the Treaty of Guadalupe Hidalgo, but ownership had to be proven to the US Public Land Commission. This was problematic for many grantees. Most grants had never been properly surveyed and natural boundaries like rivers had changed course and identifying trees had died or been cut down. Costly legal fights to prove ownership were fought through lower courts and all the way to the US Supreme Court, taking an average of 15 years, many longer. At the same time, the primary income from cattle prices, which spiked during the gold rush, suddenly dropped as railroads brought in beef from the Midwest. Sheep died in an epidemic and wool prices fell. Years of drought followed by years of heavy rains and deep snow ruined crops and killed stock, leaving the Ranchos land rich but cash poor. High legal fees for fighting to keep their land forced most grantees to sell off large parts of their acreage.

The two Ranchos in Mendocino County were Rancho Sanel, granted to Fernando Feliz, and Rancho Yokaya, granted to Caetano Juarez. Mexican Governor Manuel Micheltorena granted the 17,754 acre Rancho Sanel to Fernando Feliz in 1844. It encompassed the present day Hopland and extended along the Russian River. Upon receiving Rancho Sanel grant, Feliz sold his former home, Rancho Novato, and moved to Sanel. In 1852, to omply with the treaty of Guadelupe Hildago, he filed his claim with the US Public Land Commission and Sanel was formally granted in 1860. His attorney, John Knight, received 1 league of land, called Knight's Valley, in payment. Knight appears later in this book.

Pio Pico, last Mexican governor of California, granted the much larger Rancho Yokaya to Caetano Juarez in 1845. It was about 35,541 acres along the Russian River from the southern end of Ukiah Valley to the norther end of Redwood Valley, about 18 miles long and 3 miles

Preface

wide. As required, he too filed a claim with the US Public Land Commission in 1852. His claim was rejected, appealed and confirmed by the Supreme Court in 1864 and finally patented to him in 1867, fully 15 years after his application. Shortly after obtaining his patent, Juarez sold 974 acres to brothers, James Huston and John William Burke. They too figure in the later murderous history.

Mendocino was among the original 27 counties formed in 1850 by the California State Legislature. It was administered by Sonoma County until 1859, when its population became large enough to support itself and the administrative center was established in Ukiah.

Mendocino's early days were filled with Indian massacres, stagecoach robberies gone bad, murderous jealousy and fatal fights over land. This was a lawless time when most men, and many women, carried guns and settled their problems with violence. The earliest white settlers had to establish laws, create a government and its systems, including taxes to pay for lawmen and judges. The men with the most money controlled the government, the news, the lawmen and the courts and used these tools to control others.

In current times, the term Native American is more properly used than Indian. However, when these events happened, everyone, including Native Americans, used the word 'Indian'. When 'Indian' has been used in this book, it is to reflect the statements, point of view and reporting of the time. My use of this terminology is not meant to be, in any way, disrespectful and I apologize if anyone finds it offensive.

This book tells the stories of real people with real strengths and failings and their history is echoed in the history we are creating today. I have tried to show the actual people behind the news of each incident and what happened to the victims' families as well as the perpetrators. I hope you enjoy discovering more about the gold rush and Wild West years and the people who lived through them as much as I did.

Chapter 1 – Genocide

Mendocino Indian War

Among the earliest settlers in what became Mendocino County were ruthless men whose determination to amass great wealth at any cost led to a horrendous chapter in California history.

Before white men arrived, Native American groups resided relatively peacefully in Mendocino, Humboldt, Trinity and Lake Counties. The Elem Pomo had lived around southeastern Clear Lake for at least 10,000 years and the 56 acre Rattlesnake Island was their ceremonial center and burial grounds. Artifacts excavated from Rattlesnake Island date to 14,000 years ago, and are among the earliest documented evidence of human occupation in the western hemisphere. These Native Americans were hunter-gatherers. Seeds were cultivated by burning the grass and spreading the seeds. Acorns were a staple, gathered and stored in granaries. Men hunted deer using snares and bows and arrows and fished for trout and salmon with nets. Shells were used as money and they bartered with handmade items. Obsidian made strong arrowheads, ax heads and ornaments. Beads and jewelry of magnesite were popular and the Pomo's intricately patterned, watertight baskets were highly prized. They had strong communal institutions and great respect for family. Leaders were expected to share their wealth with others. Unlike the Plains tribes, the California Native Americans were generally peaceful.

Americans began flooding into Mexican owned Alta California in 1845 looking for land and later gold. Trouble soon followed. The concept of 'Manifest Destiny'[1], widely published and promoted by politicians, preached that Americans were special and had a divine right to build a new heaven on earth, destined by God to appropriate all the land from coast to coast and impose their concept of society and economic opportunity on all.

This belief led to the Mexican American War from 1846-1848. Mexico lost the war and the Treaty of Guadalupe Hidalgo ceded 525,000 square miles of Mexican land including Arizona, California, Colorado, Nevada, New Mexico, Utah and Wyoming to the US.

Murders in Mendocino

When the first California Constitutional Convention met in 1849, Native Americans, who had under Spanish and Mexican Rule retained their ancestral lands and were considered full citizens with the right to vote, were completely disenfranchised. They were not allowed American citizenship and could not vote. This did not change until the Federal Citizenship Act of 1924 was passed 75 years later.[2]

California passed the "Act for the Governance and Protection of the Indians" in 1850. This law included a rule that no white man could be convicted by testimony of an Indian, and made it legal to arrest Native people "on complaint of any resident citizen". Any arrested Native American could be hired out for 4 months without pay, as punishment. In reality, if a settler needed workers, he would accuse several Indians of theft, pay a small bail and the Indians would be sentenced to work for him for free. But the most devastating part of this law, authorized the indenture of any Indian child "with permission of their guardians" until they were 25 years old. This law legalized the kidnapping of thousands of Native American children who were sold into slavery, completely ending the lineage of several tribes. It was not revoked until 1867.

The California legislature, hearing only from wealthy settlers who wanted the Indians' land, became convinced that the Indians were 'on the warpath' raiding cattle and killing whites. With the Civil War raging back east and US soldiers needed there, the California legislature authorized civilian Militias. California paid over a million dollars for Indian Expeditions, despite the fact that the Northern California Indians made no resistance.[3] The first Governor of California, Peter Burnett, in his address to the Legislature in 1851 stated, "That a war of extermination will continue to be waged between the two races until the Indian race becomes extinct, must be expected." [4]

In 1850, Mendocino County had only 55 white people. By 1860 the white population was 3,967 and by 1870 it had risen to 7,545. Most had endured attacks from Plains tribes and believed "the only good Indian was a dead Indian".

Genocide

Kamdot Massacre – 1843

When Mexico won independence from Spain in 1822, Mariano Vallejo was made Commander of Mexico's Northern Frontier. In 1834, Mariano moved the Mexican Army to his 44,000 acre Rancho Petaluma and laid out the town of Sonoma where he had local Indians build his La Casa Grande on the town plaza. His brother, Salvador, had a ranch in Big Valley near Clear Lake (later Lake County). The Vallejo brothers married the Carrillo sisters and all lived in La Casa Grande Adobe.

In 1839, Salvador received a land grant to Rancho Napa, 22,718 acres in Sonoma County. He went to his ranch in Big Valley in 1843 with 80 other Sonoma ranchers all looking for vaqueros. They could not persuade the 230 Koi Village Elem Pomo on Rattlesnake Island to join them so the group went to the larger village of Kamdot at Anderson Island. That Ha-Be-Na-Po Clan village had about 340 people who also refused to move south. In fury at their refusal, they killed the chief and set the village round-house on fire, with over 300 people inside. Only a few survived to tell of the horror. Fearing retaliation, the Vallejo group hurriedly returned to Sonoma.[5]

In 1844, Salvador received another grant, Rancho Lupyomi in Lake County which included Clear Lake and his smaller ranch at Big Valley. The Indians, remembering the Kamdot massacre, raided Vallejo's cattle so often that by 1847 Salvador Vallejo gave up and moved his cattle back to Sonoma, leaving herds of wild cattle and horses behind.

The Indians, having driven out the intruders, felt victorious and considered the wild livestock theirs. Times were peaceful in Clear Lake for a while until Vallejo sold grazing rights and the 15,000 head of wild cattle and 2500 wild horses to a group from Sonoma that included E. D. Shirland, Andrew and Ben Kelsey, and Charles Stone.

Andy Kelsey and Charley Stone moved to Clear Lake, bringing a herd of domesticated cattle with them.

Murders in Mendocino

Andy Kelsey and Charley Stone – 1849

When they first arrived in 1848, Kelsey and Stone hired local Indians to work as vaqueros and agreed to pay them in food. The Ku-La-Na-Po Clan, about 400 people led by Suk, known as Chief Augustine, moved their village close to a house they built for the white men. It was the first adobe in Lake County, a 40' long x 15' wide building with two rooms and a loft, beside Kelsey Creek on the west side of Clear Lake. Under Vallejo's men, Indian vaqueros and domestic servants had been paid in cash or with meat and produce. They lived on their own Rancheria and continued their normal hunting and fishing. Kelsey and Stone soon created a far different situation.

The Indians were not happy when they realized that Kelsey and Stone were claiming 'their' wild herds of horses and cattle. Stone and Kelsey, concerned about a possible uprising, confiscated the village's weapons and locked them in the loft of the house, forcing all the Indians, not just the vaqueros, to depend on them for food. They made the Indians build a stockade fence around their village and locked them in at night. The 20 vaqueros were given no meat and were provided with only a pot (about 4 cups) of wheat gruel boiled in water each day. The rest of the clan got no food and many soon began starving to death.

Fury rose higher when the two white men forced Pomo parents and husbands to bring their young women to be sexually used by them and their guests. Upee, Chief Augustine's 15 year old bride, and a younger girl were forced to live with Stone and Kelsey. Anyone who refused was whipped to death. When Stone found out that Upee had given her young nephew a ration of wheat for his starving mother, he killed the boy as a lesson to others.[6]

In 1848, Andy Kelsey took 144 Pomo men from Clear Lake to attack Indians that he suspected of stealing cattle. The stolen cattle were not found, but they did catch a man in Blue Lake Canyon. He was tortured until he led Kelsey to his village. Kelsey set fire to the village destroying everything, and this entire clan was marched as slaves back to Kelsey's Ranch.[7] They lived in another village west of the Kelsey adobe.

The brutalities continued. Later that year, Andy's brother, Ben, a co-owner of the ranch, forced 172 Clear Lake men to go to Sonoma to build adobes. After several months there, Chief Augustine escaped but was captured when he returned to Clear Lake. As punishment, he was hung by his arms, able to touch the ground with only his toes, for a week with only bread and water and viciously whipped.[8]

In 1849, Ben took 26 Indians from Clear Lake to Kelsey's Diggings in the Feather River gold fields. They mined a bag of gold "as large as a man's arm". All returned safely and received "a pair of overalls, a hickory shirt and handkerchief in payment." Ben Kelsey bought 1000 head of cattle with that gold. That fall, Ben and Sam Kelsey, Governor Boggs, Salvador Vallejo and 4 other men, took 100 Pomo on another gold expedition. This one became a disaster.

Despite bringing a flock of sheep for food, the Pomo were not fed and 2 died of starvation on the way. When the Kelsey group arrived, they found the miners suffering from a malaria epidemic so Kelsey sold the sheep and all the mining supplies for $16,000 and hastily returned home. They left 98 starving, sick Pomo men behind in enemy Colusa territory with no weapons, food or blankets in the brutal winter. Between malaria, starvation, heavy snow and enemy tribes, only 3 men returned alive.[9] Two of those survivors were Miguel and Big Jim.

Back in Clear Lake, with so many workers missing, Kelsey and Stone decided to sell off all the non-productive Indians, the youngest children of the recently widowed mothers and the oldest adults. We can imagine the tears that fell as mothers and old people were forced to work for 2 weeks making ropes to tie their babies and toddlers to their grandparents for the long walk to Sacramento to be sold into slavery.

During the brutal winter of 1849, over 20 of Kelsey's Indians starved to death, 97 died in the gold expedition and 4 were whipped to death. The Indians were not allowed to hunt as they had no weapons and could not leave the village, so there was no meat. Women foraged

Murders in Mendocino

for acorns, mushrooms and seeds or trapped rabbits, squirrels or birds with snares or nets. Faced with mass starvation, the desperate villagers finally asked the 2 headmen to steal some cattle.

The two leaders, Xasis and Suk (Chief Augustine), were foremen over the 18 vaqueros. One night, they took Stone and Kelsey's horses and rode out to the herd. They tried to lasso a large steer but it spooked starting a stampede. Stone's horse suddenly bucked off his rider and ran off with the wild horses. Xasis and Suk returned to the village empty-handed on Kelsey's horse. Everyone panicked. They knew when Stone discovered his prize horse missing, people would die. The clans debated all night about what to do. They considered paying for the horse but knew Stone would still kill them. They finally decided to kill Stone and Kelsey. Suk (Chief Augustine), Xaxis, Ba-Tus and Kra-nas agreed to do it. Xasis, headman of the captured clan, snuck up to the house and whispered to the girls who went up to the attic and quietly handed the Indian's weapons out the windows. Chief Augustine's wife, Upee, poured water on the gunpowder and into gun barrels. As the designated executioners walked to the breakfast fire in the morning to collect their gruel, another man Ma-La-Xa-Qu-Tu, joined them.

When Stone came out to start the morning fire and saw the five men waiting he asked what was going on. Kra-nas shot an arrow into Stone, who ran back into the house, where he died. Kelsey came to the door and was stabbed but climbed out a back window and ran through the forest and across a creek. There he saw Ju-Luh (Joe Sefeis) and Big Jim, survivors of the tragic gold expedition, and begged them to help him. They told him it was too late and held him while Da-Pi-Tauo, Big Jim's wife and mother of the boy Kelsey had killed, stabbed him in the heart with a spear.

The Pomo then gathered all the provisions, caught a few horses and cattle for food and left to join clans in Scott's Valley and Upper Clear Lake. They had about 3 weeks of freedom before the revenge began. There were now many whites in the valley and they began a program of extermination that lasted for the next 25 years.

Genocide

Ben Kelsey

The Kelsey boys, Sam, Ben, David and Andrew, were born in Kentucky. The four brothers and their families came to California in the Bidwell-Bartleson Wagon Train, the first overland trip from Independence, Missouri to California in 1841. At Fort Hall, Idaho, brothers Sam and David and their families continued north on the well-known Oregon Trail with about half of the wagon train. Andy continued with Ben, his 18 year old wife Nancy, and one year old Martha Ann on the unproven route to California with Bidwell and Bartleson.[10] This party of 36 faced terrible hardships, abandoning their wagons and finally eating the pack animals. Nancy, carrying Martha Ann, walked the last miles barefoot before collapsing at the John Marsh Rancho near San Francisco after 170 days of walking through the mountains.

The Kelseys settled in Calistoga and built the first house occupied by whites there. Ben and Andy built up a herd of cattle which they drove to Oregon and sold, using the proceeds to buy dry-goods to sell back home. They reunited with Sam and David in Oregon and they all returned to California. David settled at French Camp where he died of smallpox. The rest of the family settled in Napa Valley and became friends with their neighbors, Mariano and Salvador Vallejo.

In 1846, the Kelsey brothers joined John Fremont in the Bear Flag Revolt and captured Vallejo at his Casa Grande where they declared California's independence from Mexico. Despite this, the Vallejo brothers remained friends and, in 1847, Salvador Vallejo sold the grazing rights and wild stock on his Clear Lake rancho to Andy and Ben Kelsey, E. D. Shirland and Charley Stone. Ben went to the gold country and founded Kelsey's Diggings on the Feather River while Nancy remained in Sonoma. Andy Kelsey and Charley Stone moved to Clear Lake to manage the ranch, where they were eventually killed.

When Ben and Sam Kelsey received word of Andy's murder in February they immediately retaliated. Ben organized a group of settlers in Sonoma who rode to Napa and ordered Napa settlers to separate their own Indian slaves from any "strange" Indians. They then brutalized, shot and burned to death several hundred men, women and children, who had absolutely no connection to the clans from the Clear Lake Rancho. Ben and his group were arrested for the Napa killings and released on bail. They jumped bail and fled to Humboldt County.

Ben and Nancy Kelsey moved to Mexico in 1859 and then Texas in 1861. During a Comanche raid in Texas, their daughter Martha Ann was partially scalped. She survived but became deranged. Ben and Nancy moved back to California in 1865, settling near Fresno where Martha Ann died. Ben died of cancer in 1889 in Los Angeles and Nancy, who had sewn the Bear Flag, died in 1896.[11]

Sam Kelsey

Sam gathered a different group of 40-50 settlers, including Mormon Joseph Smith, to avenge Andy's death. They started near Yountville, far south of the murder site, and rampaged through the countryside, killing every Indian they could find and burning their villages. In Sonoma they baldly announced they would "hunt and kill every Indian, male and female, found in the country."

Sam and six others, known as the "Sonoma 7", were finally arrested and held for trial by the new CA Supreme Court, presided over by Judge Serranus Hastings. California was not yet a state and had no laws or court system yet. Judge Hastings released the 7 men on $10,000 bond pending trial. The all jumped bail. Most of them, including Joseph Smith, jumped a fast sailing ship headed for Humboldt Bay. The Kelsey brothers went overland and reunited with the Sonoma group to form the Union Company and establish a town called Union (later Arcata). Within a year, this group had burned 2 Wiyot villages and killed more Indians there. Ben and Sam built large mansions, but later defaulted on their loans, and lost everything.

Sam was married to Lucretia Applegate and had 7 children. After losing their property in Arcata, Sam and Lucretia moved to San Bernardino in 1861 where Sam formed a band of Confederate sympathizers. He disappeared when a warrant was issued for his arrest, and is believed to have died in Arizona between 1860 and 1866.[12]

Genocide

The Bloody Island Massacre - 1850

Despite the deaths of hundreds innocent Indians by Kelsey vigilantes, the deaths of Kelsey and Stone were still not legally avenged so the 1st Dragoon Regiment of US Calvary was sent out. They captured 2 Elem Pomo men to act as guides. The first Indians they saw were in a village on Bad-On-Na-Po-Ti Island near Robinson Point in Clear Lake. Rifle shots couldn't reach the island, so the Army went for reinforcements, returning with 2 boats, 2 howitzers, two companies of soldiers and more settlers. The group now numbered well over 300 men. They met at Anderson's Ranch at Lower Lake. Lt. Lyon's group rowed the cannons up the lake by boat. The mounted soldiers and vigilantes, led by Lt. Stoneman, rode up the west side of the lake. They met at Robinson Point and set up the cannons on the north shore facing the island. Boats of soldiers quietly lined up on the south side of the island.

It was a hot sunny day, that 15th of May in 1850. Ni'ka, a curious 6 year old, was playing with her cousins in the cool shallow water among the tule reeds while her mother, aunts and the old ones quietly fished, cooked and collected rush for baskets. Suddenly, a cannonball exploded in the middle of the village, sending shrapnel everywhere. Women screamed and ran to find their children. Before she could get out of the water, Ni'ka heard a volley of shots from the south where a line of soldiers suddenly stood up from the reeds and mowed down the screaming women and children. She saw her mother fall from a shot so the frightened little girl hid underwater, breathing through a hollow tule reed as the soldiers and settlers rampaged through the village, shooting, bayonetting or clubbing to death even the smallest babies until the water was opaque with blood. When night fell and it finally became quiet, the shivering child finally found the courage to come out of the bloody water and became hysterical when she found everyone dead. She remained there alone until the village men returned from the hunt. Ni'ka grew up to become Lucy Moore and lived 110 years. Her terrible experience was preserved as part of her tribe's tragic history.

Murders in Mendocino

The soldiers killed over 400 unarmed people in the surprise attack that day, almost all women, children and old people, as the men were out hunting. Those killed were members of the Ha-Be-Na-Po band of Upper Lake and the Robinson Rancheria who had no connection to the murders of Kelsey and Stone. The Army took no prisoners. Two Indian hunters were caught, tied to a stake and burned to death. The soldiers also killed their 2 guides, shooting one and hanging the other.[13] The island was forever after called Bloody Island.

Chief Prieto – 1850

The soldiers and vigilantes then rode up to Potter Valley where the clan there, who had been warned, had dispersed to avoid trouble. Not finding anyone there, they rode on to Ukiah Valley. They were met in peace by Prieto, Chief of the Yokia Ha-Be-Na-Po who had no expectation of trouble. Without any warning, the soldiers suddenly surrounded his clan on the morning of the 19th. They killed Prieto and shot, bayonetted or bludgeoned over 200 members of his band.[14]

Chief Suk Augustine and Upee

Suk, known to the whites as Chief Augustine, was born about 1830 and had been a headman for Vallejo under Mexican rule before Kelsey and Stone arrived. He and his band killed Kelsey and Stone which sparked the start of war on the Indians.

1 -- Pomo Chief

He survived all the atrocities and gave many interviews before he died. He was widely appreciated as "an intelligent man, known for his truth and honesty."[15]

It is not known what happened to his first wife Upee. He did marry again and his descendants became the core families of the Scotts Valley Rancheria created in 1911.

Genocide

Broken Promises

The US Senate sent 3 men to negotiate treaties with the California tribes. The Native Americans, horrified by the massacres, negotiated 18 treaties, bartering away millions of acres of ancestral land in exchange for the US Government's promise to provide large, defined tracts of their ancestral homelands to the Indians "for their sole use and occupancy forever". These promised lands would have contained 7.5 million acres (less than 8% of the land in CA). The Indians, believing they had valid treaties, began moving to their promised lands only to find that, due to the political influence of wealthy Californians like Judge Hastings and T. J. Henley, the US Senate had gone into secret session and would not ratify the treaties. Despite a report by Senator John Fremont to the President and Congress that "Spanish law clearly and absolutely secured to Indians fixed rights of property in the lands they occupy and that some provision will be necessary to divest them of those rights", the Senate rejected the treaties and they were in placed in secret files which remained classified for the next 53 years.

Instead, Congress established a California Reservation system, appointing Edward Beale as first Superintendent. He was replaced in 1854 by Thomas J. Henley who, through his corruption and greed, almost singlehandedly destroyed northern California's Native American population.

California reservations were not like the eastern reservations. The Government owned 5 'military reservations' not to exceed 25,000 acres total – a huge reduction from the 7.5 million acres originally promised. The Indians had **no** ownership of the land and no control of tribal affairs. They received none of the promised tools or training, medical care or food. Corruption by the white reservation employees was rampant. Worst of all, it became 'normal' to kidnap and sell into slavery Native American women and children.

Murders in Mendocino

First Round Valley Massacre – 1854

The Asbills were born in Missouri. In 1854, Pierce, his brother Frank and their neighbor, Jim Neafus, joined Ben Kelsey and others going to the gold fields. They camped in Round Valley and carved their names on a tree to claim it. That night, Indians fired arrows into their camp attempting to frighten them into leaving. The next day, this small group of white men killed 32 Indian women gathering grasshoppers.

About 20,000 Native Americans lived in the Round Valley before it was discovered by the Asbill brothers. Two years later there were only 12,000 natives left in Round Valley. Things soon became worse.

Pierce and Frank Asbill

The Asbills and Neafus wintered in the Hettenshaw Valley about 70 miles north of Round Valley. The following spring, in 1855, 18 year old Pierce took 1000 pounds of hides on a 5 day journey over the uncharted Coastal Range. In Paskenta, he met a Mexican vaquero with a herd of fine horses. When Pierce tried to trade for a horse, the vaquero offered to trade him 3 horses for every Indian girl he could supply. Seeing a new business opportunity, Pierce sold his hides at the George Kingsley place and bought 2 muzzle loading rifles. He returned with an attack dog, chains and padlocks and told his brother Frank and Jim Neafus their new business plan. They went back to Round Valley for their 'trade goods'.

2 - Pierce Asbill

That first day in Round Valley, the dog treed 2 women. They kept a girl they named Black Raven and let the older woman go. They then captured a boy they named Buckshot and another girl and these 3 children were kept chained up and fed 'beans and syrup' until they were 'tamed'. They named another captured boy Injun and both boys were trained to shoot and dress deer and to lure young girls to their camp.

That fall, the Asbills and Neafus marched 35 young girls in chains to Paskenta, where they traded them to the Mexican for 105 horses including the black stallion Pierce had originally wanted. The Asbills and Neafus continued their profitable slave trade and Buckshot and Injun remained with them for several more years.

By 1870, Frank Asbill's woman, Henocme Wonta Kakini, had died leaving him with a young son, so Frank and his son John B, moved to Long Ridge and young John B lived with Jim Neafus, his Indian wife, Lydia, and their daughter Mary.

By 1879 the Asbill Ranch had 15,000 sheep, 200 dead of cattle and 200 horses. High wool prices had made Pierce wealthy. So in 1880 Frank and 12 year old John went to live with Pierce and the rest of the family, including their mother Sarah, in Covelo.

Pierce married Katie Robinson in September 1880 and had three children with her. Frank married his 2nd wife, a white woman Mary E. Frost, the following year, 1881, and had another son named Frank M. Asbill in 1882. They divorced in 1893. Frank, credited as the first white man in Round Valley, died in 1912 and is buried in Covelo.

By 1890 Pierce was facing financial problems. He was drinking heavily. The severe winter of 1889-1890 had decimated his herds, wool prices had dropped and his gambling debts were insurmountable. He left his family and moved to Mexico. His 5000 acre ranch in Trinity County was sold for $6 an acre to settle his debts.

Kate moved to Ukiah, put their children, Frank, Irma and Sybil, into Sacred Heart Convent School there, and filed for divorce. She married B. M. Cox, a successful local rancher. Pierce would periodically visit the Cox's to see his children. Sadly Cox died in 1893 only 3 years after they married. Kate then leased out the Cox ranch and opened a boarding house in Eureka.

Pierce died in 1902 in Fortuna, Humboldt County.

Murders in Mendocino

Nome Cult – Round Valley Reservation

When the Nome Cult Farm (later renamed Round Valley Reservation) was established in 1856 near Covelo, there was great prejudice against the Indians. White settlers saw only the news spread by Henley, the Asbills and other prominent men. The newspapers, supported by these advertisers and politically popular men, wrote frequent articles in lurid terms telling of Indian depredations to agitate the settlers and justify the killings and removal of Indians. It was widely accepted that the Indians would have to go. One editorial suggested, "Extermination is the quickest and cheapest remedy, and effectually prevents all other difficulties when an outbreak of Indian violence occurs".[16] Politicians up to and including the Governor supported this policy.

Soon, Indians of different tribes, often traditional enemies, were rounded up and herded like cattle by mounted white men with rifles and marched to Round Valley Reservation. Most went voluntarily because, after so much killing by white settlers, they thought it would be a safer place. Unfortunately, nothing was further from the truth.

The Indians were forced onto 5000 unproductive acres, far from hunting or fishing areas, leaving 15,000 acres of the Reservation open for stockmen to graze. In 1858 a San Francisco newspaper pointed out the horrible conditions on the Reservations. "Some of the agents, and nearly all the employees, we are informed, on one of these reservations at least, are daily and nightly engaged in kidnapping the younger portion of the females, for the vilest of purposes. The wives and daughters of the defenseless Diggers are prostituted before the very eyes of their husbands and fathers, by these civilized monsters, and they dare not resent the insult, or even complain of the hideous outrage."[17] Girls as young as 8 or 10 were routinely kidnapped and raped. Two years after the reservation was established, 20 percent of the residents suffered from venereal disease.

The Indian Agents at Nome Cult-Round Valley were horribly corrupt. Ben Arthur testified to the Indian War Commission in 1860 that in 1857, "About 300 men died on the reservation from the effects of packing them through the mountains in the snow and mud...they were worked naked with the exception of the deer skin around their shoulders...they usually packed 50 pounds if able; if not able, a less load."[18] Each worker was allowed 6 ears of corn per day. Those too old or young to work were fed only twice a week.

Children were kidnapped and sold into slavery so often that local newspapers ran ads for them. Those who could cook fetched $50 and a 'likely young girl' cost $100. The Reservation Agent himself built a false bottom in his wagon to take kidnapped children off the reservation to sell. Between 1850 and 1863, whites kidnapped and enslaved 10,000 California Native Americans, over half of them children. Several tribes became extinct when all their children were taken.

The traditional hunting grounds were ruined by herds of cattle and sheep. Deer and elk were hunted almost to extinction to make leather for gold rush miners. Provisions, sent by the Federal government to feed the Indians, were sold by the Reservation Agents for personal profit, leaving them to starve. Vigilantes continued raiding any Indian Rancheria they could find and even attacked Indians on the reservation.

In 1857 a few Indians finally retaliated to the widespread depredations of locals like Dryden Laycock who boasted that he and other settlers were killing "50-60 Indians" per raiding party.[19]

William Mantle was shot by an arrow while he crossed the Eel River in 1858. His partner Stevens drowned. Despite the fact that he was infamous among the whites for treating Indians badly, fourteen Yukis were killed in retaliation for his death.

In September 1858, John McDonald was shot. He was notorious for recreationally shooting Indians at ever increasing distances to challenge himself. He had enslaved and mistreated a number of Indians and one finally shot him with his own gun. The Army reported his death as retribution for crimes against Native people and refused to go after the killers. But settlers wanted revenge – and took it.

Murders in Mendocino

Round Valley Massacres – 1858-1859

The three wealthiest settlers in the area were Thomas J. Henley, Superintendent of Indian Affairs, Judge Serranus C. Hastings, a State District Attorney and former Chief Justice of the California Supreme Court and Hasting's ranch manager, H. L. Hall. Hastings and Henley eventually owned the entire Eden Valley.

Judge Hastings was worth over $1,000,000, equivalent to over $28 million today. He lived in Napa while Hall, his foreman, ran his ranches. Hall was notorious for mistreating Indians. At the Mendocino War Council Hearings a rancher testified that "Hall of Eden Valley employed 13 Indians in place of pack mules to go and pack loads from Ukiah City to Eden Valley, and promised to give each one a shirt in payment; the distance, I think, is about 40 miles." When they arrived, Hall refused to pay them. When the Indians protested, Hall whipped two of them.[20]

In 1858, Indians killed Judge Hasting's prized stallion, probably in retaliation for Hall's mistreatment. Hall collected a gang of men and "commenced killing all the Indians they could find in the mountains; when Hall met Indians he would kill them. He did not want any man to go with him to hunt Indians who would not kill all he could find, including children, because a knit (sic - nit) would make a louse. Mr. Hall said he had run Indians out of their Rancherias and put strychnine in their baskets of soup, or what they had to eat." Hall is known to have killed over 240 Yuki Indians to avenge that horse.

When questioned about the treatment of women and children, Hall said, "I saw one of the squaws after she was dead; I think she died from a bullet. I think all the squaws were killed because they refused to go further. We took one boy into the valley, and the infants were put out of their misery, and a girl ten years of age was killed for stubbornness."

Claiming the Indians were "on the warpath", settlers petitioned the Army for help, so the 6th US Infantry sent 20 men to Round Valley under Lt. Edward Dillon. Dillon reported back to his commander that settlers had completely misrepresented the situation. Indians were not on the warpath. Instead settlers had killed hundreds of unarmed Indians, mostly women and children and that Superintendent of Indian Affairs Henley himself was organizing and leading these raids.

Henley and Hastings held frequent town-hall meetings, telling settlers false stories about Indian raids and stock stealing to encouraged retaliation. The frightened settlers, many of whom had recently survived attacks by the Plains Indians, were easily convinced. Newspapers printed only Hasting's version of events, including frequent articles about Indian raids and depredations that never actually occurred.

Eel River Rangers

In the extremely harsh winter of 1858-1859, the starving Indians did kill some free range cattle for food, since the Reservation Agent had sold their provisions for his own profit. In response, in June 1859, the "Citizens of Nome Cult Valley", petitioned the Governor for protection and requested approval to form a Militia. This petition, one of more than 12 received from the 39 settlers in Round Valley, was written and promoted by Supt. Henley and Judge Hastings. It clearly stated their intention to wage a "war of extermination"; claiming Indians had caused over $40,000 in property damage and killed over 70 people. Governor Weller asked the Army what was going on and was informed that only 2 whites, not 70, had been killed but that over 600 Indians had been murdered that year alone! A bitter animosity soon festered between the Army and the settlers, angry because the Army refused to attack the Indians.

While the Governor was deliberating what to tell his prominent voters, Judge Hastings organized the 20 man Eel River Rangers Militia and made Walter Jarboe Captain. Hastings and Henley agreed to pay this Militia themselves. By the time Jarboe's commission arrived in September, committing the State to pay them, the Rangers had already killed 62 Indians and captured 70 more. Despite the fact that the Indians had no guns, Jarboe and his Rangers turned Round Valley into a war zone.

Murders in Mendocino

John Bland – 1859

The next white to die was John Bland, a hunter who lived in a cabin in the highlands outside Round Valley. The Army considered him a "lawless ruffian". He returned from a hunting trip one day and found food and clothes stolen from his cabin. He furiously rode to the reservation and saw several Indians wearing his clothes. Instead of reporting this to the Army or Reservation Agent, he kidnapped the men and marched them back to his cabin where he tied them up and beat them. When the Army came to rescue the Indians, Bland escaped before they could arrest him. The soldiers brought the kidnapped Indians back to the reservation along with a young Indian woman they found at Bland's cabin who begged to be taken back too. Several nights later, Bland tried to forcibly kidnap her from the Reservation. She broke free and ran away. She was never seen again. Bland was killed while searching for her in the mountains.

In an effort to rile up the settlers, his death was widely publicized. Sensationalist stories of his burned body, found bound to a stake filled the newspapers in Oct 1859. Burning at the stake was a Plains Indian tradition, unknown to California Indians. It was later determined that, while Indians had killed Bland as punishment for mistreating the girl, whites had burned his body to incite the settlers. This it certainly did.

Capt. Jarboe and his Eel River Rangers immediately went hunting again. They killed 11 men and took 98 Yuki to Round Valley Reservation.[21] Another group of settlers kidnapped a young Indian from the reservation, tortured him, cut his throat and shot him. An employee of the Reservation later testified that third group of vigilantes came onto the reservation, selected 20 random Indians and began shooting them. Eight were shot, 5 were hung and the seven managed to escape. Reservation authorities did nothing despite the fact that the killers were well known local men.

Genocide

Eden Valley Massacre – 1859

In September of 1859 the Alta California paper in San Francisco reported that Jarboe's Rangers had attacked a Rancheria in Eden Valley. They "rushed down upon them, blowing out their brains and splitting their heads open with tomahawks. Little children in baskets, and even babes, had their heads smashed to pieces or cut open. Mothers and infants shared the same phenomenon....Many were chased or shot as they ran...the children, scarcely able to run, toddled toward the squaws for protection, crying with fright, but were overtaken, slaughtered like wild animals and thrown into piles." Finally, in January 1860, due to these reports of the indiscriminate killing of women and children, the Governor disbanded the Eel River Rangers, over great opposition from the settlers.

In February, 1860, Jarboe submitted a claim for back pay, stating that in 23 engagements he and his men had killed 283 warriors (not counting the women and children killed), captured over 500 prisoners and suffered 5 casualties. The California legislature paid Jarboe's Rangers $11,143.43 for 5 months of expeditions and congratulated him.

The San Francisco Bulletin later said "The pretext upon which these butcheries were perpetrated is that 19 settlers had been killed and 600 head of stock stolen. Now, we have the testimony of Major Johnson and Lt. Dillon that not one white settler had lost his life in that region at the hands of the Indians except a person who was killed in revenge for outraging an Indian woman. In fact all these tales of Indian hostilities, when sifted, are proved to be arrant fabrications. As to the stock said to have been appropriated by the starving savages (far less savage than their persecutors) what does it amount to? Six hundred head taken by 9000 Indians, driven from their lands and fisheries, and starving literally to death, were worth at the outside, $12,000. Let the State pay it, or double or treble the sum, and call upon the Federal government to repay the sum." [22]

Bloody Rock Mass Suicide – 1860

Despite growing concerns, the depredations continued. In 1860, 65 Native Americans were driven by Henley and 8-10 of his men onto a 150 foot high spit of rock with a sheer drop off on 3 sides. The Indians, knowing they were to be killed, sang their death song, joined hands and jumped off the rock in a mass suicide. Many years later their bones were still in evidence at the bottom of Bloody Rock.[23]

In 1860, the law of 1850 was amended to state that Indian children and any vagrant Indian could be put under the custody of Whites for the purpose of employment and training. Under the law, it was possible to retain the service of Indians until 40 years of age for men and 35 years of age for women. This continued the practice of Indian slavery and made it legal for Indians to be retained for a longer period of time and be taken at a younger age.[24]

The California Legislature finally responded to concerns of citizens outside Mendocino and created a Special Joint Committee on the Mendocino Indian War in 1860 to investigate. "Accounts are daily coming in from the counties on the Coast Range, of sickening atrocities and wholesale slaughters of great numbers of defenseless Indians.....For an evil of this magnitude, someone is responsible. Either our government, or our citizens, or both are to blame."[25]

Chaired by J. B. Lamar, the Committee met at Storm's Ranch in Round Valley to take depositions from over 45 witnesses, all local settlers. Lamar wrote a minority report proposing a system of slavery where Indians would be allocated as servants to white settlers and prohibiting interference by third parties to the "relations between master and servant."

The majority report recognized that "the Indians are killing cattle for subsistence and the white men punish that with death. A humane policy would have protected the Indian in his undeniable rights to the hunting grounds. No provocation has been shown…to justify such acts...We are unwilling to dignify by the term 'war' as slaughter of beings...who make no resistance and make no attacks either on the person or residence of the citizen." They further commented "that in 4 months of 1860, more Indians of Mendocino County had been killed that in a century of Spanish and Mexican rule."

Judge Serranus Clinton Hastings

And who were these instigators? Born in Watertown, NY, Hastings became an attorney in Iowa, a Representative to Congress and Chief Justice of the Iowa Supreme Court. The politically prominent Hastings was appointed to the California Supreme Court as Chief Justice a few months after he arrived in California in 1849. When his term ended he became Attorney General of California, allowing him to practice law and make a fortune, which he invested in land. In 1859 he owned the entire Eden Valley, hundreds of horses and large herds of cattle making him the wealthiest man in the state. He also owned large tracts of land in Solano, Napa, Lake and Sacramento counties when he sent a letter to Gov. Weller demanding protection from the Indians. He founded the Hastings School of Law in San Francisco with a donation of $100,000 in 1878 and became Dean of the Law school. He also published 2 books on Pacific Coast Botany.

3 - Judge Serranus Hastings

Hastings was widely respected and was eulogized as a philanthropist when he died at the age of 78 in 1893 in San Francisco. He is buried in Santa Helena.

Henry Luther Hall

H. L. Hall became foreman of Judge Hastings ranches when he was just 23. He was born in Connecticut about 1834, the oldest surviving son of Abraham R. Hall and Hannah Ann (Fowler). He was a huge man, 6' 8" tall and 280 pounds. Hall is believed to have personally killed more Indians than any other American, including Kit Carson.[26] In 1859 he led the raids that were responsible for killing over 240 men, women and children as retaliation for killing Judge Hastings horse. Army Lt. Dillon wrote that "the monster Hall has well-nigh de-populated a country which, but a short time since, had swarmed with Indians." After these particularly brutal attacks made the San Francisco papers, Hastings fired Hall and he joined Jarboe's Eel River Rangers. During the next 3 months Hall was responsible for killing over 100 more Indians, almost all women and children.

He was drafted for the Civil War in Eden Valley in 1863, noted 'single, absent from home'. In 1870 he lived at the Washington Hotel in Petaluma. That was the last he was heard from.

Thomas J. Henley

Thomas J. Henley was born in Richmond, Indiana to Jesse and Mary (Bower) Henley in 1808. He practiced law and served as a member of the Indiana House of Representatives. He then served 3 terms in US Congress before moving to California in 1849. He was a member of the first CA House of Representatives and was appointed as Indian Commissioner in 1856. After years of complaints, he was investigated and fired in 1859 for fraud for using reservation funds to purchase land for his own ranch, much of which he had also falsely claimed was unusable swamp land to lower the sales cost. By 1859, he and other settlers had claimed 10,350 acres, and there were 15-20 more people claiming another 3200 acres of the Round Valley Reservation. Most had settled on Reservation land based on Henley's assurances. Unresolved land ownership issues would later lead to the Round Valley War.

Henley was married to Belinda Fouts who died in 1862. They had 8 children but only 3 sons survived him. When Col. Henley died in May, 1875 at his Round Valley Ranch he was widely admired by the local white population. At his eulogy he was called a man "full of love and kindness for all" and "all he said and all he did was seeking to do good for others."

Genocide

Captain Walter S. Jarboe

Capt. Walter S. Jarboe was born in 1834 in Kentucky to Stephen and Susannah (French) Jarboe. He fought in the Mexican American War and was a partner with Grizzly Adams in the Tuolumne Mountains, capturing bears for bull and bear fights in the mining camps during the early 1850s.

He bragged about being an Indian killer. He was arrested for assault in Sonoma in 1858 and apparently moved to Mendocino later that year. He became well enough known in Round Valley that he was chosen by Henley and Hastings to be Captain of the 20 man Eel River Rangers. The men of this company included James A. Mead, H. G. Hall, William J. Hildreth, William Robertson, E. M. Heard, William M. Pool, William O. Robertson, S. S. Danny, William M. Cole, William Wall, T. S. Stout, Jonathan Heacker, John D. Aeaskins, Antonio Garoillo, W. J. Graham, William Daley, James P. Watters, William T. Scott (left early in disgust), Charles Bourne, B. S. Berch and J. Alexander. They were active for the last 5 months of 1859, during which Jarboe's final report indicated that he had led 23 raids, killed 283 warriors (not counting the women and children he also killed) and took 292 prisoners.

Killing Indians was very profitable. After deducting for expenses, including medical care for the wounded, each man got over $50/month. In today's dollars that is roughly $8,400 per month, strong incentive indeed to join Militias and exterminate the Indians.[27]

Jarboe married Cynthia Winchester, daughter of the rifle family, in Sacramento in 1860. They moved Ukiah and he became Ukiah's first Justice of the Peace in 1862 and 1863. He died there in 1865 at the age of 36. It was probably of natural causes because no news reports could be found about his cause of death. His funeral was the largest in Ukiah history and over 300 people attended. His obituary noted the community was mourning the loss of a great man. He left a large estate, 500 head of cattle and 800 acres and nearly $20,000. He is buried in Ukiah Cemetery. He was survived by his wife and 3 sons.

Murders in Mendocino

Genocide

Bloody Run Creek – 1861

Most California tribes were peaceful but a group of Wylackie did get guns and learn how to use them. They killed a few horses and cattle in Round Valley, but no people. When Jack Farley's prize Palomino stallion was killed by some Modoc, enraged settlers went to Supt. Short at the Round Valley Reservation who forced several Concow, Wylackie tribal enemies, to track and help kill the Wylackie band. A group of settlers, led by Farley attacked a Wylackie village in Horse Canyon, near Laytonville and killed over 230 people, again mostly women and children. The creek in Horse Canyon became known forever as Bloody Run Creek because the creek ran red with blood.[28]

Mendocino Indians were being killed in wholesale massacres, their children kidnapped and sold into slavery often as prostitutes, and their women forced to live with white men and bear their children. In Ukiah in 1862, "there were few families in town that did not have from one to three Indian children". Starving Indians were shot for killing hogs and cattle for food. Finally, a few younger Indians did retaliate.

In the summer of 1862, 3 men including Henley's Indian cook, an Indian at Lemuel D. Montague's ranch and an Indian teamster named Pike who worked on George E. White's ranch, plotted to kill the three men and hoped others would join them to kill all the whites in Round Valley. Montague known as an Indian fighter, arrived in Mendocino in 1860. He later started a hotel in Covelo.

Pike stole weapons and provisions from Montague and White. Their plot was discovered when Henley's cook put quinine instead of strychnine in his coffee. All 3 Indians fled and during their escape they killed a group of Concow women harvesting wheat in a field, enraging everyone.

Henley hung his cook from an oak tree. The Concow killed Pike and put his head on a pole.[29]

Nome Cult Reservation Massacre – 1862

Following the Bloody Run Creek Massacre, a group of Wylackie moved to the reservation, believing it safer than remaining off reservation. By all accounts they were living peacefully near the house of one of Short's sons, also a reservation employee.

Superintendent Short, in a conversation with Martin Corbett, leader of an Indian hunting group, asked him why he was chasing Indians into the mountains when there were "plenty right here on the reservation." Martin Corbett, J. B. Owens and 28 other well-known settlers then arranged a raid on the reservation and killed 20 Wylackie men, 23 women and a small child on Aug 6, 1862. Capt. Douglas of the US Army investigated this massacre when he arrived at the reservation in December. Apparently everyone but the victims knew it was to happen. One of Short's sons even lent his pistol to use in the massacre, and another son moved his family to his father's house "to prevent his wife from being frightened during the affray."

Capt. Douglas also charged that agency employees were grossly negligent. Provisions receipts showed food that should have been sufficient to feed over 1500 people but the 300 Indians on the reservation were starving because Short sold the provisions for personal profit. Douglas charged that Agent Short had no idea how many Indians were in his custody, but that "this was apparently not necessary because he did nothing for them anyway". Short frequently left the reservation for personal business. Later reports noted this business was selling kidnapped Indian children. When a reservation employee tried to help Indians build fences to protect their crops from the settlers' illegally grazing cattle, Short reassigned the Indians to useless jobs elsewhere. "Utter neglect of duty" is how Capt. Douglas summed up the Indian Agency's performance at Round Valley."[30] That was putting a tactful face on it, to avoid an interagency feud.

George Bowers – 1863

The next white man killed was 32 year old George Bowers a rancher in Williams Valley north of Covelo. A band of Yuki was bound to him, allowing them to live off reservation if he was responsible for them. Bowers was a notorious thief and murderer. He ordered 'his' Indians to steal stock from other settlers, an offence they would be killed for. When they refused, he told them in Yuki to sit down then calmly shot several of them without warning. Bowers forced a young girl to be his "squaw" and they had a child. Due to his mistreatment, the Indians on Bowers' ranch decided to run away and the unhappy young girl escaped with them, leaving her infant daughter behind.

The furious Bowers forced 15 year old Yuk-Numth-Til known as Hope-No-Clan, to track the group. They found a different band but Bowers killed them all, swearing to kill every Indian he could find. Hope-No-Clan, fearing he would be next, killed Bowers by hitting him in the head with an ax one evening as he was bathing his daughter.[31]

When news of Bowers murder reached him, Capt. Douglas and 15 of his men searched for the run-away band of Yuki. They first captured 2 old women who had fallen behind their group due to heavy snow. They came upon the rest of the small group and, when they refused to surrender, the soldiers killed all 6 of them, and brought the 2 old women to Round Valley Reservation.[32] Frustrated because they could not find Hope-No-Clan, they captured a number of random Yuki and threatened to hang them one at a time until the young man surrendered. Hope-No-Clan was finally turned in. He confessed, explaining why and how he had killed Bowers and was hung on 7 December 1864.[33]

Bowers' run-away "squaw" was never heard from again. His half-Indian daughter, Anna Bowers, was taken in by Antone and Julia Lazier (Lazaro), a Portuguese family in Covelo who raised her. She married Jesus Castello in 1881 in Mendocino.

Murders in Mendocino

Concow Death March – 1863

Conditions on the reservation became so bad that in September 1862, Concow chief Tome-Ya-Nem led 500 Concow and Atsugewi back to their northern California homelands where they received permission to camp about 5 miles from Chico. Of course, there soon was trouble. A group of whites, claiming some horses were missing, shot the first Indians they saw, three men, a woman and her 10 year old daughter. This group was on an errand with a pass from their owner. Enraged settlers then shot and scalped 2 more Indians. None of the murdered Indians had anything to do with the missing horses.

In July, Mill Creek Indians retaliated, killing Richard Morrison and Mrs. Blum and kidnapping 3 children of Sam and Mary Lewis. The 2 boys were killed but the brave little girl was able to escape and tell her story to rescuers. A group of angry settlers met at Pence's Ranch to form a vigilante committee. The following week, this group killed 611 Concow Indians and demanded that the Army remove every Indian from Butte County or they would kill them all. To prevent further bloodshed, the government sent troops out to convince Indians to surrender and to gather at Bidwell Ranch to be taken to the Reservation. Capt. Starr of the 2nd Cavalry and his men were detailed to help Indian Sub-Agent Eddy escort them all to Round Valley. The Indians were to be provided with flour, meat and potatoes, and water. Fourteen wagons were loaned for their use. This march became the Concow Trail of Tears.

On Sept 4, 1863, Capt. Starr and 23 mounted soldiers began the 120 mile march from Chico to Round Valley with 461 Indians. Many were already ill from camping in close quarters with poor food at Bidwell's and unable to hunt for fresh food for weeks before the trip. The sick rode in wagons with the small children and elders. The first day the group walked 10 miles to a campsite with good forage, wood and water. The promised food was not provided so soldiers hunted and the unarmed Indians foraged for food.

On Sept 5th, they walked 10 more miles across the blazing hot valley to Kirkpatrick's Ranch in Colusa. According to the official Army report, "the Indians suffered much for want of water." The water at Stoney Creek was bad and made those who drank it sick. They spent the cold night with no food, water or fire to warm them.

Sept. 6th they walked 12 miles from Kirkpatrick's Ranch, crossed Stoney Creek, and on to James Ranch in Tehama, where there was "abundant wood, good water and forage".

Sept. 7th they left James Ranch and walked 6 miles to Laycock's on Thom's creek. Dryden Laycock was a notorious Indian killer, so stopping here was not at all reassuring to the exhausted, sick and hungry Indians. He refused to provide any food so the Army "obtained some forage from Mitchell's ranch". The next day the 14 wagons returned to Chico, leaving everyone on foot. The pack train with food and water from Round Valley, on the other side of the mountains, failed to arrive so after waiting 4 days with little food, they moved on.

On Sept. 12th Capt. Starr ordered them to walk 3500 feet up the steep trail to Mountain House where they again waited. The long awaited pack train finally arrived with food but many of the Indians were now too weak to walk so 150 were left behind at Mountain House with Sub-Agent Eddy. This group kept almost all the provisions from the pack train as they had no weapons to hunt and were too ill to forage.

On Sept 14th the walk resumed with 300 people. The small children were placed in the now empty food wagon and older children and elders rode mules or doubled up on soldier's horses. They walked 7 miles up the mountain to "camp at Cedar Creek, no forage but wood and water abundant, little grass." There they ate the last of the food but at least had a fire to warm the cold mountain air and water to drink.

On Sept 15th they left "Cedar Springs and traveled 6 miles to Log Springs and camped, "water and wood abundant, no forage, grass scarce. Road from Mountain House steep and difficult to travel with wagon." This was the halfway point. They had now been traveling for 12 days in extreme daytime heat and frigid cold fall nights with little water and almost no food. Once again there was no food at Cedar Springs.

On Sept 16th, they left the wagon behind and walked 10 miles to Log Cabin, "wood, water and grass abundant, no forage." Still no food! Starving, thirsty mothers struggled to carry their children up the rugged almost impassible path over the 6000 foot summit. Those who could not keep up were just left behind. Starving, some frantic mothers killed their children, afraid to watch them be eaten alive by the wild hogs that were now following the group.

On Sept 17th, they left Log Cabin and walked 13 miles to camp between South and Middle Forks of Eel River. "First 3 miles was ascending, next 10 miles was steep and descending. Some water about half-way down, wood, water and grass at camp, no forage." Still no food!

On Sept. 18th, the barely living group staggered the last 8 miles out of the mountains to the reservation in Round Valley desperate for water, food and shelter only to find that no preparations had been made for their arrival! Capt. Starr's report noted that his men and horses were in good condition, though.

Meanwhile, the group left at Mountain House ran out of food and began walking. Captain Douglass knew almost 200 Indians were coming, starving along the trail. He ordered Short to conscript every mule on the reservation and take food and water to rescue them. Short spent the next 13 days picking up survivors, reporting that "150 sick Indians were scattered across 50 miles of trail, dying at a rate of 2-3 per day. They had been given nothing to eat, and had no water. Wild hogs were eating them where they fell, even before they died."

Capt. Douglass wrote "all the Indians from Chico were in an almost dying condition through sickness and gross neglect of duty of the present supervisor. There had been no preparation for their arrival." On Oct 1, a report from Camp Bidwell in Chico noted that "the means for transportation provided by those in charge of Indian Affairs was entirely inadequate".

Genocide

Johnson Heacock – 1866

The next white to die was Johnson Heacock. He had settled in Leggett Valley and, with Jerry Bailey, began trading with the Wylackie Indians. Heacock formally asked to marry Lillie, young daughter of Ishoma, a minor chief. Her father was pleased but Lillie was young and frightened and ran back to her tribe, refusing to return unless Heacock also married her sisters. Ishoma was delighted at this protection for his tribe so all 3 girls married Heacock and bore him eight children.

Heacock later decided to marry a new white settler named Agnes Stokes. She accepted, knowing nothing about his Indian family, and he sent the 3 girls and their children back to their tribe. This was a major insult. As cast off wives they could never regain their social standing. Their half white children could never marry into the tribe. To make matters worse, one sister had been promised to a prominent young warrior who agitated for revenge over her dishonor.[34]

One morning, Agnes woke up to find eight small children sitting on her doorstep. After she learned the truth, she wanted to raise the children but Heacock refused and sent them back again. Word got back about the tribe's growing anger at these insults, so Heacock sent Agnes to her family. Days later, the Indians attacked. They tortured him for the location of his gold before killing him and putting his head on a pole in the village. The Indians who committed his murder left the area till things cooled off.

Jerry Bailey, later saw one of the murderers and shot the man, leaving him for dead before fleeing. Standley, a young Deputy Sheriff at the time, captured Bailey for this attempted murder. Standley later interviewed the Indian who had survived Bailey's shots. He was in prison for killing a member of his tribe, a rare occurrence. Standley knew the man to be honorable and asked why he had killed his fellow clansman. He explained that the man had dishonored the clan by stealing part of Heacock's $20,000 stash of gold, which had been saved for the 3 cast off sister wives and their children.

Extermination

The original Yukia Pomo inhabitants of Round Valley lost more people than any other tribe. They had about 20,000 members before the Indian War started. By 1864 the Indian Affairs Superintendent counted just 85 men and 215 Yuki women at Round Valley. White settlers lost fewer than 10 people during the same period.[35]

In 1870 President Grant finally agreed to earlier suggestions that the entire Round Valley be dedicated as a reservation, but it was far too late for that. Settlers had been illegally claiming the land, building ranches, running cattle on government land for free and making a fortune. They violently protested and took their anger out on the Indians. They deliberately drove their herds onto the reservation fields and trampled their crops just before harvest.

Congress eventually did expand the reservation to more than 100,000 acres but Indians were still restricted to only 5000 acres in the unproductive northern end of the valley, with no hunting or fishing areas. Then the Dawes General Allotment Severalty Act of February 8, 1887, created even greater problems. Under this Act, individual Tribes lost legal standing as a tribe and all the communally held tribal lands had to be divided among tribal members. In exchange Native Americans were to become American citizens and receive land; 160 acres to family heads, 80 acres to single adults. However, full ownership would come only after another twenty-five years of federal oversight.

It soon became clear that most of the Round Valley Reservation was already lost to illegal settlement. Only 1,240 allotments were granted to 42,163 acres. These allotments were widely scattered making it impossible to combine parcels and too small and unproductive to support a family. Almost 60,000 of the reservation's original acres had been lost to white settlement. As a result, most Indians lost their allotments through lack of tax payments, or to outright occupation by the larger wealthy settlers.

Slaves and Concubines

Starting with Pierce Asbill in 1850, it became 'normal' to kidnap and enslave women and children. Between 1860 and 1865, over 25% the families in Northern California had multiple Indian 'servants'. In Ukiah the proportion was even higher. Newspapers openly posted prices for Indian slaves. While many girls worked as domestic servants, much of the demand came from unmarried white men. The Mendocino Herald finally acknowledged this "crime of the darkest dye" noting that "around 50 single white men in the county were living in concubinage with squaws from 10 -14 years old." This slave traffic thrived throughout Northern California where likely young girls were sold for $100, more than twice the price of young boys. By 1860 large numbers of Native women had been forced into relationships with white men.[36] While a few of these relationships became affectionate and lasted, the majority did not. These women and their children were frequently "put away" when the man married a white woman.

Genocide

And this is just what happened in Mendocino County. Similar massacres happened in Humboldt and Trinity and all the way up the state. This chapter was very painful to research and is hard to read but these stories must be told. Literally thousands of Native Californians were massacred. Wealthy settlers made clear their intention to exterminate the Indians and they were supported by the state politicians all the way to the office of Governor. The US Senate was complicit in taking away the land negotiated in treaties and destroying a way of life and a group of people whose only crime was to live on land others wanted.

A few people like Army officers Dillon and Douglass attempted to protect the Indians and reported their concerns up the chain of command. Reporters like Brett Harte in Humboldt County and others in San Francisco exposed the atrocities. But they were few and most were threatened until they left the area.

Murders in Mendocino

It is important to understand that not all the settlers knew of, or supported, these atrocities and some whites treated Native Americans fairly. Most settler thought of the Native Americans as simple and uneducated people who needed help to live among the smarter more industrious whites. Most whites simply had no idea what was actually going on because news was controlled by the wealthy landowners. The only news they saw and heard was about Indians killing livestock, robbing or killing people. Everyone agreed that needed to stop to protect their families. Indians outnumbered the widely scattered settlers who were led to believe the Indians were trying to kill them all. The Civil War was going on for much of this period and southern secessionists with their dismissive views about non-whites were abundant in California. The Army was stretched too thin, opening the door for Vigilante Militias to gain public support.

Most settlers thought the reservations would help feed, train, educate and support the Indians who had been displaced from their lands. Unaware of the corruption and abuse on the reservations, they didn't see reservations as a bad solution. Most whites just did the best they could with the information they had.

Native Americans had moved north from San Francisco fleeing the white encroachment. This served to further concentrate them in northern California leading to the genocide that occurred here. The Committee on the Mendocino Indian War recommended laws to protect the California Indians but not one of these laws was ever put in place.[37] It wasn't until 1979 that scholars began to acknowledge that the systemic abuse of the Northern California Indians did, in fact, constitute the clearest case of genocide in America.[38] A way of life and the Native American people of California, here for thousands of years, were wiped out in just 25 years. For further reading, the book "When the Great Spirit Died: The Destruction of the California Indians 1850-1860" by William B. Secrest is highly recommended.

Genocide

Chapter 2 – Claim Jumpers

Murders in Mendocino

William B. Poe - 1858

Nov 15, 1858 was a windy blustery day in Long Valley. Jerry Lambert and Bill Poe were wrestling to get a barbed wire fence built. Digging post holes in the frozen ground was hard work but fencing was necessary to protect crops from free range cattle, and keep their stock from mingling. Suddenly, neighbors George and Edwin Dutton galloped up, demanding angrily to know what they were doing. Poe continued digging and ignored them. This infuriated Ed Dutton who declared the land was his. Poe, who had a valid claim and been working it for about 3 weeks, replied that the land was legally his. As the argument grew more heated, Poe accused Dutton of moving the boundary markers. George Dutton said *"he did not care a damn if he had moved the lines"* and punched Poe in face, knocking him back about 2 steps, then drew a revolver and fired at Poe but missed. Unarmed, Poe picked up a hoe and hit George Dutton with it, knocking him down. Dutton got up and fired at Poe again. His brother, Ed Dutton now came running with a knife in his left hand and struck Poe with his right fist under the ear. Five shots in all were fired at the un-armed Poe, one finally hit and lodged in his abdomen. Poe lived until the 20th of November before dying a painful death.

William B. Poe was born in North Carolina about 1809. He arrived in Long Valley around November 1857 and settled with his wife Nancy (Johnson) Mulky Poe and children Robert, Julia and James on land near Cahto, adjacent to the Dutton brothers claim. He was one of the few married men among the first settlers in the valley with Jerry Lambert and his family and Jackson Farley and his family. The others like Robert White, John P. Simpson, George Woodman, Harry Schroeder, and George and Edwin Dutton were all unmarried.[39]

After his death, Nancy and their children remained on their ranch in Long Valley for many years. Their oldest son Robert Hardin Poe married Louisa Lambert, whose father, Jerry, had witnessed the murder. Robert and Louisa had 11 children and farmed in Long Valley for many years. Robert died in 1907 at the age of 72 in Laytonville, Mendocino.

Their 2nd son, James Poe also remained in Long Valley. He married Susie Grimes in Mendocino in 1897,[40] and was noted in a newspaper clip as living in Cahto in 1901.

Sadly, daughter Julia A. Poe did not have a peaceful life. She married Solomon Harmon in Long Valley on 13 Feb 1890. In a tragic twist, her husband was also shot, just a year after their marriage, leaving her pregnant.

George and Edwin Dutton

George and Edwin Dutton were both arrested.[41] They were the sons of Evelyn and Almira (Hough) Dutton. Evelyn farmed in Long Valley with sons Edwin (30) and Evelyn Jr. (21).[42] Evelyn Sr. died on January 4, 1867 in Long Valley.

George Dutton was charged with murderer and Ed was charged as an accessory. With Jerry Lambert as witness, they were certain to be convicted, so both jumped bail and moved to Santa Cruz where George enlisted in Co K of 5th CA Infantry in 1861. After the Civil War, George and Edwin remained in Santa Cruz until 1870.[43] Edwin apparently died before 1876 when his brothers, George and Evelyn Jr., moved to the small town of Jolon.

George Dutton married Deborah Dodge of Watsonville and purchased the old Ramirez-Dodge Adobe and 100 acres for $1000 in Jolon in 1876. This building, the earliest in town, became the Dutton-Tidball Hotel, Livery Stable and post office.[44]

George and Deborah Dutton lived in Jolon from 1876 until their deaths. George Dutton died in 1905 at the age of 80 having gotten away with murdering Bill Poe.

Sol Harmon - 1891

Julia Poe, daughter of William B Poe murdered by George Dutton in 1858, married Solomon Harmon in Long Valley on 13 Feb 1890. Sol was known as a bully and brawler. One Wednesday afternoon, March 11, 1891, he and his brother Will went into Laytonville about 4 p.m., both quite drunk. Will went to James Capell's saloon and ordered a drink. When he ordered a 2nd drink without paying for the first, Capell refused to serve him. Will left the saloon and walked across the street to Branscomb's blacksmith shop and returned to the saloon with a sledge hammer over his shoulder.

As he strode in, Capell pulled a 44 pistol from under the bar and warned him to stop and drop the sledgehammer. As Will moved towards the bar, Capell fired at him, the ball going through his wrist and into his left breast.[45] Will turned and walked outside, and dropped the hammer on the porch of the saloon. Capell followed him, still carrying the pistol. Sol, sitting on a water trough about 20 feet from the saloon, ad heard the shot. He saw Will bleeding and rushed towards Capell. After several warnings that Sol ignored, Capell shot again. Sol was hit in the abdomen and soon died.[46] Will survived his shots.

James Nathan Capell
James Nathan Capell was arrested and charged with Sol's murder. At his trial, many people testified that Sol had made threats to kill Capell. A large number of good citizens from Laytonville testified to Sol's bad reputation and Capell's reputation for peace and quiet. Despite this, Capell was convicted of manslaughter and sentenced to 5 years in San Quentin because Sol had not been armed.[47]

Capell was granted parole in 1893. Most of the people involved in his prosecution had recommended his release.[48] He returned to tending his bar in Willits and in 1895 he married Mrs. Dorinda Holman of Willets. He became a successful tavern owner and discovered a vein of gold. They later separated and he moved to Idaho. Dorinda remained in Mendocino until her death.

Julia (Poe) Harmon

Julia (Poe) Harmon was pregnant when Sol was killed and had their child about 6 months later. She named him Solomon Francis Harmon. She married again two years later in 1893 to James Robert Downing and had 6 more children. Julia (Poe) Harmon Downing died in 1925 in Laytonville, CA and is buried in Little Lake Cemetery in Willits.[49]

Sadly, her first son with Sol Harmon, Solomon Francis 'Frank' Harmon also died young. He was killed in an automobile accident in 1928. He is buried with his father in Laytonville Cemetery. He left a 12 year old son, Oliver F. born 1915, from his first marriage to Bessie Quinliven. He had been married only 9 months to his 2nd wife when died leaving her pregnant. His widow, Emma B (Fawcett) Packard Harmon, bore their son Eldon soon after his father's death. Emma died in 1966 and is buried at Memory Gardens, Concord, Contra Costa, CA.

Solomon Jr.'s first son, Oliver F. 'Red' Harmon, died in 2006 in Ukiah at the age of 91.

Emma's son, Eldon E. Harmon, has a plaque on his side of Emma's grave with a birth date of 30 June 1930. Since his father died in Nov 1928, this date must be incorrect and should probably be 1929. He is apparently still alive.

Murders in Mendocino

Rench and Catherine Angle

Wealthy cattlemen were used to intimidating white settlers as to get their way, but in Catherine (Orender) Angle they met their match. Mahulda Catherine Orender was born in Illinois about 1843 and came to California with her parents Joel and Mary and her siblings when she was about 10. Rench Angle was born in Pennsylvania in 1829 and moved to Placerville about 1850. They married in 1859 in Sonoma when she was just 16 and moved to Walker Valley where Rench bought 40 acres of land called the Ridgewood Farm south of Willets at the far north end of Little Lake Township. They started raising cattle and, at Catherine's insistence, also bought sheep, which proved to be better stock for the weather and terrain. They also raised hogs and poultry.

State law required all Indians to be working for a white person or to live on the Reservation at Round Valley. The Ma-se-li clan of the Ma-sut Pomo didn't want to leave their home, so Catherine had the entire Ma-se-li Rancheria bound to her. Catherine treated the Native Americans well and they called her "*Kakan*". They took the Angle eggs and chickens to market in Calpella or Ukiah and bartered them for the Angle's groceries. They were paid for their services with flour. The Ma-se-lie continued their lifestyle of hunting and gathering, supplemented with food from the ranch.

4 - Catherine Orender Angle
Drew Christy

Due to her husband's alcoholism, Catherine was widely acknowledged as the ranch manager. She rode out daily, in all kinds of weather, to supervise ranch activities. Long Valley is 36 miles North and 18 miles West of Ukiah a little south of Round Valley. It was settled by George E. White, John P. Simpson, George and Edward Dutton and

William Poe (killed by the Duttons). These cattlemen became Catherine's enemies. As we saw, the Duttons were dangerous men, not afraid to commit murder. There were only about 6 white families in the Valley then, two or three houses and a store in Calpella. The original Angle Ridgewood ranch in Walker Valley was only 40 acres but grew over the next 12 years to 16,000 acres of valley land with 20,000 sheep plus hundreds of cattle, horses and hogs. Another 20,000 acres was timberland. As the sheep multiplied, Catherine decided to lease small herds of sheep on 'shares' to incoming settlers. This allowed her to increase her herds and bring income from the 'shares' which she could (and did) use to buy out the settlers.

Eight cattlemen who controlled Little Lake Valley and Round Valley strongly opposed her plans and threatened to shoot her sheep and run off the newcomers. Catherine, then a young woman of 26, would not be bullied. An interview published in 1894 stated that she told them: "The law won't let you hold half the land you are using and these men have a right to homes here the same as you and me. I say for them to stay and they can have sheep from me on shares as long as they like." Of course this interview was probably slanted in her favor but the truth was that she stood up to the Little Lake Cattlemen who sent a peremptory order to Catherine to join their group 'or else'. She tauntingly refused. That is when people began getting killed.

Old Charlie - 1869

Little Lake Valley soon became notorious for its murderous range war as hostilities grew between the cattlemen and newer settlers, often sheep men. Indians were shot on sight and sheep and cattle were shot, poisoned and stolen. There were several unsuccessful attempts on Catherine's life and several of her Indian vaqueros were ambushed and killed. One of Catherine's most loyal Indians, Old Charlie, was shot right in front of his family. Since Indians could not testify against whites, they acted with impunity. There were no laws to protect the Indians, or

Murders in Mendocino

Catherine. One night, she and her 2 daughters kept 3 assassins at bay with rifles until help finally arrived at sunrise, alerted by a loyal Ma-se-lis.

Rench was unmanageable when drunk, as he frequently was. The girls once sent word to Catherine in Ukiah, to "Come home quick. We have locked Pa up and hid his gun to keep him from killing Bill Johnson." Catherine raced 22 miles back to the ranch in the middle of the night, arriving at 5 AM, to find her daughters on guard at the front door with their father's gun cocked and Bill Johnson pacing up and down, swearing at the gate. Catherine negotiated with Johnson and paid him $300 to settle all accounts. Then he was hustled to his horse and commanded to "keep straight ahead till you've put 50 miles between you and Angle. Me and the girls will keep him locked in for a couple of hours longer so you'll get a good head-start." Bill Johnson was killed by a falling tree a week later.[50]

Under her management the Angle family became wealthy. When George W. Knight was killed in 1869, they bought his Long Valley Ranch and added it to the Angle Ridgewood Ranch. Both ranches were soon free of mortgages.[51] Catherine built the first saw-mill in the area, generating good income from their timber. She bore 15 children, managed the ranch and took care of her alcoholic husband. She started the first church in Walker Valley, raised several orphans and educated many local children, including Indians.

Childhood mortality was high and Rench and Catherine's first son, 2 year old David, died in 1865. An infant son, David, died in 1867. Ida M. died in 1875 at the age of 2 and Rachel died in 1877 at the age of 3.[52] Then, in 1878, there was a terrible diphtheria epidemic which took five more of her children in 2 weeks. It was believed that they got the highly contagious diphtheria from the well on the porch of the house.[53] Ella 13, Franklin 10, Samuel 8, Reuben 7, Rachel 4, and Malinda 18 months, all died between May 30 and June 13 of 1878. The Angle children and their father are buried in Angle Cemetery in Willits.

When Rench Angle died at the age of 60 in 1889, the Angle Ranch included the 9000 acre Walker Valley Ranch. The Riley English

Ranch, Two Rock and Martin Ranches contained 5269 acres and the Jones Ranch contained another 817 acres totaling 15,000 acres. It was the largest ranch in the county, with fine apple orchards, cereal, alfalfa, vegetables and fruit. The upper part of the valley contained redwood forest and a busy sawmill. A separate property, the recently acquired Haas Ranch, contained another 4897 acres, not considered part of Angle Ranch. When he died, Rench's estate, appraised at $107,238, was left to his wife Mahulda Catherine (46), daughters Euphrasia Aldrich (29) and Anna Haskett (27) and sons Carl (10), Joseph Victor (9), Basil Augustine (7) and Richard Eugene (5). Rench's will stipulated that Catherine had the right to sell or dispose of part or all of the property without court order but his wish was that the property be kept intact in trust for the children and divided to them upon her death. Catherine owned 50% outright as community property. The remaining 50% was the children's inheritance.

The 1889-1890 winter when Rench died, was so severe that almost half the stock in the area died. A record cold temperature of -20 degrees on Jan 14th in Eureka still stands. This, coupled with low wool prices, created great economic hardship for everyone. As a result, more crimes occurred, including several brazen stage robberies on the road through Angle Ranch. The extreme weather also led cougars and large bears to prey on weakened stock, and several bears were killed on the ranch which supported Catherine, her older daughters and their families and the younger Angle boys. Then the hard times came.

That spring, Catherine had to commit her 29 year old brother to the state hospital for the insane. He had been acting '*peculiar*' for several months and suddenly became homicidal. Shortly after Christmas, in January of 1891, Catherine's father also died. Then her sheep became infected and what was left of her vast herds herd had to be put down. Suddenly she was land rich but had no income. A bit of happiness did shine on Catherine when, on July 1, 1891, 48 year old Catherine married 40 year old Sylvester Edson Drew.[54] Catherine ran the Ranch and took care of her 4 little boys but the financial situation was dire and she considered selling the ranch..

In 1892, unhappy that Catherine wanted to sell Angle Ranch, Catherine's adult daughters, Euphrasia Aldrich and Anna Haskett, petitioned the court to have Catherine removed as their father's executrix, alleging that the property was $45,000 in debt and that Drew "a shiftless, intemperate, worthless character who exerted great influence" over Catherine, was squandering their inheritance.

In response, Catherine gave the court a complete accounting of the estate's income and expenses. The only debt was a $45,000 mortgage made by Rench to purchase the Haas Ranch before his death. The harsh winter and the sheep epidemic had killed her flock and income source. Without sufficient cash to restock the ranch, she could not make mortgage payments on Haas Ranch. Its owner, Schweitzer, was threatening foreclosure so Catherine petitioned the court for permission sell the larger Walker Valley ranch. Between the lost stock and the hard weather, the ranch was now appraised at only $66,000. Her half of the proceeds of this sale plus the 4 little boys' shares would pay off the mortgage on the Haas ranch and she could move there and improve that ranch which would become the boy's inheritance. The girls would receive their inheritance from their half of the sales proceeds of Angle Ranch. The court approved and Catherine found a private buyer for Angle Ranch. It was sold in 1892 to Mrs. Margaret McGuire of San Francisco for $72,500, higher than the appraised price. At the time, it was the largest real estate transaction ever made in the county.[55]. When the Angle Ranch was sold, the Ma-se-li clan was forced to move to the Round Valley Reservation.[56]

After Angle Ranch was sold, Catherine and Ed Drew and her boys rented the Edwards house on Perkins St. in Willits. She got a loan to purchase 2700 sheep to stock the Haas Ranch. Despite her good business sense, Catherine apparently made poor choices in men. Drew was badly burned when, 'dead drunk', he rolled into a campfire while asleep in December 1894. He didn't wake up until he was badly burned and despite amputation of a leg, he died.[57] They had been married about 4 years. After Drew's death, Catherine moved from Willits to Ukiah and hired a manager to run the Haas Ranch. Shortly after Drew's death, her daughters again petitioned to have her removed as executrix for the boys. The court again denied their request, but Catherine, devastated at the loss of her 2nd husband, and the estrangement from her daughters, resigned and an attorney replaced her. Sadly, hard times were not over.

In 1898, her youngest son, 14 year old Eugene, was kicked in the face by a horse. His cheekbone and eyebrow were shattered and his eye had to be removed. Dr. Linquist, practicing in Ukiah at the time, assisted in the surgery and recovery and became a family friend. In 1905, 35 year old Dr. William M. Linquist of Healdsburg, ill for several months, chose to die at Catherine's home, where she cared for him until his death.

In June 1907, Catherine, then 65, married her 3rd husband, John Henry Christy a 75 year old widower pioneer of Coyote Valley.[58] She filed for a divorce in August of 1913 for desertion and their uncontested divorce was granted in 1914. Christy died in 1927 in Sonoma.

In 1919 Catherine's daughter Anna died of heart failure at the age of 57. She was married to Guy Haskett and was the mother of 7 children. The ashes of Anna's recently deceased daughter Mrs. Ethel Shane were buried with her. Ethel had died of influenza 14 days after the birth of her first child.

Mahulda 'Catherine' (Orender) Angle Drew Christy died in 1926 in Ukiah at the age of 85. This beautiful and remarkable woman had lived through the most turbulent years of history including Indian Wars, Range Wars, the Civil War and WW1. She had built one of the largest ranches in the west despite enduring the tragic loss of ten children, a granddaughter, two husbands and a divorce. She was survived by sons Carl, Victor, Gus and Gene and oldest daughter, Euphrasia (Mrs. C.A.) Aldrich.[59]

Euphrasia, as beautiful and strong willed as her mother, died in 1929.

Murders in Mendocino

Basil Gustave 'Gus' Angle became a detective in Ukiah. Possessed of a wonderful tenor voice, he also sang in the Tivoli Theatre in San Francisco. He died of a heart attack in 1936, without issue.

Six weeks later, Joseph Victor Angle also suffered a heart attack while hunting. He was survived by his widow and brothers, Gene and Carl. He had no children.

Carl Leon Angle died in 1937 leaving no male children.

Richard Eugene Angle died unmarried at the age of 66 at Ukiah Hospital in 1950 and, with his passing, the Angle family name died out in California.

Claim Jumpers

William '*3 Finger Jack*' Atkinson - 1861

John B. and Evaline (Wood) Hargrave traveled the Oregon Trail in 1853 then to California and moved to Navarro in 1855. Capt. Fletcher had settled along the mouth of the Navarro River in 1850 where he built a small mill. The Hargraves lived on the ridge north of the river and opened a saloon and inn on the well-traveled road to Albion.

Early in the morning of Dec 13, 1861, Lou Breckenridge, who had spent the night at Hargrave's Inn, was standing on the porch when John came out with a spyglass and focused down the dusty road towards Albion. Lou asked who was coming and Hargrave said it was Destinal, Greenwood and Atkinson. Lou met the riders at the gate and all walked towards the house when Hargrave suddenly said to Atkinson, "You are the d--n son of a b----h that's been talking around that you will make me mind you and keep my place." Atkinson denied it. "You did, you d---n son of a b----h, it was brought to me direct." Atkinson stepped partly behind Jim Greenwood where, hidden from Hargrave, he pulled his pistol and took a shot at Hargrave. As Greenwood dove out of the way, Hargrave tackled Atkinson and they began fighting, each with a pistol in hand. Atkinson knocked Hargrave down and was about to shoot him when Hargrave's son, Charlie, standing on the porch, shot Atkinson in the shoulder. At that, Hargrave stood up and, while Atkinson was still on the ground, fired at him twice, killing him. There were 2 wounds found on Atkinson, one in the center of his breast (fired by Hargrave) and the other on the right shoulder (fired by Charlie). John and Charlie Hargraves were soon arrested for murder.

Their animosity had started when Atkinson and John Rector jumped a claim of Hargraves. Hargrave lost a suit against them and had to pay $1800 court costs. The day after the shooting, Moses Sanborn gave an affidavit in which he stated that Atkinson had threatened to kill Hargrave.[60] Hargrave and Charlie were released on bail and remained in the area[61] and were eventually cleared on grounds of self-defense since Atkinson had shot first. More trouble came Hargrave's way.

Murders in Mendocino

Adams - 1865

John Hargrave, in addition to his saloon/inn, worked as a butcher supplying the Albion and Navarro mills with beef. Four years later, in November 1865, he killed a man named Adams at his saloon. Apparently Adams, formerly of Cloverdale, in Sonoma County, had discussed leasing property from Hargraves but decided to lease instead from J. J. Perkins. This infuriated the hot tempered Hargrave and during a heated argument, Adams was shot and killed.

The San Francisco Alta California newspaper said that Sheriff Lewis Warden and a deputy chased Hargrave, who swore he would not be taken alive. This article claimed the Sheriff shot Hargrave who, although mortally wounded, fired several times killing both the Sheriff and the deputy. Despite this lurid news article, it was confirmed 10 days later that the Sheriff and deputy were both alive and well and it's not clear they were ever even shot.

The local newspaper called the murder of Adams "one of the most cold-blooded on record" and accused newly elected Democrats, Sheriff Lewis and District Attorney Bond, of negligence, claiming that the murderer was "allowed to escape." This was biased reporting at its worst since Hargrave had actually remained around his saloon for more than a week after the killing without trying to escape and Sheriff Lewis had never tried to arrest him.

A vigilante committee from Albion, riled up by the news articles, went looking to lynch Hargrave. They told his family to leave the county within days or they would be burned out. Hargrave gave himself up to William Heeser, Justice of the Peace, and went before the Grand Jury, which issued a bill of murder against him. He was released on bail but, with the Vigilantes after him, and politically motivated news articles whipping up prejudice against him, he feared for his life. He jumped bail and left town before his trial.

John B. Hargrave

Family troubles also pressed him to leave. He went to Hopkins County, Texas to help his recently widowed daughter Susan Westerman. She had just lost her 2nd husband and was left destitute with 6 small children and competing claims on his estate. John arrived in Texas in late 1866 and remained there for several years. After the Westerman probate was finally settled, early in 1869, John had wagons built and set off along the Southern Overland trail to return to California with daughter Susan Jane (Hargrave) (Davis) Westerman, her children and her share of the Westerman estate, which she had taken in cattle. The cattle were picked off by the Apache along the trail and the remainder of the herd, her only inheritance, was left with a local rancher in Arizona who was paid to care for the animals. When her son came back to get the cattle the following spring, he was told the cattle had all died, leaving her destitute.[62]

When John returned to Navarro in 1870, his saloon had closed, and Fletcher had built a fine Inn that he could not compete with. John gave himself up again and this time was acquitted for lack of evidence.[63] Adam's murder was never solved and he disappeared from history.

While John was gone, his wife Eveline lived with their son Charley and his family. Charley had married and gotten his own place in 1867 and was supporting his own family plus his mother Eveline and her 3 youngest children when John B returned with their daughter Susan and went to jail awaiting trial for Adams' murder. Eveline divorced him in 1871. Eveline (Woods) Hargrave died in Fort Bragg in 1894.[64] She is buried in Little Lake Cemetery in Willets.

John B. married again to Elizabeth Colston in November 1874 in Jackson County, MO but died a few months later in March 1875. A death announcement noted "John B. Hargrave, late of Mendocino, died in the German Hospital in San Francisco in 1875 and all his property, worth $3,000, was left to his wife Elizabeth and 7 children, Susan Westerman Brown, Charles, Aurelia Tuttle, Henry, William, Pittman, and Emma Hargrave."[65] His children remained in the Mendocino area.

Murders in Mendocino

Susan Jane (Hargrave)(Davis)(Westerman)Brown

Susan Jane Hargrave married a man named Thomas Davis in Texas when she was only 16. Her first child, William Franklin Davis was born the following year. The couple remained in Texas when the Hargrave family went to California. After Tom Davis died, Susan married Wilson T. Westerman in 1858, became stepmother to his young children and had 2 more sons, Pleasant B. and Henry B. Westerman.

Wilson Westerman died in 1863 of typhoid fever while with the Confederate Army. After his death, the Westerman family contested Susan's inheritance. With her father's help, Susan brought William F. Davis and her 2 Westerman children to California in 1870. When she lost her inherited cattle, Susan went to work at the Little Lake Hotel in Willits for her sister Aurelia and her husband Philo Tuttle. His partner was William Lee Brown who became Susan's 3rd husband in 1871. They had no children.

Susan's first son, William Franklin Davis, married Sarah Upp. They had 4 children in Mendocino.

Pleasant B. Westerman married first Delia Brush and had 2 children. He then married Dora Henley, granddaughter of T J Henley, Supervisor of Indian Affairs. After her death he married again to Henrietta Woods.

5 - Susan Hargrave Davis Westerman Brown

Henry B. Westerman became a lawyer but died of consumption, unmarried, in 1895 at the age of 31. They are all buried in Little Lake Cemetery in Willets.

John B. Hargrave's other children also remained in the area. Oldest son Charles Hargrave supported his mother Eveline and the younger children while his father was in Texas. He married Anna Frances Flannigan in Mendocino in 1867 and moved to his own 520 acre ranch. Charles and Annie had 9 children.

Daughter Aurelia Hargrave married Silas Osborne in 1860 at the age of 14 and had 3 children with Osborne which she brought to her marriage with 2nd husband, Philo Tuttle, a partner in the Little Lake Hotel in Willets.

Henry B. Hargrave married Elizabeth Whited in 1877 in Harrisburg, OR and moved to Mendocino. They had 2 daughters, Ora and Lena. Henry farmed in Mendocino later moving to Ft. Bragg and working as a gardener. He died in 1939 and is buried at Rose Memorial Park.

William Hargrave did not marry. He died in Willets in 1932.

Pittman Hargrave married Melissa Ann Edington in 1872 in Anderson Valley. They had a son Eugene and daughter Mary. The Edington family features in another story in this book.

Youngest child, Emma Hargrave, married Henry Baker Muir, a wealthy timber baron, son of famous pioneer Presley Muir who had settled Coyote Valley, Mendocino. Henry was in partnership with C.A. Irvine for many years and their firm, Irvine and Muir, became the largest business in the county. Henry Muir died in 1942 at his daughter Ora's house in Berkeley. Emma died in 1947 and is buried in Little Lake Cemetery in Willits, Mendocino with her husband and deceased children.

Chapter 3 - Money

Jerry O'Cain - 1863

About the 18th of October, 1863, Jeremiah O'Cain of Sanel was found murdered by a friend he had invited to join him on a hunting trip. His friend arrived on Wednesday the 21st as planned, to stay the night for an early start the next morning. Jerry wasn't around and the door was padlocked shut. His friend waited outside until dark then broke the padlock, started a fire and cooked his supper. When he went into the bedroom to go to bed, he saw the mattress and blankets on the floor. He was shocked to find the body of Jerry O'Cain under them. He had been shot in the back near the heart and there were bruises on his head. He immediately rode to Cloverdale to report the murder.

Two or three weeks before the murder, Jerry had sold his sheep ranch on Sanel Creek and moved to this new place, 3 miles from McDonalds. He was known to have $300 or S400 in cash from the sale. A few days before his murder, he had hired a stranger to shear sheep for him. On Tuesday morning, this stranger passed through Cloverdale, riding O'Cain's horse. It was later presumed that this man was the killer but he was never found.

Jerry O'Cain died intestate. He left about 556 head of sheep, two horses and 450 pounds of wool, a cow and calf, a field of barley and personal items worth about $1000. Frank McElaney, a creditor, was appointed his executor.

No one was ever arrested for his murder and the crime remained unsolved, but O'Cain's murder did figure in a later trial.[66]

Money

Francis Holmes - 1865

On June 12, 1865, Frank Holmes, a rancher living just north of Cloverdale, was killed. Folks first noticed he was missing on the 13th and search parties went looking. He could not be located until John Hawks, assisted by Indian trackers, found his body on July 4th. He had been shot through the head from behind and his head was bashed in with a heavy weapon. His body was carried a considerable distance to a gulch and covered up with stones and brush.

Holmes died intestate. He was not married and had no local heirs. At his death he owned about 573 sheep which were first taken by W.H. Crowell who filed letters of administration to be executor. The court had appointed as executor, E. M. Pierson, who objected to Crowell's petition. The matter went to trial and Crowell was ordered to surrender the sheep, worth almost $8600. Holmes also owned a mare, colt and yearling worth $45, and a ranch worth $325. All were to be sold by the court.

Then another objection was raised to the sale. George W. Strong claimed he owned the sheep and had branded them with his brand and he refused to release them for sale. Strong claimed that he had bought the ranch and stock from Holmes before his death. That matter was resolved when Strong was convicted of his murder, and executor Pierson finally sold the 582 sheep at $2.10 each amounting to $15,000.

William Holmes, Frank's brother, finally arrived in town and was made the executor of the estate, claiming it for their father, John Holmes (65). He was given the $15,000 from the sale of the stock. He sold the 400 acre Ranch, bounded on the south side by the Jerry O'Cain Ranch which was now owned by McElaney, for $400.

But who killed Holmes?

Murders in Mendocino

George W. Strong

George W. Strong had worked on the Holmes ranch that spring, and soon became the chief suspect. Holmes hired the 24 year old to shear sheep. The men struck up a friendship and he and Holmes told folks that Strong was going to buy the ranch and stock. Strong was arrested in Petaluma and claimed he was looking for Holmes, not trying to escape. He provided a bill of sale for Holmes' ranch and insisted to everyone that he was innocent. During his trial, Strong appeared intelligent and self-assured and was in constant conversation with his lawyers. The case against him was entirely circumstantial.

His defense attorney gave an eloquent closing statement. He reminded the jury that Strong had a bill of sale and Holmes had confirmed the sale to several people. He claimed that it was logical that Strong would have earlier concealed his money because he was living in a remote and dangerous locality, near where O'Cain had been murdered for a similar sum. Strong clearly had not planned to leave town because he had loaned $100 to Mr. McDonald two days before leaving, and had another balance of $80 due from a store. The case was given to the jury between 1 and 2 o'clock Saturday morning, and at 6am they returned with a verdict of "Guilty." Eleven of them decided the verdict without ever leaving their seats. Judge Southard sentenced Strong to death. Strong appealed to the California Supreme Court, which upheld the guilty verdict in in July, 1866.

Despite his attorney's belief in his innocence, before his death Strong wrote a biographical sketch of his life, in which he made a full confession of his commission of the murder. On the day set, at about 2 pm, "he was led from the jail to the scaffold and, after a brief speech to those present, signified his readiness to meet his fate, the trap was sprung and he was hurled from time to eternity and, for once in Mendocino County, the law had taken its course".[67]

Israel Millett Millay – 1865

Someone really wanted Israel Millay dead! Millay, living about three miles from Ukiah, was shot as he and Mr. Hathaway were riding together on the road near Mr. Williams' farm. The report of a gun was heard from a thicket of bushes, and the ball pierced his arm. Millay was at odds with several of his neighbors and it was believed that one of them had tried to kill him. Silas E. Gaskill, a leading citizen, was arrested but was released when no evidence could be found to implicate him.

Millay went home to his cabin to recuperate and Hathaway stayed to help him. Millay appeared to be recovering when, two weeks later about nine o'clock on Saturday night, someone fired a double-barreled shot-gun, loaded with buckshot, through a crevice in the chimney. Millay was lying in his bed on the floor near the fire. Four to six shots hit his breast, passing through his heart and lungs, killing him instantly. Hathaway, lying a few feet away was not injured. On Monday W. P. Bovay, and on Tuesday Silas E. Gaskill, were again arrested. On Thursday J. J. Bell was also arrested.[68]

Israel Millett Millay had been born in 1815 in Maine. He married Elonia Crockett Butler there and had six children, three of whom had died before he left them all behind and came west to mine gold in 1852. Israel decided to stay in California and filed for divorce from Elonia. She was apparently fine with this decision and agreed in 1862, leaving her with 3 children to support. At least she had family nearby in Maine.

Millay's estate was about $1500 when he died and consisted mostly of perishable crops. His 24 year old son, Israel Millay Jr., traveled to Mendocino and was named executor, noting that the heirs were himself, his brother George A. Millay (21) and their sister Ellen M. Millay (16), all of Maine. There is no record of what might have led to Millay's murder. The men who were arrested were all leading citizens.

Murders in Mendocino

Silas Gaskill

Silas Gaskill was from Michigan, a blacksmith and gunsmith by trade. He was quite prominent in the area and there is no indication what evidence there was against him for the murder. He was released on bail of $1,000, but he forfeited bail and fled. A reward of $500 was posted for his capture, describing him as 5' 10" tall, with dark hair and whiskers and dark piercing hazel eyes and a dark complexion weighing about 160 lbs. His wife quietly settled up their affairs in Mendocino and joined him in southern California.[69] Jumping bail was apparently a wise move as Silas went on to have a long, productive life. He went first to San Bernardino County where he and his brother, Luman, built a large successful farm.

They sold that land and moved to southern San Diego County in 1868 where they purchased immense tracts of land near the Mexican border and built a compound with a general store, gristmill, vegetable garden, blacksmith shop and a hotel with a Post Office and Telegraph. The place was known as Campo and was the first town in the US across the border from Tecate, Mexico. Their general store contained everything from needles to crosscut saws, liquor and medicine. Luman became Postmaster and Justice of the Peace and built the first schoolhouse there. Luman's wife ran their hotel.

Silas was reputed to be able to make or repair anything made of wood, iron, brass or steel and the family was well respected. They owned 5000 Angora goats and their store was famous for its angora socks knitted by local women. They had large herds of stock and their range extended into Mexican Baja California. Luman lived part of the time in Ensenada, Mexico where he supervised their cattle interests and managed a meat market. They also became the 2nd largest bee apiarists in the US.

The Campo location on the border was lawless and dangerous. Because they were so successful, it was known that they had plenty of cash as well as food, guns and ammunition. The original store spanned a creek in which they would store items to keep cool in the hot desert. But bandits from both countries made such frequent raids on the original store that the Gaskills built a stone house, which still stands today.

The surviving members of the notorious Tibercio Vasquez gang decided to rob Campo, planning to kill the Gaskills and the telegraph operator before looting the place. Since Vasquez had been killed, the new gang leader was Cruz 'Pancho' Lopez. The gang gathered in Tecate and sent Rafael Martinez into Campo as their lookout. Cruz took 3 men to rob Luman in the store and sent 3 to kill Silas in the blacksmith shop. The remaining gang members waited across the border with wagons to load up the loot. Fortunately, Silas had been tipped off about the plot and the brothers had stashed guns around the property.

On the clear sunny Saturday morning of Dec 4, 1875, a group of armed horsemen rode into Campo, led by Lopez. Two of the bandits went into the store where the advance man, Rafael Martinez, was hanging around. As Lopez, the gang leader, stood in the doorway and lifted his hand to signal the others, a Frenchman (probably Basque) sheepherder rode up. Inside the store, Cota and Alvijo saw Lopez's signal and reached for their guns. Luman yelled "Murder!" and grabbed his shotgun from under the counter. Cota jumped over the counter and fired a bullet point blank into Luman's chest. It hit his lung but missed his heart. Luman slumped to the floor unconscious and bleeding from the mouth and was left for dead.

Silas Gaskill was in the blacksmith shop. He heard his brother Luman yell and grabbed his shotgun just as Teodoro Vazquez ran in with his gun drawn. They fired at the same time. Silas was wounded in the side and arm but his shot killed Vasques. Alvitro and Martinez ran behind the blacksmith shop as Silas came out the back door and shot Martinez with the 2nd barrel of his shotgun. Silas ran for the house as Alvitro took cover.

The Frenchman began firing at Lopez using his horse for cover. Lopez, shot in the neck, continued firing from the store. Cota and Alvijo in the store also began firing at the Frenchman. Luman regained consciousness, dragged himself to his shotgun and shot Alvijo.

Murders in Mendocino

Silas came out of the house and saw Alvitro coming at him, gun drawn. Silas grabbed an empty shotgun and pointed it at Alvitro who turned and ran – right into Luman's sights. After Luman shot Alvitro with his 2nd barrel, Luman dragged himself to the trapdoor and slid into the cold stream under the house, where the terrified telegraph operator was hiding. During the 5-6 minute gunfight, Vasquez was killed and Lopez, Martinez, Alvijo and Alvitro were all wounded. As the gang was escaping, Lopez killed the badly wounded gang member, Alvitro, with a bullet to the brain. Martinez and Alvijo were captured and lynched the next morning. Lopez escaped but died from his infected wounds months later. Cota escaped uninjured and returned to the gang in Mexico. The brave French sheepherder died several months later but Luman and Silas Gaskill survived to tell the story.

Luman and Silas both moved to the nearby city of San Diego in 1900. Luman was married and had 6 children. He moved to Los Angeles where he died in 1914.[70]

Silas E. Gaskill became a well-known hero in San Diego when stories of the Campo shoot out were publicized by the newspapers.. He died in San Diego in October 1914 at the age of 85. His obit noted that he had been born in New York and his funeral was held by the Pioneers Society. He was survived by his 2nd wife, Catherine, whom he married in 1881, and children, May (Gaskill) Sasey of San Diego, Charles J. and Henry L. Gaskill of South Bend, Indiana, and a stepdaughter Mrs. Mary J. Morse of San Diego.[71]

Back in Mendocino, the other accused men, Bovey and J. J. Bell were soon released and no further action was taken in the murder of Millay. It is not clear why any of these men had been arrested in the first place as there appeared to be little or no evidence against them.

William H. Bovey

William Henry Bovey and his wife Martha (Spargo) came from Cornwall, England. They lived in Grass Valley with their 5 children. Bovey was a miner and found a new quartz ledge in Grass Valley in 1868. His orchard was known for fine peaches and pears. He also drove the stage between Grass Valley and Nevada City for many years.[72]

Bovey died on 9 Dec 1889 in Grass Valley at the age of 56 and is buried in Forester's Cemetery there.[73]

Joseph Jones Bell

Joseph J. Bell also led a productive and successful life. Years before Millay's murder, Bell had built a ferry across Clear Creek in Shasta County. He became well known for building a toll bridge and the Mansion House Hotel in 1859. A small community grew up around his hotel called Bell's Bridge and he became the first postmaster of the town. This is near where the Asbill family originally settled.

His Mansion House Hotel became an important stage-stop on the road to the gold fields and figured in the Long March of the Concow to Round Valley Reservation. It was a 3 story house built of massive hand hewn and pegged timbers. The first floor held an office, dining room parlor and 2 large bedrooms. The 2nd floor featured 6 bedrooms for female travelers and a 'corral' room with rows of beds for men. The 3rd floor was another large room for men. Bell became a prominent and wealthy citizen in Mendocino and Shasta Counties. His elegant hotel and stage stop even offered a horse racing track. It remained a local landmark for many years, finally collapsing in March 1998.[74]

Bell and wife Mary moved to Santa Clara County in 1881. He died there in Nov 1882. His will left his entire estate to his nephew William Jackson of Shasta County. He was survived by his brother Thomas Bell and sister Rebecca Bell of Huntington, PA. He left a house, a few tons of hay, a horse, a watch and some household furniture.[75]

The murder of Israel Millay was never solved.

Chapter 4 – Revenge

Captain George W. Knight - 1867

On the morning of Friday, December 13th, harsh words passed between Henry and his son Joe Fairbanks and their neighbor George Knight. Captain George Knight had purchased a large ranch but, shortly after taking possession, Fairbanks began claiming and fencing part of Knight's land. That day, Knight rode to where Fairbanks and his son Joe were taking rails out of a Knight fence, told them to stop tearing up his fence, and allegedly attacked Joe Fairbanks. Knight had a pistol in his hand but did not fire. Henry Fairbanks fired his rifle, hitting Knight in the leg, hitting an artery and Knight died an hour later.

Capt. George W. Knight was a master mariner from Maine. After his death, his large ranch was sold to Rench and Catherine Angle, and became part of their large Angle Ranch.

Henry Fairbanks gave himself up to the Justice of the Peace in Arena Township. On the 4th of March, 1868 the Grand Jury indicted him for manslaughter, but his trial ended in a hung jury (7 for acquittal and 5 for conviction) and he was released. He was never retried despite the fact that most of the local population believed he was guilty of manslaughter in killing the well liked Captain Knight.

The Fairbanks family did not live happily ever after. Joe Fairbanks, the son whose testimony helped result in the hung jury, drowned in a pond near his residence in 1870 at the age of 20 under suspicious circumstances.[76]

Then Henry W. Fairbanks himself was murdered in 1873.

Revenge

Henry Fairbanks – 1873

On 13 May 1873 Henry Fairbanks, of Point Arena, was assassinated in his own house.[77] He was a native of New York, about 48 years old, and had lived in Point Arena since 1849. Many people disliked the quarrelsome man who frequently argued over land and sued his neighbors. He had been involved in several violent altercations, including the shooting of Capt. Knight and local antagonism had grown against him in the 6 years after the hung jury at his trial. Most people believed he had provoked the fight that resulted in the killing and were angry that he was not re-tried. They believed his skillful attorney, Judge McGarvey, had gotten him off despite his guilt.

On the night of his murder, his wife and 3 children had gone to bed. He had been reading and carried the lamp to the kitchen for a drink of water before bed, as was his custom. He placed the lamp on the left side of the sink and began pumping water when five shots were suddenly fired through the window over the sink in rapid succession. He was shot in the head and died of his wounds the following morning. Oddly, bullets found in the window casing and inside the house were from different guns, indicating that 3 or 4 different people had shot at him simultaneously.

It was soon reported that ten days before his death, Henry Fairbanks been arrested on the charge of raping the 10 year old stepdaughter of his brother, William Clark Fairbanks. Henry had made bail of $2000 and immediately contacted a lawyer to defend him on the rape charge. He was murdered before he could go to trial.

It was widely believed that his brother's family, fearing he would again escape justice, took matters into their own hands.[78] The general sentiment of the community was that Fairbanks deserved what he got and no one was ever arrested for his murder.

Henry left a wife, Mary, and 3 children, Frank, William and Harriet Fairbanks.[79]

Ella Snider

The little girl who made the accusation of rape had already been through much in her short life. Her mother Elizabeth Jane Antrim was born in Iowa before her family moved to California. Elizabeth married Charles Snider in Sonoma when she was only 14. Her first child, Ella's older brother, died shortly before Ella was born. Her father died when Ella was only 1, leaving the 22 year old Elizabeth Jane almost destitute.

Elizabeth Jane soon married 44 year old Aquila Barton Aull, a widower with 2 young children of his own. Elizabeth Jane and Aull had 2 more children, before he too died in 1869. Shortly after his death, 29 year old destitute Elisabeth brought Ella and her 2 younger daughters, Bertha and Jessie Aull to Mendocino to live with her parents, Aden and his wife Mary (Windsor) Antrim.

A year later, Elizabeth Jane married her 3rd husband William Clark Fairbanks and they all moved to Clark's house where she soon became pregnant with Hettie. It was there that 9 year old Ella was raped by her new stepfather's brother, Henry Fairbanks. Terrified by his threats to kill her mother and unsure of her step-father, it took her almost a year to gather the courage to tell her mother. Her parents, very surprising for the time and the family situation, both supported her and brought her to the Sheriff to file charges. She told her story in such a straightforward way that there was little doubt of the horrible truth and the sheriff immediately arrested Henry Fairbanks.

After Henry's murder, most likely by her husband, Elizabeth Jane was stricken with epilepsy and Ella became primary caretaker for her 6 younger siblings. She also had to overcome the stigma of a rape and murder that everyone knew about.

Ella Snider married Hiram Olney Hillman, at the age of 22 in 1884. Hiram was from Maine and came to Mendocino about 1879. He worked as a shingle sawyer in Manchester. Sadly, Ella died just 4 years after their marriage at the age of 26. After Ella died, Hiram moved to Eureka. He died in there 1924 and is buried in Evergreen Cemetery with Ella. He never remarried.

Chapter 5 – Family Feud

Murders in Mendocino

Coates Family

The Coates families had arrived in the area in the mid 1850's. They were well respected and strong abolitionists, siding with the Union in the Civil War.. They had migrated from Pennsylvania to Indiana and then to Wisconsin before arriving in Little Lake Valley.

Benjamin and Anne (Longstreth) Coates were the grandparents of the families who came to Mendocino. Their son Abner A. and Margaret (Tussy) Coates were the parents of Abner C. and Thomas Johnson Coates, brothers who migrated west together.

Abner C. and Isela Celia (Wilson) Coates farmed in Rock Tree Valley and had the following children: Sarah Ann (Coates) Endicott, John P., Margaret (Coates) Endicott, Mary (Coates) (Daniels) (Snuckles) (Bessee) Munn, Joseph A., Abraham T. and Charles C. Mary's husband Samuel Bessee was killed by her brother John P.

Thomas J and Elizabeth (Knox) Coates came with their children: George W, Mary Jane (Coates) Laughlin, Rebecca Amelia Coates. He worked as a teamster and owned a ranch in Scotts Valley.

Great-grandson George Ivestor Coates and his wife Loretta Jane (Lytle) came west too. Grandpa Ben's youngest son, Benjamin and wife Elizabeth (Ivestor) Coates were the parents of George Ivestor Coates. George and Loretta had the following children: Mary E. (Coates) Traber, Wesley, Martha Ann (Coates) Berry, Adaline (Coates) Boyd, Henry, Laura J. (Coates) Say, 'Nellie' (Coates) Sherwood, James B, Fanny E. (Coates) Southard.

George Coates ran a gristmill in town. He also owned a ranch with a house and cultivated fields and a tannery.

Family Feud

Frost Family

The Frost family arrived in Little Lake Valley about 1858 from Davis County, Missouri. The patriarch of this family was 'Old Elijah' Frost and his wife Elizabeth (Brown). The children who came with them included Elijah Jr., William, Louisa (Frost) Gilliam, Catherine (Frost) Duncan, Martin, Isom and Elizabeth 'Lizzie' (Frost) Cox.

Elisha Jr., a rancher, married Amanda (McCully) and had Elijah 3, Taylor, Sarah, Asbury, David, James G. and Mary (Frost) Smith. After Elijah Jr was killed his sons, Elisha 3, Taylor, David and James got into trouble with the rest of the family and the law.

Daughter Catherine married Frank Duncan who was in the brawl that set off the Frost-Coates Shootout.

Son Martin married Alice Whitcomb and had a daughter Jane.

Son Isom never married. He was convicted of murdering his nephew James.

Daughter Lizzie figures in several of the stories in this book. She married James Cox in 1868 when she was 16. They had 5 children but divorced in 1879. Cox married Annie (Parks) Kell in June 1880 and they had a child, James Tolliver Cox, in March 1881. Meanwhile, Lizzie married Claudius E. Ramey in Nov. 1881 but quickly divorced him. In Oct. 1883, after the death of her cousin Ben, with whom she had been having an affair, she married Samuel Burgess. She did not have children with Ben or her 2nd and 3rd husbands. In 1884, James Cox, was murdered by his 2nd wife, Annie and Schemmerhorn Johnson.

Lizzie and Sam Burgess moved to Washington where Sam was a quartz miner. Lizzie died in Humboldt County in 1915 at the age of 63 and is buried in Ferndale Cemetery and shares a headstone with Alice E. Brown and Jerald L .Brown, relatives of her mother Elizabeth (Brown) Frost.

The Frosts were successful sheep and hog raisers and strong anti-abolitionists. These great differences in political beliefs led to high levels of tension and anger between all the families in the area.

Coates – Frost Shootout - 1867

On the 16th of October, 1867, the bloodiest shootout in the history of the west occurred in Little Lake Valley. Two families, Frost and Coates, had been at odds with each other for a number of years. The underlying animosity stemmed from Civil War loyalties. The Coates were northern abolitionists and the Frosts were southern sympathizers. Tension between these two families erupted over a schoolyard fistfight between a Frost and Coates boy, probably over politics. The teacher intervened and thrashed both boys equally for fighting on school grounds. When the parents complained, the School Board upheld the teacher. The Coates family let the matter go but the Frosts were determined to have the teacher removed and withdrew their son from school. People in the valley began taking sides and tensions continued to build. In the five years after the schoolyard fight there were periodic fistfights between Frost and Coates family members. Everyone knew this was a powder-keg waiting to blow.

Oct 16, 1867 was the date of elections, which drew all the local men to Little Lake (later Willits) the center of Little Lake Valley Township. The village had a town hall suitable for the election, a hotel, a school, several houses and Baechtel's general store. A new School Board was to be elected and the Frosts were determined that the old Board would be replaced. Both families had done a lot of politicking with their neighbors over the election. Frank Budd, editor of the Mendocino Herald was in Little Lake for the election and wrote that it was a breathless hot day. People were sitting outside, in the shade of the porch at Brown's Little Lake Hotel, when Abner Coates' wagon arrived. Abner always carried a rifle and his sons Wes and Abe Coates were also armed.

Three Frost men were already in town, hanging around in Baechtel's store after voting. Brothers Elisha, Mart and Isom Frost were talking with their brother-in-law, Frank Duncan, who was sitting on the counter, when young Henry and James Coates walked into the store and "exchanged words" with the Frosts. Their father, George Coates, hearing the argument said, "Henry, it's time to leave."

Outside, Henry told his older brother, Wes Coates, that Frank Duncan was inside. These two men hated each other so Wes went into the store and began trying to pick a fight with Frank Duncan. Wes Coates made finally one remark too many and Duncan jumped off the counter and walked outside with Wes following.

As Wes was removing his jacket, Frank Duncan rushed him and struck him over the head with his pistol. Wes got up and Duncan hit him over the head again, this time hard enough to break the pistol, which he dropped to the ground. Fists began flying and the crowd decided to let them fight it out. Wes Coates suddenly grabbed a knife from Duncan's belt and stabbed him several times with it. Duncan tried to run away from Wes Coates who followed, stabbing him again in the shoulder. Duncan's brother-in-law, Martin Frost (22), pulled his gun and yelled "Stand Back" trying to stop the fight but suddenly all hell broke loose. Unbelievably, 20 shots were fired within 15 seconds!

As the dust cleared the bystanders, who had taken cover, came out to find 6 men dead or dying and 3 others seriously wounded. The dead included Abner's sons, Albert (22) and Abraham Coates (21); George's sons Henry (25) and Wesley Coates (33) and uncle Thomas Johnson Coates (63). Albert Coates had exclaimed "My God!", the only words spoken.[80]

James and Abner Coates and Frank Duncan all survived their wounds.[81]

Elisha Frost (43), the only Frost to die in the shootout, was buried in Little Lake Cemetery in Willits, with the Coates.[82]

Abner, Martin and Isom Frost quickly left town after the shooting, chased by the Sheriff. They were arrested but were acquitted on the basis of self-defense.[83]

Frank Duncan survived 15 knife wounds and 2 bullet wounds. He wisely moved to Chico.[84]

But trouble continued to follow these families.

Samuel Bessee – 1872

Mary (Coates) (Daniels) Snuckles had married Samuel Bessee in 1865, several years before the shootout. She was the daughter of Abner Coates who survived the shootout. Abner had given Sam and Mary Bessee half of a government claim of 160 acres, and the other half to his sons John and William. Sam and Mary got the 80 acres with a house on it. This arrangement continued for several years.

Samuel Bessee was born in Pennsylvania in about 1831 and worked as a miller in Mendocino in 1863. He was a difficult man with a bad temper. He was known locally as a bully and had been indicted for assault with intent to commit murder, although not convicted.

When Abner died in 1870, matters became heated because Sam tried to fraudulently prove the entire claim in his name to cheat her brothers. John and Will Coates went to Tompki on Feb 8th, 1872 to serve notice on Samuel Bessee, demanding possession of their half of the claim. Bessee was in the woods hauling rails. Sam tore up the legal eviction notice, drew a butcher knife and, according to John and Will, attacked John Coates with it. John then fired 5 shots, killing Bessee.

John and Will rode to the Bessee house and told their sister Mary that John had shot her husband, Sam. John then rode to Ukiah and surrendered to the Sheriff and was held on $1000 bail.[85]

Mary and her neighbors went to collect Sam Bessee's body and later testified that they found him lying on the ground with his coat buttoned and gloves on. Mary had lost her only means of support and the claim and she was furious. She insisted that Sam had no knife. The coroner believed her version although a knife was found 15-20 feet from the body.

Her brother, John Coates, was found guilty of manslaughter and sentenced to 3 years in state prison. He developed tuberculosis there and was pardoned on March 4, 1873.[86] He died at home soon after his release.

Family Feud

Mary Coates

Mary certainly had bad luck with husbands. She married young and had Sarah Emma Daniel, before divorcing her 1st husband, Frank K. Daniel, in Wisconsin and moving west with her family in 1860.

Her 2nd husband was John Snuckles with whom she had two more children, Edward and Ida Snuckles before he too died.

Her 3rd husband, married in Mendocino in 1865, was Sam Bessee, with whom she had children Celia, Charles and Margaret before he was killed by her brother, John, in 1872. She was pregnant with Albert at the time of his death.

Sam's death left Mary, still only 34, destitute, pregnant and with 6 small children to support with no help from her family who were furious over her testimony against her brother John. In 1876 she moved to South Union, Thurston County, WA where she operated a boarding house and soon married her 4th husband, John Munn. They had a daughter named Mary they called May. Unfortunately, Munn was sued for unpaid loans. They separated and were living apart when John Munn died in 1885 at 47 years old leaving Mary widowed for the 3rd time at 47.

She kept the boarding house until youngest daughter May married. Mary died at the home of her daughter Maggie, Mrs. Frank Moyer, at 1903 Franklin Street, Olympia, at the age of 86 in 1922. Her obituary noted that she was an honored pioneer who had come to California by ox team in 1860. She was survived by five daughters; Mrs. Emma (Daniels) Hunter of Hunter's Point, Mrs. Ida (Snuckles) Curtin, Mrs. Celia (Bessee) Littlejohn and Mrs. Margaret (Bessee) Moyer of Olympia, Mrs. May (Munn) Tunin of Keechelus and two sons; Charles A Bessee of South Union and Albert M Bessee of Spokane. Their old home in Union was always noted for its hospitality. She was buried under Christian Science auspices.[87]

At least she got away from her feuding family. It seems the Frosts and Coates families were just not destined to have peaceful lives.

Murders in Mendocino

Elijah Frost III – 1879

Elijah Frost III was lynched at Willets on 4 September 1879. He had seen his father Elijah Jr. killed in the Frost Coates Shootout of 1867. His mother had died in 1870 and Elijah and his siblings became the wards of James McKindley, husband of their oldest sister. McKindley had his hands full when Elijah went completely off the rails.

First he and a friend stole $50 worth of apples. They were caught but charges were dropped. Then he talked his brother Taylor into stealing some hogs. Again they were caught but released. In September 1875, Elijah (26) convinced his young wife Mary (Brown) and his 14 year old brother Jimmy to steal 16 horses in Red Bluff. Mary and Jimmy were released but Elijah was finally convicted and sent to San Quentin.

When he came home in 1878 his problems continued. He was 26 and, with his gang, Abijah Gibson and Thomas McCracken, both 19, was burning barns, stealing, and raising all sorts of hell. One night they were caught stealing a saddle. The Sheriff locked them up in Brown's Little Lake Hotel to wait for the circuit judge.[88] The boys were blustering and swearing loudly, threatening to get even with everyone. The younger two were handcuffed together and all 3 were in a small room off the office, guarded by Deputies Tatham and Davis.

Vigilante justice in Mendocino was frequent and harsh. A group of about 25 "Regulators" met at the Willits Masonic Temple. About 2 AM, they walked into the Little Lake Hotel, tied and gagged the two guards and marched the boys to a bridge about 400 yards away. Ropes were placed around their necks and their pockets were loaded with rocks. The two younger boys, handcuffed together, were pushed off one side of the bridge and Elijah Frost went off the other. One agitated man in the vigilante group was heard to say to a companion "I know, I know, but I refuse to save a thief. Swing him off."

It was widely known that Martin Frost, Elijah's uncle, was the leader of the Regulator's. Anger festered within the Frost family against each other as well as outsiders.[89] Mart began drinking heavily.

Family Feud

Benjamin Franklin Frost – 1882

On March 12, 1882, Mart Frost rode into town with his nephew, Ben, dead on the saddle in front of him. Mart told the Mendocino Beacon that he and Ben were drunk and that he and John Robertson had tried to keep Ben from falling off his skittish horse when a pistol in Robertson's pocket discharged, accidentally killing Ben. His explanation to the Coroner's Jury was a bit different. They heard that Ben's hat fell off and he tried to pick it up without dismounting. The horse shied and the drunk Ben fell off. While Mart and Robertson were helping him, a pistol fired from a saddlebag on Robertson's horse because the horse was stamping and shaking.[90] The coroner's jury returned the only verdict ever of "accidental death by horse". Most folks, including his own family, believed that Mart had shot Ben because there was family animosity over Ben's intimacy with Mart's youngest sister, Lizzie.[91]

Long after Mart's death, a great grandson of John Robertson Jr. shared what really happened that day. John Sr. was riding back from market and eleven year old John Jr. was driving the wagon when they encountered Mart and Ben Frost, both drunk, who had their guns drawn, planning to rob them. They ordered John off his horse, but ignored John Jr. in the wagon. Eleven year old John lifted a pistol from the wagon seat and shot Ben. Mart's horse reared at the shot and Mart fell off. By the time drunken Mart got to his feet both Robertsons had both their guns on him.

Robertson fearful that Ben's crazy brothers would take revenge against John Jr., made a deal with Mart. Robertson agreed not to report the attempted robbery if Mart agreed not to tell about John Jr. shooting Ben. Mart kept his word. John Robertson moved his family from Little Lake to a ranch near Albion. Afraid of the Frost family's reputation for revenge, John Jr. used his first paycheck to buy a long barreled revolver which he carried with him everywhere for many years. John Jr. lived a long peaceful life without the public, or the Frosts, ever knowing he had shot one of the notorious feuding Frosts.[92]

Murders in Mendocino

Martin Van Buren Frost – 1883

On December 29, 1883 Mart Frost himself was shot and killed by James Frost, a brother of Ben and Elijah. Elijah III had been lynched by Mart's Vigilantes and most in the family believed that Mart had also shot Elijah's brother Ben. As if that wasn't enough, Jim Frost and his brothers wanted land claimed by Mart and his partner, Andreas Hamburg.

Andreas Hamburg was a peaceable family man. One night, Jim and his brothers went to Hamburg's house, calling for Andreas to come out. His wife, Martha, asked who was there and the reply was Martin and Isom Frost. Andreas suspected an ambush so his wife told the men that Andreas was asleep and to come back in the morning. The next morning Andreas went to see Mart and Isom, who confirmed they had not been the night visitors. They all suspected that Jim and his brothers were planning trouble, so Mart and Isom went to see their nephews. The discussion escalated into an argument and Jim

6 - Martin VB Frost

Frost suddenly drew his pistol and shot his uncle Mart in the forehead. Jim immediately went to Ukiah to surrender, no doubt believing he'd be safer in jail than free where the rest of the Frost family could get revenge.[93] Jim Frost admitted at his trial that Mart had not drawn his pistol first saying, "No, if he had, I would not be here to tell it." He claimed he felt his life was threatened and drew first. Strangely, given this confession, James Frost was acquitted of killing Mart Frost on the grounds of self-defense, despite many who believed it was cold blooded murder.

Martin was survived by his wife Alice Amelia Whitcomb Frost, son Fred (3) and daughter Jane (5). His estate was $473. She married William D Heath the following year and moved to Oregon.

Jim's uncle Isom, Mart's brother, of course vowed revenge.[94]

Family Feud

Jim Frost and Andreas Hamburg – 1885

In April 1885, Jim Frost, and Andreas Hamburg (50) were both killed while herding sheep on Hamburg's ranch. Brothers Jim and Dave Frost were in the herding party despite Jim's murder of Andreas's partner, their uncle Mart Frost, 2 years earlier.

Mart's brother, Isom, vowing revenge, involved two men in a plot to kill his nephew, Jim. Isom, Ed Jewell and George Gibson hid on a hill about 130 yards above Andreas's ranch. Isom fired his rifle, hitting Jim Frost who suddenly threw up his hands and shouted "Jesus Christ, I am shot". Jim, thinking he had been shot by Andreas, pulled out his gun

7 - Isom Frost

and shot Andreas in the abdomen before dying. Dave, thinking Andreas had killed his brother, also shot Andreas in the heart killing him instantly. Meanwhile Isom Frost, Gibson and Jewell escaped unnoticed down the back side of the hill. Poor Andreas Hamburg had never even pulled his gun.

Sheriff Doc Standley knew Andreas had not fired his gun and was determined to find out who shot Jim. The coroner pulled the bullet and it was from a rifle not a pistol. Using the angle of the bullet, Doc determined that he had been shot from the nearby hill and had a pretty good idea who could have made that long shot.

After the shooting, Ed Jewell had left for Marysville and Isom Frost went to Trinity County. The Sheriff, convinced that Isom had planned Jim's murder and used Jewell and Gibson as accomplices, sent a deputy to get hired where Ed Jewell was working. The deputy befriended him and got Ed drunk enough to confess the whole plot. Sheriff Standley then went to Trinity County and disguised himself as a prospector to catch Isom. He surprised Isom walking on a trail and was able to disarm and arrest him. Once Isom was in custody, Doc telegraphed his deputies to arrest George Gibson and Ed Jewell.

Murders in Mendocino

George Gibson

Poor George Gibson got the worst of it. He had been harassed by Jim and his brothers for years. They had burned down his house with everything in it and stolen his claim. They continued to harass him and threaten his life. Isom used George's frustration to convince him to join his plot. Gibson didn't want to get involved, but Isom threatened that he'd be dead either way, so he reluctantly agreed to help.[95] The unfortunate George Gibson got 17 years in San Quentin because he pled guilty without a lawyer, wrongly believing that he would receive immunity for testifying against Isom. He finally received a pardon in 1889 after 4 years in San Quentin, signed by over 800 Mendocino residents, who firmly believed he had been coerced by Isom.[96]

Ed Jewell

Ed Jewell was found guilty as an accessory and sentenced to 30 months.

Isom Frost

Isom Frost received a life sentence for the murders. His 200 acres of land was sold at public auction in 1897 to Gordon Baechtel for $700. He was finally released from Folsom Prison in 1904 after serving 18 years. He received a full pardon from Governor Gillette and went to live with his older widowed sister, Louisa Gillam before moving to the old family home in Willets.[97] He lived there many years and worked in a livery stable. Luckily, he was visiting relatives in Humboldt County when the old home, built in 1866, and several outbuildings burned to the ground in 1926.

Isom Frost died in April 29, 1928 at the State Mental Hospital in Talmadge where he had been living for four months, in ill health with his mind failing. He was 85 years old and the last survivor of the Little Lake Massacre. He had never married and had no known descendants. He is buried on the Hospital grounds.[98]

Chapter 6 - Impulse

Murders in Mendocino

John Rector - 1867

John Rector, a partner of '3 Finger Jack' Atkinson whom John B. Hargrave killed in 1861, was himself murdered on April 28th, 1867. A man named Somers was fixing his wagon by the side of the road one afternoon when Rector came by on his way home from his mill job. Somers wife was struggling to carry a heavy bucket of water from a nearby spring so John stopped to help. Somers yelled "You are just trying to insult me because I don't help my wife." Thinking he was kidding, Rector just laughed and was still carrying the water bucket when the enraged Somers ran up and struck him in the head with the king bolt from the wagon. Rector lived 5 hours before dying, leaving a pregnant wife and 5 small children. Somers was never found.[99]

John Rector was originally from New York. He married Elizabeth Caroline (McGimsey), the daughter of Judge John Cox McGimsey, an early settler in the Christine/Philo area. John and his family lived in Big River. He worked at the Albion mill and ranched in Anderson Valley.[100] After his murder, his wife Caroline and their 6 children Charles, Harriet Ann, Mary Louise, William, Edward and Emma Rector stayed on their ranch. Caroline never remarried. She died in Marin County in 1914. She and her family are all buried in Evergreen Cemetery.

Charles was 9 when his father was killed. He supported the family as a sheepshearer. He married Sarah McReynolds in Mendocino in 1883, and owned a farm in Honey Lake, Lassen County. He died in 1948.

Harriet Ann (Rector) Main died in 1901.

Mary married William Singley in Mendocino. She died in 1944.

William Lynard Rector died in 1945 in Sonoma. He apparently never married.

Edward M. Rector died in Mendocino in 1908.

Emma married William Virgil Ornbaum and had 7 children. She died in 1937 in Mendocino.

Irvin R. Wright – 1868

Irvin Russell Wright was in debt and Constable J. Dodson had a warrant for his arrest for hiding property from his creditors. Unable to locate him, Dodson got a group of neighbors from Point Arena to form a posse on July 18, 1868. Among them was Calvin Stewart. They hunted all day for Wright and, about 10 pm, they found him hiding in the straw of his brother's barn above Mal Pass.

When he was flushed out, Wright ran out of the barn towards Deputy Cal Stewart, who told him to stop several times. Ignoring the warning, Wright kept coming, and said "G-d you, what are you doing here?" Stewart said, "Stand back!" to which Wright replied, "I'll blow your G-d brains out!" and continued to advance so Stewart fired, killing Wright instantly. When the body was searched, it was discovered that Wright had left his weapons in the barn and was unarmed.

John Calvin Stewart

Cal was arrested for manslaughter. Calvin Stewart had been arrested before. Only 16 at the time, he had been briefly arrested in the murder of L.D. Helm in Salt Point to force the surrender of his older brother, accused of firing the deadly shot. He was released and had moved to Point Arena in 1864 and became successful. He had volunteered to help the Sheriff in the posse. Despite the fact that he had been deputized and had fired in self-defense the jury returned a verdict of guilty!

His attorney immediately filed a motion for a new trial. His second trial was finally held in April, 1869, and the verdict was not guilty and he was released.[101]

So what became of Calvin Stewart? He became a wealthy, well-known businessman in Mendocino. He and James Hunter erected a saw-mill in Mill Creek 1875 and by 1880 Stewart and Hunter were listed among the wealthiest men in Mendocino.

Murders in Mendocino

Calvin married Julia Francis Cooper on Nov 18, 1877 in Mendocino. When C.R. Johnson joined Hunter and Stewart, their company was renamed the Union Lumber Company.

The Union Lumber Company moved to the old MacPherson mill site in Fort Bragg, with plenty of land for a plant and a harbor where boats could load alongside a wharf. The new Fort Bragg mill commenced operations November 16, 1885 and the town of Fort Bragg was incorporated in 1889.

8 - Calvin Stewart

For the next 100 years Fort Bragg was essentially a company town for Union Lumber which pioneered enlightened conservation policies, established a reforestation project, and provided continuous employment for generations of local men. Mill workers could buy lots of 100 x 150' for $100. By 1965, over 27% of the county's tax revenue came from Union Lumber.

In 1969 Union Lumber was sold to Boise Cascade, and in 1973 Boise Cascade was sold to Georgia Pacific. The mill closed in 2002.

Calvin Stewart was also a founder of the Fort Bragg Railroad Company in 1885 and an original principal of the Bank of Fort Bragg in 1891. He became a county supervisor and later moved to Petrolia, Humboldt County where he died on 30 Nov 1938, at the age of 95. He was survived by 4 sons and 3 daughters.[102]

John Ketchapaw - 1868

On the 20th of March, 1868, Harrison Standley, the father of future Sheriff Doc Standley, shot and killed a man named John Ketchapaw near Hopland, in Sanel Valley, south of Ukiah.

Harrison Standley's testimony said that as he rode towards John Ketchapaw and got within four feet of him, he had his hand on the horn of the saddle and no gun in his hand. Standley claimed he called out, "John, stop; I want to see you a minute." Rather than stopping, Ketchapaw pushed back his coat with his left hand and pulled his revolver with his right hand. Standley then drew his own revolver, cocking it as he drew. Ketchapaw's horse ran and Standley chased him. They ran by Wash Higgins on his horse. Standley said that when he saw Higgins, he took his eyes off Ketchapaw and said to Wash, "Excuse me Wash, I am not shooting at you." He looked back to see Ketchapaw point and fire his revolver at him. Standley then kicked his horse towards John Ketchapaw and they both went around the barn.[103] Apparently this unlikely explanation was believed instead of the witness account of Wash Higgins.

George Washington Higgins, eye witness to the shooting gave a statement that, on the day of the shooting, Standley met Ketchapaw and Higgins on the road coming towards Sanel. When he came within about six feet of them, Standley drew his pistol and pointed it at the head of John Ketchapaw, and said to him, "Johnny, just a word", repeated it once or twice, then fired his pistol. Higgins claimed that Ketchapaw dodged down on his horse and galloped by Higgins with Standley chasing him. In all five shots were fired, two by Ketchapaw who fell from his horse and soon died.

The jury decided the shooting was in self-defense, and Harrison Standley was found 'not guilty'. Nothing is known of John Ketchapaw.

Harrison Standley

Harrison Standley was an old pioneer in the Mendocino area, arriving about 1853. He was born in East Tennessee on 15 May 1814 and moved first to Missouri. He arrived in California in 1852, went back to Missouri and then returned to California gain crossing the plains with his family. He stayed in Petaluma until 1858 when he went to Ukiah. There he established the first general store in town. He built the first hotel, the Ukiah House, in 1859 and traded it for the Fountain House Ranch in Nov 1860.

Fountain House Ranch was located on the road from Ukiah to Cloverdale, south of Hopland and contained 1970 acres of grazing land for sheep, cattle and horses. He also became the first postmaster.

He died in 1886 at the age of 72. The ranch was sold after his death for $12,120 to Mrs. Cooper of Santa Rosa.

9 - Harrison Standley

He had married in 1836 and had 9 living children. These were hardy people. Harrison's wife, Elizabeth Gladde (Shelton) Standley, of North Carolina was still spry at 89 years old when, in 1903, she traveled overland and slept out in the woods at night on a visit to Harrison, Jr. She was reported as "chipper as a girl of 16". She was the mother of 15 children, 6 of whom died in infancy. She died in 1909 at the age of 96 and was buried beside her husband in Ukiah Cemetery.[104]

Impulse

Lazare Landecker – 1879

The city of Ukiah was thrown into great excitement on the morning of April 3, 1879, by the announcement that Mr. Lazare 'Louis' Landecker, the new partner in the downtown store recently re-named Marks and Landecker, had been stabbed to death by Elias Marks.

Louis was a nephew of Abraham Blochman and had worked for many years for Blochman and Cerf, a well-known general merchandise store in San Luis Obispo where he became a $1/4^{th}$ owner. His sister was married to Moses Cerf, the other partner of the store. His wife, Alice (Hirsch) was the sister of Ernest Cerf's wife. All were from well-known prominent Jewish families.

10 - The Landeckers

After twenty years with Blochman and Cerf, Louis decided to go out on his own and purchased a partnership in the B. Marks Store in Ukiah. That store was owned by well-known retailer, B. Marks and his nephew Abraham Marks who was the managing partner.

B. Marks had started a store in Santa Rosa in the late 1850's and expanded, opening other stores in different locations. He helped Abraham Marks open the Ukiah store, and retained part ownership. When Abraham sold his managing interest to Louis Landecker, Louis became the new managing partner of the store, now renamed B. Marks and Landecker, on the corner of State and Perkins Street in Ukiah.

Abraham Marks younger brother, Elias Marks, born in Poland about 1845, was known to be a mentally deficient and emotionally unstable young man. Abe had employed him as a general handyman at the store, but Louis had found him defiant and rude and had discharged him the day before the murder.

Murders in Mendocino

Louis went to work about 7:30 that morning and found 25 year old Elias Marks sweeping the floor. Since Elias had been dismissed the day before, Louis told him his services were not wanted anymore and to get his wardrobe and leave, remarking that "when he was a boy, he left in a minute when a man told him he was no longer wanted." Elias became defiant and said he'd stay until his uncle, B. Marks, came to tell him to go. Louis replied that he was the store manager now and that if Elias didn't leave he would call the Marshall. A witness then heard Louis say, "You put your hand in your pocket to me?" Then he heard "Oh! Oh! Oh!" The witness, Mr. Hocker, a clerk in the store, walked around the counter and saw Louis staggering and Elias with a knife in his hand. Hocker went up to Elias and quietly told him to give him the knife, which Elias did, saying "I have no trouble with you." As Hocker took the knife, Louis fell to the floor. Hocker ran to the door calling out for a doctor and help. The Sheriff took possession of the 5" knife that had been on sale in the store.

C. H. Ackerman, another witness, was at his own shop nearby when he heard Hocker yell for help. He immediately ran over and found Louis on the floor and Elias holding a pair of pants. Hocker, standing on the other side of the counter, wordlessly showed him the knife. Ackerman got water to bathe Louis's head but realized he was bleeding heavily and quickly left to get B. Marks. By the time they returned, Louis Landeker was dead.

Elias Marks said at his trial that he had come in at 6 as usual. Louis had arrived and come over to him where he was folding and displaying pants and told him to leave. Elias told Louis to "wait until B Marks came in and if he said so, he'd leave". He claimed that Louis had slapped him and kicked him three times before he grabbed a knife and stabbed him. The other employee disputed this, saying he heard no such altercation. Louis had a wound on the left side of his head just above the ear another wound in his scalp about 3" long and a fatal wound in his abdomen.

Alice Landecker had only recently moved to Ukiah and knew no one there. Louis's brother, William, rushed to Ukiah, and brought Alice and the 6 children, aged 1 to 8, back to their former home in San Luis Obispo where they had the support of many friends. Louis was well known there, having held several public positions.[105] At his funeral there was a large procession with nearly 1000 people walking and almost 100 carriages. Burial ceremonies were performed by both the Jewish rabbi and the Masonic fraternity. The city had never seen such a large turnout, showing the high regard in which he was held.[106]

Just five months after Louis's death, Alice had to bury her youngest child Jacob, just 1 year old, beside his father and sister when he died of diphtheria. She moved from San Luis Obispo to San Francisco with her children, Rachel, Mark, Harriet, Fannie and Pauline. Moses and Ernest Cerf were named as co-guardians of the children. Alice was the sole heir to their property in San Luis Obispo totaling about $30,500, not including the value of his partnerships in both stores. Tragedy struck this family again when Louis's brother, William B. Landecker, hung himself in 1894 after losing a fortune in speculation.

Louis was enlightened for the time and had started a journal for his wife to teach her how to make business decisions. He wanted his children to become entirely self-sufficient, both girls and boys.[107] His will stipulated that each daughter at the age of 18 be emancipated from her guardian and receive her portion of his estate. His sons were to receive their inheritances at the age of 21.

Elias Marks

Elias Marks was found guilty of murder in the second degree. Two days later he was sentenced to hard labor in the State prison for the term of twelve years. When he arrived at prison he refused to eat for 7 days.[108] He was conditionally pardoned and discharged on 10 April 1883, but was returned two days later for violating conditions of his parole.

He was finally discharged on 24 April 1887. He apparently moved to Los Angeles and died there in 1892.[109]

James Harvey Carter – 1889

Jim Carter was born in Virginia about 1842. His wife Elizabeth (Marshall) Carter was born in Missouri. His wife had died and he and his children settled in Potter Valley about 1886. He boarded his 15 year old daughter, Vienna, in town with the Lownes family who had no children. Centerville held an annual Christmas Ball but Mr. Carter had refused permission for Vienna to go. The Lownes attended and brought Vienna with them. Mr. Carter heard that his daughter had been at the dance and angrily confronted his daughter and Mrs. Lownes on the street in Centerville. He loudly chided her for taking his daughter to the dance against his wishes and ordered Vienna to pack her belongings and return to his house immediately. Mrs. Lownes loudly claimed there was money owed for Vienna's board. Carter walked towards the store of T. J. Compton to get money, followed by the highly agitated Mrs. Lownes. In front of the store, Mrs. Lownes slapped Jim Carter in the face and he grabbed her wrist and told her to go home and mind her own business. Furious, Mrs. Lownes went to find her husband, who had not seen the quarrel, and told him that Carter had slapped her. They returned to the store and Frank confronted Jim Carter, demanding to know why he had struck his wife. Mr. Carter denied he had struck her and said that she had actually slapped him, but Lownes pulled out a pistol and, with the exclamation "No --- --- --- can strike my wife!" shot Jim Carter. Lownes and his wife immediately left and he rode to Ukiah to surrender. Carter died at the store about 20 minutes after he was shot.

According to his obituary, Carter was considered a man of unquestioned integrity and veracity and his death left his orphaned children in poor circumstances. Feelings ran high in town over this killing. Most agreed that Mrs. Lownes had started the argument by going against Carter's wishes, then slapped him and lied about it, provoking her husband to shoot. She was greatly disliked by the townspeople.

Impulse

Franklin Pierce Lownes

Frank Lownes was charged with Jim Carter's murder and held without bail. Mrs. Lownes was also arrested but made the $5000 bail and was released pending trial.[110] Frank Lownes was convicted of murder in the 2nd degree and sentenced to 21 years.[111] He was a 37 year old farmer who had never been in trouble before he was sent to San Quentin. Frank was released on March 16, 1903, after serving 13 years of his sentence, and returned to Mendocino.

Luzena V. (Scott) Murie had received the final decree of divorce from her first husband Thomas Murie in Feb 1887. She promptly married Frank Lownes the following October in Mendocino.[112] Luzena divorced Frank the year after his release from prison in Feb 1904.[113] Her grounds for divorce were that he had committed a felony. Rather ironic, since she waited 15 years to divorce him, especially since she was the direct cause of the murder he committed. In her divorce, she asked to resume her maiden name of Scott.[114] She left town and was not heard from again.

11 - Frank Lownes

After his release, Frank Lownes lived a quiet productive life. In 1916, he applied for legal guardianship of a niece who had been abandoned by her parents, and was granted guardianship. He put Nellie under the care of his sister and paid for her upkeep and schooling for many years.

Frank married Elizabeth Shelton in 1923. His happiness was brief. Franklin Pierce Lownes died three years later on 21 Feb 1926 in Ukiah. His widow, Mrs. Elizabeth (Shelton) Lownes and a sister, Mrs. William Hopper both of Potter Valley survived him. He never had children of his own. At the time of his death, he was much esteemed by all who knew him and the sympathy of the entire valley went out to his bereaved relatives.[115]

Carter Children

Several of the older children had been married before the murder of their father in 1889 so the younger children moved in with their married siblings.

Annie Carter had married John Freeman in 1879.

Margaret Jane married James Dunbar Scott in 1880. She had 4 children by 1889 and was pregnant with another when her father was killed.

Mary Alice married Thomas Willard Scott in 1883, James Sherman Hunter in 1890 and John T. Keenan in 1907.

James Harvey Jr. married Addie Hubbard about 1895

Richard Harrison married Etta Jane Hubbard in 1895.

Vienna married John Green Hardwick in 1891

John was called Jack.

Ida May married Enoch Jackson Lane in 1895.

William Henry married Dolly May Redfield in 1902 and Mary Lena Oakes in 1911.

Wardie Ellen married Daniel C Groscup in 1896 in Mendocino. She lived in Longvale.

Vienna, the daughter who had defied her father to attend the Christmas Dance, married John Green Hardwick, 25 years her senior, about a year after her father's murder on 11 Jan 1891 in Mendocino.[116] She and John had 6 children before she died in 1903 at the age of 29 in Mendocino, possibly in childbirth.

Her husband died in 1916 at the age of 66. Both are buried in Little Lakes Cemetery in Willets along with his parents, and two of John and Vienna's children, Laura and Reuben who also died young.[117]

Garrett Fitzgerald – 1889

Garrett Fitzgerald was driving about 200 head of cattle across Andrew Clark's land with his son Thomas (19), stepson William Kelly (14) and another man. Clark's cattle were grazing on the same range and Clark and another man angrily came up in an effort to prevent the two herds from mingling. Clark had previously denied permission to Fitzgerald to drive his cattle across his land and he was furious at this blatant provocation. It was hard to keep the cattle separated and more work would be needed to cut out those that mingled. Clark and Fitzgerald argued. Both were on horseback but Clark was on a better horse and had a Winchester rifle. Fitzgerald had a stick which he was using to drive his cattle. Clark shot, killing Garrett Fitzgerald on 11 June 1889.

Fitzgerald was born in Kerry, Ireland in about 1838 and was in Round Valley by 1866. He and his wife, Mary, were both listed as stock raisers (oddly, as most women at the time were listed as keeping house). At the time of his death he owned 1500 head of sheep, 200 head of cattle, 50 horses and mules and some real estate.[118] He is buried in Valley View Cemetery, Covelo. His wife Mary later re-married to William Stuart in 1909.[119] They divorced in 1926.[120]

Andrew Clark

Clark claimed that Fitzgerald advanced on him 3 times, aggressively brandishing his stick, and that he had retreated each time. At the 3rd approach, Clark drew his rifle and ordered Fitzgerald to stop. Witnesses agreed that both men were swearing at each other. Fitzgerald ordered his stepson to get his pistol but he refused. On Fitzgerald's 3rd advance, he attempted to strike Clark with the stick but missed, hitting Clark's horse instead. When he raised the stick to strike again, Clark shot him. Clark said Fitzgerald had a grudge against him because Clark had leased land that Fitzgerald had used for free in prior years. He claimed

Murders in Mendocino

Fitzgerald was trying to provoke a confrontation and trying to intimidate him into leaving the pastureland.

The prosecution claimed that a lack of powder burns on the deceased clothing indicated that they were not in close proximity as Clark had claimed, and that Clark was not being attacked.[121] Andrew B. Clark was convicted of murder in the 2nd degree. He was born about 1834 in New York so was about 55 when he went to prison. He was relatively new to California at the time of the murder. His prison record says he was discharged on 25 Aug 1890 after only 1 year of his sentence.[122] After his release, Andrew and his wife Martha moved to Siskiyou where they lived with their daughter Mattie and her husband, farmer Thomas Robinson and their family.

In August 1900, about 10 years after the shooting, Andrew Clark was committed to the California State Hospital, a mental institution. Hospital notes claimed that he had been kicked by a horse in 1872, 17 years before the murder, and his mind was affected for about 18 months after that incident. He apparently had periodic bouts of rage for years afterward. About June of 1900 he began exhibiting signs of being homicidal. He was also suffering from dementia and believed someone had stolen his horses and frequently threatened to kill the thieves. He also claimed that an Indian told him where a quartz mine was located on Squaw Creek and he was frequently found wandering around there looking for this mine, acting irrational and violent. He died at the State Hospital for the Insane on 17 April 1901 of apoplexy. His wife Martha Clark of Wanncastle, Siskiyou was noted as next of kin.

Impulse

Chapter 7 - Kidnapping

James Valentine Crowey - 1872

The headline read, "On Thursday last Joseph Gschwend, of Anderson Valley, together with his family, among whom was a daughter aged 16 or 17 years, started for Texas. After travelling a short distance their wagon was overtaken by two young men, one named William Addington (sic – Edington) and the other George Cleveland, who managed to abduct the Gschwend daughter and bring her back to Anderson Valley, it is said, for the purpose of marrying Addington. The affair created a lot of excitement in the valley. The next Sunday night Cleveland was approached by a young man named James Crowey, a resident of Napa and a distant relative of Miss Gschwend. Cleveland immediately raised his pistol and fired, killing Crowey almost instantly. Witnesses said that Crowey approached Cleveland with a pistol drawn, others said he was unarmed. Cleveland is to be brought to Ukiah tomorrow by Constable Goss, who has a warrant for his arrest. Crowey was the son of a wealthy and respectable citizen of Napa. Cleveland is the son of Jasper Cleveland who owns a flouring mill in Coyote Valley and is one of our most respected citizens."[123]

The Mendocino Democrat of Dec 19th, 1872 confirmed that 2 young men had abducted a young girl from her parents and subsequently got into a quarrel outside a house and that James Crowey, hearing the dispute had stepped out to ask what the matter was. He was immediately shot, the ball entering near the mouth and exiting at the base of the skull, causing instant death. It was believed that Crowey was not connected with the dispute or the girl's abduction. In an apparent attempt to save the reputation of Christine Gschwend, her name was not mentioned in this article, and the abduction was never mentioned again.

The Crowey boys were infamous for drinking and rowdy behavior. A few months before his death, James had shot off his own nose while trying to shoot his brother-in-law and business partner, Peter Hogan.

Kidnapping

William Riley Edington

John F. Edington and his brother Luke T. Edington, their sister Jane and her husband George Washington 'Wash' Crowey came from Tennessee. John and Luke Edington's families originally settled on a farm adjacent to the Gschwend's in Anderson Valley but soon moved to Napa where George and Jane (Edington) Crowey had located. William was Luke's son. His aunt, Jane and George Crowey were the parents of the murdered boy, James Crowey, his cousin. The families all lived on the Crowey Place north of Napa.

William Edington was the black sheep of the family. He developed a serious drinking problem. In 1870, a few years before the kidnapping, he got drunk and fired his pistol in his parent's house. The shot hit his 20 year old sister Martha in the shoulder.[124] In 1871 he was arrested in Napa for being drunk and disorderly. Apparently the family had enough and, shortly after this event, he moved back to Mendocino where he came up with his crazy plan to kidnap Christine Gschwend and convinced his friend George Cleveland to help.[125] William was released without charges in the killing of Crowey on the 8th of March 1873. He was never prosecuted for the kidnapping that started this series of events.

William Edington died on 27 Dec 1875 at the age of 33 in Mendocino. There was no notice of his death in the Mendocino or Sonoma County papers, highly unusual for such a prominent family, especially one that had been involved in a recent murder scandal, implying his death was perhaps a suicide. Another clue supporting suicide is the fact that he is buried in Evergreen Cemetery in Booneville, the only Edington buried there.[126] The family did not bring his body to Napa where other family members lived and were buried.

The Edington family moved to Oregon in 1884 where his parents are buried.

Note: A cousin, William Riley Edington (34), died on 13 Aug 1872 near Yountville. He was the son of Wade H. Edington and is not the same person.[127]

Murders in Mendocino

George William Cleveland

George Cleveland fired the shot that killed Jim Crowley. He was the son of William 'Jasper' and Tennessee (Owen) Cleveland who arrived in the Mendocino area about 1857. After the death of his wife in 1853, Jasper married Sarah Owen, a cousin of his 1st wife, and had 2 more children. Jasper Cleveland owned the Coyote grist-mill and was a prosperous farmer, well known in Coyote Valley. He supported his son during the trial and paid for his expensive legal defense. On Dec 26, 1872, George petitioned the court to reduce his bail from $10,000 because this was more than his family could get. The judge refused and he remained in jail until his trial.[128] He pled 'not guilty' to murder and the jury took 4 days to convict him of the lesser charge of manslaughter. He was sentenced to 15 years in prison at the age of 25 in 1874.[129] He was pardoned three years later, in June 1877, and returned to Mendocino.

Four months after his return, he became the 3rd husband of Rebecca (Potter) Gordon Hildreth, following the death of her 2nd husband.[130] This marriage brought him into another old and respected local family. Rebecca was the daughter of Nancy (Anderson) and John Potter and the sister of William Harrison Potter, founder of Potter Valley. Her uncle, William Anderson and his stepbrothers Henry and Isaac Beeson were among the earliest settlers of Anderson Valley in the early 1850s, and all were well acquainted with the Gschwends, Gaskills, Rectors, McGimseys and others. They also knew the Edingtons from their time in Mendocino before their move to Napa.

George and Rebecca Cleveland had a son, William Jasper, in 1879 in Mendocino but the couple divorced. He married his 2nd wife, Laura in 1888. George Cleveland later owned a saloon in Mendocino and lived on property adjacent to his father. He died in 1912.

Rebecca (Potter) Cleveland died in 1905 in Arizona and is buried in Potter Valley Cemetery in Mendocino.

Kidnapping

John Gschwend Family

So was Christine really kidnapped? Yes – it appears so. John Gschwend did file a legal complaint against William Edington and George Cleveland on Dec. 13, 1872 alleging that they had 'willfully and maliciously assaulted him with a pistol' apparently during the kidnapping attempt. On the back of the complaint it was noted that Edington was held on $500 bail.[131] There is no further record about a trial and it is presumed that charges were dropped to keep the abduction a secret to protect Christine's reputation.

12 - John Gschwend

John and Elizabeth (Guntley) Gschwend were among the earliest pioneers in the Anderson Valley. Both were from Switzerland and married in Madison County, IL. They arrived in Anderson Valley about 1855, with his brother, Joseph, and Elizabeth's brother, Andrew Guntley. Andy built a distillery which flourished until 1866 when temperance taxes closed it. John built the first split timber house in 1855 and the first sawmill in 1856.

They planted orchards and established fruit drying firms. John became a County Supervisor. He sold subscriptions to build a road from Boonville to Ukiah to take products to market. When money ran out, he completed the road himself and charged a toll until it was paid off. He built another road over Navarro ridge connecting Anderson Valley with the coast. Early in 1872, John was in debt from building these roads and made a court ordered agreement to turn over his sawmill, gristmill and saloon to J. B. Estes, with the profits to be paid to his creditors until all were paid. All were paid off by November 1872 and his property was returned to John shortly before this kidnapping incident.[132] John and Elizabeth had 11 children and he died in 1891 in Philo (originally named Christine after his daughter).

Christine Gschwend

Christine was the 2nd white child born in the Anderson Valley on Aug. 23, 1857. The old town of Christine, later renamed Philo, was named after her. She was 16 at the time of these events. No word was ever mentioned again about the abduction, and Christine did not marry Edington who died in 1875, possibly by his own hand.

She married James E. Reilly in 1877.[133] Following their marriage, the couple moved to Sonoma County. Her husband died in 1898. Christine lived to be 102 years, 5 months and 37 days old, dying in Santa Rosa on 20 Feb 1960. She outlived her siblings and all her children. She was survived by 4 grandchildren, 7 great grandchildren and 1 great grandchild and is buried in Evergreen Cemetery.

Christine grew up during the pioneering days of wild California. She survived a kidnapping that would have ruined her reputation and could have forced her into a marriage with her abductor. She endured the gossip of a murder scandal involving people she knew well. She saw the world change with the Mexican American War, California statehood, Indian Massacres, the Civil War and World Wars I and II. She lived through the advent of national railroads, cars, telephones and airplanes. What stories she must have told!

Chapter 8 - Jealousy

Murders in Mendocino

John Benton Owens – 1873

John William 'Bill' Burke, a wealthy resident of Mendocino County, shot and killed his brother-in-law John B. Owens (25) about 4 miles below Ukiah on the Cloverdale Road on Tuesday, Feb 22nd, 1873, the newspaper proclaimed, startling everyone.

Bill and his brother Huston Burke were early settlers in the area, well known, hard-working and respected. Originally from Missouri, they arrived in Mendocino in 1857 and purchased 974 acres of the Yokayo Rancho land grant from Caetano Juarez. Their ranch was south of Ukiah extending from Robinson Creek to Burke Hill. In 1872 they had just sold their first crop of hops, providing enough cash for Huston to buy Bill out for $20,000. That April, 34 year old Bill Burke married 20 year old Anabelle Florence Owens, daughter of 'Old Man' Owens, in Mendocino.[134] Old J. B., another early settler, had basically sold his daughter. On the day of the wedding Burke gave his new father-in-law $500 in gold.

Burke put aside his '*squaw*' wife just weeks before the marriage. Burke soon became insanely jealous of his pretty young wife, even accusing his own brother Huston of having an affair with her. She became pregnant and Bill tried to force her to agree that if the child resembled his brother, she would give the child to Hus and his Indian wife Lizzie. She indignantly refused.[135]

That cold Tuesday in February, her father, Old J. B. and her brother John came to Ukiah and visited the couple at the house of Bill's parents. Old J. B. and John planned to take Florence and the baby back to Anderson Valley with them to visit her mother. Old J. B. went to visit a neighbor and John was talking with his sister and her in-laws, Alex and Susan Burke, when Bill came in and belligerently told his parents he needed to speak in private with his wife and her brother.

Burke, who had been drinking, angrily confronted the two, shouting: "This thing has got to be settled right now. Didn't Florence tell you that this baby was not mine?" John replied that the child

Jealousy

certainly was Burke's! Burke drew a revolver and threatened to kill them both. Florence, in tears, said he "must be crazy to act in such a manner" and he replied that he "was neither crazy nor drunk and knew perfectly well what he was doing". John said "Bill, if I have ever done you any wrong, you are big enough to whip half a dozen men like me without using a pistol." [136] Burke kept ranting that the child wasn't his, insisting that Florence had been unfaithful and John knew it and was making a fool of him. He was waving his pistol at Florence, threatening to kill them both when John lunged for the pistol. They struggled together out the front door where the pistol fired without hitting anyone. John burnt his hand grabbing the barrel, threw it as far as he could and ran. By the time Burke found the pistol, John was too far away for a pistol shot, so Burke mounted his horse and chased him. He caught up with John along the road about 400 yards from the house, near the creek, and shot him point blank with both barrels of the shotgun holstered on his horse.

Florence, terrified by her husband's rage, saw her brother grab for the pistol and heard it fire as the men struggled outside. Not knowing if her brother was hurt and fearing that she would be shot, she quickly bundled up their 5 week old baby, and ran out the back door to the creek. We can feel her panic as she recounted staggering across the 50 foot wide, rushing creek, trying to hold her newborn baby dry above the waist high, icy water, terrified of slipping on the rolling rocky bottom, struggling against the current, her long heavy skirt dragging her down. On the other side, soaking wet, freezing, and half drowned, she ran to the Weller house. She was telling her father and Weller that Burke was going crazy when they all heard 2 shots. A few minutes later, Weller and Old J. B. found John by the creek, shot in the back of his head with another shot in his back. He lived 6 painful hours before dying.

John B. Owens Jr. was only 25 when he was shot, leaving a widow and young child. His widow, Hattie (Clay) Burke later married Isaac B. Crispin, a rancher in Manchester, and had 9 more children. His daughter Evelyn Leota Owens married John Peck, became a schoolteacher and died in Sonoma in 1953.

Murders in Mendocino

Owens Family

On July 8th, 1873, four months after the murder, Florence Burke and her baby were with her brother William when a stage coach capsized. They all received severe but not life threatening injuries.[137] In May of 1874, after her husband was sentenced to life in prison, Florence (Owens) Burke obtained a divorce. She apparently left the area and was never heard from again.

Her father, old James B. Owen, born about 1794 in Kentucky, had been with the first settlers and stockmen in Round Valley. He arrived about 1856 with his family, Dryden Laycock, the Asbills and others. Old J.B. became part of fraud to illegally acquire Reservation land by falsely swearing the land was swampy and unfit for crops led by Superintendent Hastings.

Seventy nine year old J. B. still lived near Ukiah with his wife Louisa when his son was killed. His children included: James, William, John Benton (murdered man), Joseph, Anabelle Florence (Mrs. Burke), Louisa, Jasper, and Owen.

James Huston Burke

The Burkes were all born in Missouri. In 1857 Hus and Bill bought 974 acres of the Yokayo rancho. Their parents, Alex and Susan (Shelton) Burke bought a ranch near his sons where he farmed and raised sheep with younger children. Bill and Florence were visiting his parents when he killed John.

13 - James Huston Burke

Huston was married to Lizzie, an Indian woman, with whom he had two children, son Greene Curtis and daughter Nellie. He put aside Lizzie and married a white woman named Amber Lard in 1889. They had no children and she divorced him in 1892. He married his 3rd wife Anna M. Wilming in 1912. Huston died in 1918 at the age of 83 and is buried in Ukiah Cemetery.

Lizzie Burke, who died in 1919, is buried there as well.

Jealousy

Bill Burke

Bill rode back to his parent's house and tore it apart, looking for Florence. Unable to find her, he jumped on his horse and fled. Sheriffs Chalfont and Standley and a 35 man posse tracked him.[138] They captured him 5 days later on the Round Valley Indian reservation near Huston's house. He had no gun and was cold and hungry.[139]

The citizens of Mendocino were furious. There had been 24 murders in Mendocino in the past 7 years and only 3 of the murderers had been lightly punished. Burke and 7 other accused murderers including George Cleveland were in jail. The sheriff quietly transferred them all to Santa Rosa before vigilantes could get to them.

14 - John 'Bill' Burke

Burke's trial was in Santa Rosa. He hired excellent attorneys who called doctors to testify that he had 'monomania', a mental illness. The jury didn't buy it. After deliberating 1 hour and 45 minutes, they returned a verdict of "murder in the 1st degree" and Burke was sentenced to life in prison in 1874.[140]

His father petitioned for a pardon in 1878. The petition contained the signatures of 900 citizens of Mendocino County and 400 from Sonoma County, including 9 of the jurors who tried the case and the prosecuting attorney. This plus an accident at San Quentin where his foot was crushed, got his term reduced to 10 years, plus time off for good behavior, and he was released.

Before the murder, Bill Burke had been worth about $20,000, but the expense of his trial left him practically penniless. He returned to Mendocino and married Elizabeth Erwin, a daughter of D. Erwin, in 1888 and had another child with her.[141] They lived in relative poverty for several years before separating.

He died in August 1896, alone in a cabin about 4 miles south of Ukiah, of blood poisoning from his crushed foot, which he had refused to have amputated.

Chapter 9 - Stealing Land

Murders in Mendocino

Mrs. Katherine Strong - 1874

Rensellaer G. and Katherine Strong bought a 200 acre farm in 1868, near Willits on Sherwood Ridge where they built a lovely home on the main road with extra rooms for occasional travelers. They didn't own much; 160 acres, 40 in crops, 18 head of horses, some cattle and hogs.

D. H. Geiger and James Alexander purchased the adjoining ranch. They owned about 1700 acres four miles from the Strong's and another 8000 acres three miles further with 2500 head of sheep. The pair offered to purchase the Strong Ranch but Strong declined as he and Kate were too old to start over elsewhere. So Geiger and Alexander framed George Strong for butchering their cow. They led a lynch mob to Strong's house and arrested him without a warrant. Fortunately, Strong escaped and got back to his ranch. He sent a message promising to surrender when the constable showed up with a proper warrant. That move saved his life, but with perjured testimony by Geiger and Alexander, he was sentenced to the State Prison for 5 years in 1873. While he was away, their feud with Mrs. Strong intensified.

Kate was determined to not be driven off her land. After her husband was sent to San Quentin, she managed the ranch alone. Geiger and Alexander did everything they could to drive her off, openly herding their stock onto her place. Katie, then 58 but appearing much younger, would mount a horse (often wearing men's clothes), grab her gun and with her dog, would drive their sheep off her ranch. She wrote several times asking Constable Hughes for protection and advice, complaining that the men were continually driving their sheep onto her land and trampling her crops. Alexander had drawn a pistol and threatened to shoot her, and had whipped her horse to make it bolt to cause an accident that would injure or kill her. One letter claimed that she had driven their sheep off her land 4 different times that day alone. She asked the Constable to arrest the men. The constable, cowed by the financial power of Alexander and Geiger, did nothing to help her.

Stealing Land

On Jan 30th, the last time Kate was seen alive, she asked Ed Saunders, the stage-driver, to bring her a bag of flour. The next day he brought it but she wasn't around. After four days without seeing her, he raised the alarm and her neighbors began looking and Deputy Sheriff Doc Standley was sent to investigate. The entire community was now thoroughly aroused, and several Indians were brought from Cahto to help track. One found a woman's hair comb and followed tracks showing that a horse with a load had been led along the rough trail. The horse's body was found in a deep ravine. It had been shot through the head and footprints indicated that 2 men had pushed the carcass over the edge before riding away. Looking into the canyon, he saw a pile of stones under a waterfall in the creek. He climbed down and spotted something white. A few of the rocks had fallen from the pile exposing a naked foot. It was Kate's body, found about 3 miles from her home on the 22nd of February, 1874. She was in her night dress, calico wrapper, shoes and stockings. She had been taken from her bed in the early morning hours in the middle of a snowstorm, placed on her horse and taken to a bluff where she was shot in the back left side of her head. Her body was then covered with large stones. Heavy water flow after a storm had dislodged the stones, partially revealing her body.

Geiger had tried to form a Vigilante Committee to drive the Strong's off their land, people knew of his feud with them and suspected his testimony had been perjured to send George to jail. He had joined the search party and tried to direct them to areas away from where the body was found.

To the credit of the people of Mendocino County, as soon as it was known that Mrs. Strong had been murdered, a petition was sent to the Governor to release her husband, signed by every man in the county who had an opportunity to do so. He was pardoned on March 17, 1874 and returned to his ranch.[142] There had been 5 murders in 15 months in Mendocino including Crowey, a stabbing in Pt Arena, John Owen, Henry Fairbanks and now Katie Strong. Folks were fed up.

Murders in Mendocino

David Henry Geiger

Sheriff Doc Standley and a deputy arrested Geiger and Alexander. They and the prisoners were surrounded about halfway to Ukiah by a lynch mob but were able to outride the mob in a race to town. As Doc remarked later, "seldom were two men more eager to get into jail". They had separate trials in Santa Rosa. Geiger boasted he would never serve time saying, "I have a million dollars back of me. I'm all right."

Geiger was tried first. At his trial, Catherine Strong's letters, describing Geiger driving their sheep onto her property and threatening her were entered into evidence. She had written to her husband how she planned to "put them under bonds" and sue them for damages of $25 per day for every day their sheep were on her property.

The bullets from his gun matched those in the head of Mrs. Strong and her hours. No other pistols of that pattern were known to be in the valley, and none used that special size of ammunition. The jury quickly returned a verdict of guilty, and he was sentenced to State prison for life. His case was appealed all the way to the Supreme Court which sustained his conviction. Three hours after his sentence was affirmed on May 26, 1875, Geiger used a saw and file to break out of the jail in Santa Rosa with another prisoner named John Jones. They were never caught.[143]

E M Bailey

Many years later, in 1898, a neighbor from Mendocino named E. M. Bailey went camping at Registration Flats in Yosemite. He had known Geiger in Mendocino. One evening an old man wandered down to his campsite. They chatted and, because Bailey could see there was another man watching, he didn't let on that he recognized Geiger. He left before other members of Bailey's party returned.

A few days later Bailey was out looking for his pack mules and came across a cave. No sooner had he entered the cave than the sharp click-click of two Winchesters stopped him. One man stepped forward and Bailey saw it was Geiger and a younger man. "Hello, Geiger" Bailey said, explaining that he was no threat. The two men talked about the old times. Geiger told Bailey that he had never left California. He had plenty of money and showed Bailey a menu from the first class Russ Hotel in San Francisco, dated 15 Aug 1897. He also had a program of a Wagner Opera which he had recently seen in a San Francisco Theatre. He was living well for a man on the lam. The cave was well equipped with provisions and clothes, nice beds, books, guns and other small luxuries. There was a stream running through it and smaller side caves with exits. The men could not be starved out and could see anyone coming from a good distance.

Geiger was well preserved for a man of 70. His long white hair and beard were neatly trimmed. He was dressed comfortably and bragged of his cleverness. Geiger asked Bailey to say nothing for 6 months. "By that time I'll be fixed again just as safely as I have been any time during the past 25 years and none of the old Mendocino people will be able to tumble on my old hiding place as you have done". Bailey kept his promise and didn't say a word for 6 months. Then he told his story to the newspapers.

Geiger was born in Virginia about 1825. He left behind his wife Elizabeth Jane Byrnes and 5 children. She and the children moved to Sonoma by 1880. That was the only time Geiger was recognized. He was never heard from or seen again.[144]

James Alexander

When Jim Alexander's trial started, Geiger was still in jail awaiting his appeal trial. Alexander's defense successfully claimed that no conspiracy could be proven between Geiger and Alexander. Without a conspiracy, the evidence used against Geiger could not be presented at Alexander's trial. He was acquitted.[145]

James Alexander had been born about 1812 in Louisiana. In 1890 he registered to vote in Long Ridge, Trinity County. But he moved back to Covelo where he registered to vote in 1892. He was still living there in 1898. He never married.

So, two more Mendocino murderers escaped justice.

Southard and McCoy – 1880

This killing took place at the South Fork of the Eel River, about twelve miles east of Usal, and about three miles from the Humboldt county line on July 2, 1880.

Marshall Howard had purchased and stocked a sheep ranch but part of his claim had been jumped by Frank Southard. Trying to avoid trouble, Howard bought Southard out with cash and a promissory note. Southard took the money and agreed to leave but he had scarcely gotten the money in his pocket when he moved right back onto Howard's land and began building a house. Shortly after this, Marshall Howard's house was burnt down and his life was threatened. Southard was trying to drive Marshall Howard out.

Marshall heard that Southard had bought building materials, so on Friday, July 1, 1880, Marshall went to where Southard was building a house - on the land that Howard had paid him to leave. Marshall Howard was angry and when he saw Southard on the top of the house nailing on roof shingles, Howard raised his gun and, without a word, shot him. Welburn McCoy was carrying lumber towards the house and, when he saw Southard get shot, he started to run, but Howard turned and shot him twice, fatally wounding him. McCoy lived long enough to make a statement.

Immediately after the shooting, Marshall rode off and found men to guard the scene and sent a telegram to Kibesillah for an officer to come take him into custody. Deputy Sheriff Banker responded and, on Tuesday, the 6th, he returned to Ukiah with Marshall Howard in custody. He was held to appear before the Grand Jury on a charge of manslaughter (an odd charge given that he had shot 2 unarmed men) and bail was set at $3,000, which was furnished with Messrs. Stewart, Banker, Frazier, and William Bonee.

There was no record of a trial. He probably jumped bail and left town.

Stealing Land

William Franklin Southard

There was a family connection in all this. Marshall Howard's wife, Nancy, was a daughter of Hiram Bonee, an early settler in Greenwood-Elk.

Hiram Bonee, a widower, had married his 2nd wife in 1876, several years before these shootings. She was Maria M. (Callen) Southard, mother of the Frank Southard that Marshall killed.[146] Marshall had paid Frank to leave his land to prevent a family feud. The William Bonee who put up Marshall's bail was his brother-in-law.

Frank Southard's probate papers listed the $1000 promissory note from Marshall Howard secured by Howard's 160 acres of land. The note was to be paid within 10 years from date of issue, Dec 6, 1879. William Franklin Southard never married. Hiram Bonee, his step-father and executor, noted that the issuer of the note, Marshall Howard, was then insolvent and absent from the county and the promissory note was now worth only $600. Southard's heirs were listed as Maria Southard Bonee, his mother, 57, Charles E Southard, a 14 year old brother and Mary E. Hunt, a sister aged 30.

Welburn McCoy

Welburn 'Webb' McCoy was a farmer from Tennessee who had been living in Blue Rock, Mendocino. In his household were Welburn (50), Julia (20), Spruce (4) and Henry (1) listed as Wilburn's sons. Julia and the boys were listed as ½ Indian. His claim was next to Marshall Howard's. There is no probate record for him. It is assumed that his claim was not proven, and that Julia and her children went to live on the reservation after his death.

Marshall Howard

Marshall Howard was born in 1848 in Illinois, son of Squire Dealing Howard known in California as "Square Dealing" Howard and Elizabeth Canfield. He was 32 at the time of this shooting. He, his father and his brother Orville came west with his uncle Joseph Howard and his family. They all settled in Cloverdale, Sonoma where he met and married his wife, Nancy Bonee.[147] By 1871 Marshall had moved to Cuffey's Cove in Mendocino, and in 1880 he and Nancy were living in Blue Rock where he was a 30 year old sheep rancher, Nancy was 27 and they had 3 sons named Henry (6), George (3) and Newell (1).

Marshall disappeared from records for several years. He apparently jumped bail and fled to Idaho where he was later found with an uncle and brother. He died in Grangeville, Idaho at the age of 87, never having married again.

Marshal and Nancy (Bonee) were divorced in April 1882, 2 years after these shootings. It is assumed from the speed with which she remarried that Howard had been gone since the shootings, as 3 months after the divorce was final, Nancy married James F. Murphy in Mendocino.[148] The Murphy family had no children.

Nancy married her 3rd husband, William J. Scott, in 1896 and moved to Oregon where she had 2 more children.[149] Nancy (Bonee) Howard Murphy Scott died in 1919 in Oregon.

Stealing Land

Gardner and Fitch Boys – 1880

The year of 1880 was certainly a bloody one for Mendocino. The inhabitants of Little Lake Valley were horrified on Saturday evening, July 10, 1880, to hear that two young boys, Marion W. Gardner (12) the son of John H. Gardner, Constable of Willits, and his stepson, Henry D. Fitch (11), son of the J.B. Fitch, Associate Editor of the Mendocino Beacon, had been found shot to death at Gardner's claim on Manzanita Flat about 4 miles from Little Lake.

Gardner ran stock there and the boys usually stayed out there during the summer. On the day the boys were murdered, John went over to check on them, as he did every few days. Not seeing the boys around the house, he went searching for them, and about three hundred yards from the house found their dead bodies lying close together in a pasture near the road. Harry was lying on his side. He had been shot near the right nipple. Marion was lying on his back with his arms crossed, the empty revolver clasped in his left hand and a bullet through his head. It was staged to give the impression of a murder suicide and the Coroner's Jury did originally give that verdict.[150] But, at the insistence of their fathers, a more diligent investigation found tracks of a man leading away from the bodies. They were followed back towards Little Lake.[151] A pool of blood was discovered by the house with a bloody handprint on the side of the house. Drops of blood led from there to the bodies. It was clear that one of the boys had been carried and placed into the position in which he was found and it was determined that both boys had been murdered.[152]

McCoy, a blacksmith from Pomo, was arrested but released. A reward of $500 was offered by the Governor.[153] It was believed that someone wanted Gardner's claim. The boys were stepbrothers and the best of friends. They had, just weeks before their deaths, been noted in the Mendocino Beacon for shooting the largest deer ever killed in that section, weighing 140 pounds when dressed.[154]

Sadly no one was ever caught for murdering them.

Murders in Mendocino

John H. Gardner

John H. Gardner, Marion's father, was the sheriff in Willits. Born about 1836 in Virginia, he registered to vote in Mendocino as early as 1867. In 1870 he and wife Margaret had 2 children, Thomas (5) and Marion (2), and he worked as a farmer. He and Margaret filed for divorce in 1873. Five years later, in 1877, John married Mrs. Lydia J. (Hockman) Fitch. Her son Henry D. Finch was the other murdered boy. Death came back for another of John and Lydia's children. Their son Frank died in 1882 at the age of 4.

Juan B. Fitch

Henry Fitch's father was a colorful figure with his own story. Juan Bautista Fitch was born in California about 1838. His father, Capt. Henry Delano Fitch, of Bedford, Massachusetts was a handsome 27 year old sea captain when he arrived in San Diego and fell madly in love with 16 year old Maria Antonio Natalia Elijah 'Josefa' Carrillo, daughter of Joaquin Carrillo, a soldier in the garrison at San Diego. Capt. Fitch was the first American settler in San Diego and spent 2 years converting to Catholicism and becoming a Mexican citizen in order to get approval from her family to marry. They finally did give their permission but their joyous wedding ceremony was abruptly interrupted by order of Governor Echeandia, who desired Josefa for himself. Gov. Echeandia was so infatuated with the lovely girl that he would sing under her window. Josefa never took him seriously, referring him to him as a "funny ugly little bantam rooster of a man". But he determined that if he couldn't have her, no one could.

When the wedding ceremony was interrupted that afternoon on Echeandia's orders, the couple decided to elope. Josefa's cousin, Pio Pico, delivered her to Captain Fitch's ship that night and they sailed for Valparaiso, Chile where they were married three months later. This elopement, of course, created a huge scandal throughout all of California and her father, although he had approved of the marriage, threatened to kill her for the dishonor she brought to her family. When the couple returned to San Diego over a year later, Josepha reconciled with her family but the Governor was still furious and out for revenge. He had the couple arrested for 'irregularities' in their Chilean marriage documents. An ecclesiastical tribunal ruled that the Fitch-Carrillo marriage was 'valid', though 'illegitimate' due to 'technicalities'. As penance Fitch was ordered to give a bell of at least 50 pounds to the church in Los Angeles. This he never did.

Captain Henry Delano Fitch and his beautiful wife Josefa received the 48,800 acre Rancho Sotoyome land grant near Healdsburg in 1841 with the help of his brother in law, Mariano Vallejo. After her beloved Capt. Fitch died in San Diego in 1849 at the age of 51, the 38 year old Josefa and their children moved to Rancho Sotoyome. The many children of this marriage made great alliances and became part of the history of early California. One great-great-grandson of the couple was Franklin Delano Roosevelt, who later became 32nd President of the United States. Sadly, Juan Bautista Fitch was not the strongest branch of this illustrious tree.

15 - Juan B. Fitch

Juan, father of the murdered boy, was the 8th child of this famous couple, born in San Diego, CA in 1838. In 1864 he married Lydia J. Hockman in Sonoma.[155] They had 3 children but divorced before 1870. He was living in San Luis Obispo as a single publisher and Lydia was living in Healdsburg with Alfred (5), Charles (3), and Henry (1). She then married Sheriff Gardiner and moved to Mendocino.

In 1868 J.B. Fitch, then editor of the Democratic Standard in Healdsburg, and J.B. Davis, an ex-editor and his wife's uncle, had an altercation. Davis had disassembled the printing press belonging to Fitch and had hidden a piece, making publication of the paper impossible. Outside parties convinced Davis to rebuild the press, but he then chased Fitch, threatening to kill him. Fitch was standing in front of a hotel when Davis saw him and pulled a pistol. Fitch pulled his own pistol and shot Davis just below the left eyeball. Surprisingly, he survived.[156] Since Davis had threatened and drawn first, Fitch was released.

In 1876, J.B. Fitch married Bessie Ford Campbell in Sonoma.[157] John and Bessie lived in Healdsburg and had a daughter, Anita. He became editor of the Lower Lake Bulletin newspaper in 1877.[158] And in June 1880 they moved to Mendocino when he became Associate Editor of the Beacon. Tragedy soon hit this family. His 11 year old son Henry was murdered in Mendocino on 12 July 1880 and his wife Bessie died of pneumonia on 18 March 1881 in Mendocino, leaving him with an 8 month old son, John Byron Campbell Fitch and 3 year old Anita.[159]

J.B. recovered quickly however, and on Feb. 9th, 1882 in Petaluma, where he was now with the Petaluma Courier and teaching Spanish, J.B. married Libbie Graham (his 3rd wife).[160] Juan was 45 and Libby was to turn 16 later that month. She lived in San Rafael with her widowed mother Augusta L. Graham. Eight months later, Libbie filed for divorce on October 18th, 1883 stating that J.B. had 'willfully deserted her' in August 1882, just 6 months after their wedding and had failed to support her. He was summoned to appear in court but never showed up so her divorce was granted by default on Feb 20th, 1885.

The lack of a divorce didn't stop J.B. He married Anita Gutierrez (his 4th wife) in Santa Barbara on Jan. 16th, 1884 three months after Libbie filed for divorce and well before it was finalized.[161] John and Anita moved to Arizona where he took over the Arizona Sentinel newspaper.[162] He and Anita had 4 children, Grover Cleveland in 1884, Henry in 1885, Effie in 1887 and Randolph, born in California in 1889. J.B. moved to Florence, AZ in 1889 to start the Florence Advance News as owner and editor. Anita returned to Santa Barbara, California with the children. Neither filed for divorce.

On 18 June 1890, John married 18 year old Josefa Shomeker (wife 5) in Tucson, AZ.[163] A few months after this marriage, J.B. published a death notice for "a wife of J.B. Fitch" (presumably Anita) who had "died in California", noting that "the couple had lived in Yuma, Arizona for nearly 2 years where J. B. worked for the Sentinel".[164] John and Josefa had a daughter Raquel in 1891. Josefa suddenly died in 1891 after less than a year of marriage.

On 26 Feb 1892, on the eve of yet another marriage, J.B. was accused of having bigamously married Josefa in Tucson, while he was still married to Anita in California.[165] The charges were sworn to by Florencio Ruiz and Angela Orci whose beautiful younger sister, Ysidra Flores, was to become Mrs. Fitch #6 the day after the warrant was sworn out. Fitch further infuriated the Flores family by claiming that he had no intention of marrying her!

Fitch claimed that Anita had remained in California in 1888 for her health and they were estranged. He said she refused any reconciliation. At the same time he claimed she was a prostitute! He said that her father had written, telling him Anita had died, to justify his publication of her death notice. J.B. swore he had believed her dead until a few days before his arrest when he was informed she was still alive. He had married his 5th wife, Josefa Shoemaker, on 19 June 1890. He noted that his wife in the bigamous marriage, Josefa, had already died so there was no current crime.[166] He insisted the charges were in retaliation for evidence he had given in a trial.[167] He was fined $100 and released after 3 months in jail.

In 1893 he was in his room with a woman when an unknown assailant shot him with a Winchester through the widow. One shot hit his hat, another hit his arm. The wound was not serious.[168]

In September 1894 he moved to El Paso, TX to practice law and publish a paper. Later that year, he married Maria Angelina de Jesus Figueroa (his 6th wife) in El Paso, TX. She too was much younger. Angelina and Juan had 3 children: John B Fitch Jr. who died in 1897 at the age of 2, Mary Evangelina (1896) and Henry F. (1899). Fitch was by then called 'Judge' Fitch. Everything seemed to be going well until Anita, the California Mrs. Fitch (4th wife), filed for divorce in February 1898. When the Constable in El Paso serving the divorce papers saw J. B. was married, he swore out a warrant for bigamy. John's employer at the Tribune, Mr. Lowe, put up $500 bail and J. B. asked to borrow $7 to pay court expenses. J.B. then jumped bail and fled across the bridge to Juarez, Mexico where he remained, becoming an official court interpreter for $60 per month.[169] He left behind his 6th wife and children. News articles soon made him a laughingstock. Heartbroken, Maria Angelina de Jesus Figueroa Fitch filed for divorce in 1899. Before their divorce was finalized, she committed suicide by drinking carbolic acid on 10 April 1901 in El Paso. She was only 25.[170] The children went to live with their maternal grandparents Francisco and Angelina Figueroa in Las Cruces.

Less than a month after Angelina committed suicide, John B. Fitch (55) married yet again to Margarita Marcos Hidalgo (21) (his 7th wife) in El Paso, Texas in May, 1901. Margarita was from Chihuahua, Mexico. Their first daughter, Modine, was born in 1902, and Anita was born in 1903 in Forney, Texas. John claimed to be a Lawyer and Teacher and gave his age as 49.[171]

The serial husband, J. B. Fitch died in 1905 in Terrell, Texas where he was the Associate Editor of the Times Star. He was survived by Margarita and their 2 small children whom he left destitute.[172]

Anita (Gutierrez) Fitch, his 2nd wife, never remarried and despite their divorce, called herself a widow after John's death. She died in 1938 in San Francisco at her daughter's home. She is buried at Holy Cross Catholic Cemetery in Colma, San Mateo, CA.[173]

Murder for Land

Chapter 10 - Rejection

Mrs. Reynolds – 1877

Mrs. Frances (Moore) Reynolds was a young 'grass widow' in Ukiah with two young children. According to news reports, Mrs. Reynolds had been quite ill and the town Marshal, Jerome Caneza, reportedly nursed her back to health. It would have been scandalous for a single man to have nursed her at her home without a chaperone, so this news account raises several questions.

Jerome Caneza had repeatedly asked Mrs. Reynolds to marry him and, when she refused, he became furious and threatened to kill her. She believed he would, and could get away with it because he was a city Marshal. He frequently brought presents of shoes and gifts for her children. Not daring to offend the man, she reluctantly accepted the gifts, but he became so persistent she decided to leave town. She made arrangements to visit friends and start over in Lower Lake County and booked passage on the Ukiah-Lakeport stage. Caneza learned of her plans and tried to meet with her before she left town, but she refused to see him. Frightened and fleeing towards safety, she and her children boarded the stage on July 17, 1877.

About five miles east of Ukiah, Driver Ward pulled to a stop when they came upon Caneza, lying alongside the road groaning and covered with dust. Caneza said his horse had thrown him and asked to ride to the next house, claiming to be too badly injured to walk. He asked the only other passenger, to go look for his livery stable horse.

Ward let him aboard and started off but almost immediately heard Caneza say "This is what I got in here for!" Caneza grabbed Mrs. Reynolds by her hair, placed the pistol to her ear and immediately fired two balls into her head. She was sitting on the front seat with the driver, holding her baby in her arms. Mrs. Reynolds died instantly, collapsing onto the driver, her blood saturating his clothes and her baby.[174] As the horrified driver again hauled the horses to a stop, Caneza jumped off the stage, stepped to the side of the road, placed the pistol to his nose and fired again, falling dead.

Rejection

Moore Family

The Moore family arrived in CA about 1854 when Rebecca 'Frances' Moore was born. Her father, John, died in 1870 and she lived with her mother, Elizabeth, and siblings in Ukiah. She married William Reynolds in 1871 when she was 16 but William lived apart from her and was not located again in Mendocino County. It does not appear that they obtained a divorce so she would not have been free to marry Caneza even had she wanted to.

Frances's oldest sister Mary had married Bill Shields in 1865 and moved to Oregon, so was not in a position to help.

Her brother, Walter, was 21 and single, working as a printer in Ukiah when she was murdered. He later married Annie Dougherty in 1879 and moved to San Francisco.

Sister Mollie married to Tom J. Chase in 1874 and was living in Little Lake. She was pregnant with her son Walter. Frances was probably going to stay with them when she was killed.

Sister Luella was 17 and single. She married Sam Burns in 1880.

The youngest siblings, Lolla and William were living with her brother Wade Moore and his wife in Calpella in 1880.

It is not clear what happened to the Reynolds children after Frances was killed. They were not located again.

Jerome Bonaparte Caneza

Jerry Caneza, a native of Chile, was a naturalized citizen, registered to vote in Ukiah in 1869. He was appointed a City Marshall in Ukiah in 1873. Caneza had laid his plans well. He hired a horse, well-known to be difficult, from the livery stable, and made sure the stage driver saw him ride out of town on it, so his tale of being thrown would be believable. The horse was found by the helpful passenger, securely tied to a tree not far from where the tragedy occurred.[175]

At the time of the murder/suicide, he was 34 years old and a member of the Good Templars. He had always had a good reputation, and was considered an upstanding member of the community.

Andrew Jackson Shrum – 1878

On the evening of July 11, 1878, Andy Shrum heard a hello outside. He walked out to greet a visitor when he was shot and killed. He was, from all accounts, a quiet and inoffensive man living with his wife Susan Elizabeth (Helm) and 3 children on the east side of Round Valley near Covelo. It was soon revealed that Lizzie was having an affair with James Anthony. Jesse and James Anthony, and Lizzie Shrum were arrested for Andy's murder and indicted on 11 July 1878. By 1880 when they went to trial, the three were among 10 prisoners in Mendocino County jail awaiting trial on murder charges.

The Anthony Family

Jesse and James Anthony were the sons of Josiah and Mary Anthony. Their older sister Ellen Virginia Anthony married Wylackie John Wathen and Sylvester Palmer who appear later in this book.

James (30) knew he would be a suspect because of his affair with Lizzie, so he set himself up with a solid alibi out of town. Jesse actually did the shooting so, to convict James who had not been present, the prosecution needed to prove that James had conspired in the attack.

A witness named Brown testified that James had told him about the plan and was hoping the crime could be pinned on Albert Smith saying, "If we could convict anybody it would do away with the d—d noise and me and Jessie would be as much thought of as we were before we did it." Another witness, Frank Lownes, mentioned earlier in the book, testified to a conversation he had with Jesse in jail in which he discussed the improper relations between James and Lizzie.

This was sufficient to find James guilty of murder in the 1st degree and he was sentenced to life imprisonment in San Quentin. James' attorneys took an appeal to the Supreme Court where his conviction was upheld, but he was pardoned by the Governor on 2 Nov 1882, just 4 years after the murder. He returned to Mendocino, and married Alice Steinagle in Jan 1884. They had 4 children and lived in

Rejection

Mendocino until the late 1890's before moving to Lakeview, Oregon. He was an engineer.

Jesse Anthony actually fired the shot that killed Andy Shrum. He was tried first, but had a hung jury.[176] His 2nd trial ended in acquittal. Jesse married May Adaline Hughes in March 1884 but they divorced two years later in 1886. He moved to Chico, CA where he worked as an electrician.

Suzanna Elizabeth (Helm) Shrum

Suzanna Elizabeth 'Lizzy' (Helm) Shrum was the daughter of Shelby Weeden Helm of Missouri. It was never clear if she knew of the murder plan or not. She was released without trial as conspiracy with the Anthony brothers could not be proven.

Lizzie was appointed executrix of Andrew's estate. He left 120 acres of land worth about $3000 and personal property and stock worth about $1000. Lizzie (26) and her children William, Etta and a baby born in November 1878 were listed as heirs. His debts exceeded the value of their personal property which brought in only $900. Lizzie requested an allowance of $50/month for herself and her children, which was granted by the court. The ranch finally sold in Dec, 1879 for $1475 at auction. Lizzie and the children remained on the property until it was sold. She received nothing when all was finally discharged in July 1880.

She married Duncan Berry in December 1880 and apparently lived a repentant life thereafter. Duncan Berry, from Scotland, adopted the three Shrum children: William, Mary Etta and Nellie Cordelia. They had no children of their own. Lizzie and Duncan Berry managed the Chinese Mission School in Salinas, CA.[177] She became the District President of the WCTU (Women's Christian Temperance Union) and was active for many years in that organization.[178] Duncan Berry died in 1915 at the age of 76 and is buried in Pioneer Cemetery, Watsonville, CA.

Lizzie married her 3rd husband William T. Scott in 1919.[179] She died 3 years later on 25 Feb 1922 in Alameda, CA at the age of 59 and was buried with Duncan Berry in Pioneer Cemetery in Watsonville, CA.

Murders in Mendocino

David E. Shull – 1891

On May 29th 1891, Stonewall Jackson Roads shot and killed David E. Shull in Cuffey's Cove.

Rosa Thurston, a widow from Ireland, was about 50 at the time of these events. She owned a dry goods store and was raising 3 older children. They were becoming successful in their own ways. May was a 24 year old schoolteacher. Clara, 21, was also teaching school and George was 19 and studying to be a dentist. David Shull, a school principal in Cuffey's Cove also boarded at the Thurston home.

Against her mother's wishes, May had become engaged to Stoney J. Roads. Stoney was 25 and lived near Christine/Philo in the Anderson Valley. They had been engaged about 18 months when Stoney went to work in Bakersfield, hoping to save enough to purchase a home for them. May wrote him many affectionate letters and it was understood they would marry when he could afford a house.

One day, Stoney got a letter from May breaking off their engagement. Distraught, he quit his job and returned to Mendocino. The day he returned, May met him in Greenwood-Elk in the parlor of a friend. May told Stoney she had decided to end their engagement because of her mother's continuing objections, and despite his pleas, insisted she would not change her mind.

Stoney didn't take the news well. He angrily left but later waited for her at her school. After a brief angry conversation there, she went into the schoolhouse and locked the door until he finally left. Later that day he came to her house. May locked all the doors but he broke in and they argued again. He began choking her but came to his senses and left, saying he hadn't meant to hurt her, leaving May bruised and terrified.

Stoney Roads then went to find a gun. He went first to a neighbor's house to borrow a rifle, claiming he had seen a deer he wanted to shoot. They thought his behavior was odd and told him no gun was available. He then went to the next house where they did loan him a rifle. As he began walking back to the Thurston house with the gun, the woman from the first house told her son to run to May's to warn her.

Stoney, apparently trying to lure Schull to the house, asked another boy to take a message to Mr. Shull's school, saying that Mrs. Thurston had hurt her ankle and needed his help. When he got this message, Shull immediately rode to the Thurston house. May and her friend Mary Laakman were puzzled when he arrived as Mrs. Thurston wasn't home. May told him about the day's events, including the warning she had just gotten that that Roads was on his way there with a gun.

Just then May saw Roads coming down the dusty road with the rifle and insisted they should all run. May and Mary ran out the back door to escape to the neighbor's house. Mr. Shull remained in the house. Roads attempted to break in but all the doors were locked. He walked around to the back of the house and saw Shull pass an open doorway. He fired into the house, killing Shull. Realizing what he had done, he stole a horse and ran for the mountains.

16 - Stoney Roads

David E. Shull

The murdered man, 29 year old David Shull, was a well-respected, successful teacher recently arrived from Illinois. He was the principal of the school at Cuffey's Cove. Despite Stoney's irrational jealousy, Shull had no interest in May and was actually engaged to Eva McKerricher of Cleone. Their wedding was scheduled for the weekend after his death.[180] He was buried instead at Cleone on his wedding day.

His fiancée, Eva, many years later, married Joel Sheldon Cotton in 1899 in Mendocino.[181]

Stonewall Jackson Roads

Stoney surrendered to Constable Looney at Boonville on Sunday morning, June 7th and was brought to the Ukiah jail.[182] He was charged with murder, pre-meditated since Roads had gone to borrow a rifle from Mrs. Anderson before the shooting and had lured Mr. Shull to the house. Mary Laakman confirmed at the trial that she saw Roads at the Thurston house with the gun. She saw him go through the gate to the rear of the house as she and Mary ran to safety. Shortly thereafter, she heard a shot and saw Shull lying on Mrs. Thurston's back porch. Mrs. Thurston testified that she had not sprained her ankle and had not asked Shull to help her, proving that Roads deliberately lured Shull to the house.

Roads attorneys raised the defense of diminished capacity. They said that Roads mother was 'epileptic and feeble minded', her brother was an 'idiot', and her oldest son was an 'epileptic idiot'. They claimed that Roads had screaming spells in his sleep and was forced to sleep in a barn after he disturbed hotel guests. A number of people testified that he had diminished mental capacity and was subject to hollering fits. Despite this evidence of mental illness, he was found guilty and sentenced to life in San Quentin in 1892. He was released on parole in 1905.[183]

He moved to Cloverdale, Sonoma where he married a woman named Rena and worked as a farm laborer. He died in Sonoma in April 1930 and is buried in the Santa Rosa Odd Fellows Cemetery in Santa Rosa.[184]

May Lillian Thurston

May continued working as a teacher in Cuffey's Cove until 1892 when she married James Alexander McMaster. They and had 5 children and lived in Greenwood-Elk until her mother died in 1924. They then moved to Santa Rosa, where they owned a chicken farm.

May died in 1944 and is buried with James (1867-1943) in Cavalry Catholic Cemetery in Santa Rosa.

Rejection

Mrs. Julia Scott – 1892

Mrs. Julia (Thompson) Scott lived with four small children in a little house known as Perry's Photography Gallery at the edge of Greenwood-Elk. She was the daughter of Jacob and Caroline Thompson of Norway. She was well educated and of good upbringing. She married Edgar W. Scott in Mendocino on 24 Sept 1881.[185] They had 4 children before Edgar abandoned her to go 'north' in 1890, leaving his young family destitute. In 1891 she was allotted $40 from the county indigent fund.

A young Greenwood man, William H. Harris, became infatuated with Julia and repeatedly begged her to marry him. She steadfastly declined as she was still legally married to Edgar. One Thursday morning, on 9 June 1892, about 7 am, William Harris came to the Scott house and asked her daughter, Lena, to leave the room so he could discuss something with her mother. No sooner had Lena left than Harris pulled a gun and shot Julia twice. He then went into the yard, and turned the gun on himself, committing suicide.[186]

Dr. Reilly extracted one bullet from her thigh, but the other was lodged too close to her heart. Julia miraculously survived a long and difficult convalescence with the bullet still in place. Unable to work, she was granted $30 from the indigent fund in Ukiah.[187] And in April she was allotted another $80.[188]

Julia Scott remained in Greenwood with her younger children Oscar (1875) George A (1877) and Chester (1881). She married again to Arthur Edson on 11 June 1902 in San Francisco.[189] It was a 2nd marriage for both. Arthur Edson was a machinist from England. Arthur died in San Francisco in 1937. Julia died in Humboldt, CA in 1940.

Julia's first husband, Edgar W. Scott eventually died in the state insane asylum at Mendocino State Hospital in 1936. He is buried in Ukiah Cemetery.[190]

Daughter Lena Scott (20) married Joseph Rudd (20) son of Peter Rudd and Mary Sorenson of Norway, in Greenwood on July 4, 1907

Murders in Mendocino

with written consent of her father, so they apparently knew where Edgar was. Joseph and Lena Rudd lived in Delta, Shasta County in 1910. Julia and Lena were later noted as members of the Native Daughter's organization where Lena and her mother were mentioned in news articles. Julia and her 2nd husband Arthur Edson visited Lena and Joseph Rudd in Eureka in 1934. Joseph Rudd died in San Francisco on 14 Oct, 1952. Lena was listed as his next of kin.[191]

Son Oscar Benton Scott became a bartender. He divorced his wife Essie and at 37, he and daughter Lillian (2) moved in with Julia and Arthur Edson in Cuffey's Cove. They remained there for 10 years until after the 1930 census. Oscar died in Humboldt in 1964.

Rejection

Chapter 11 - Outlaws

Murders in Mendocino

Mendocino Outlaws

These ex-cons failed to commit the crime they planned for. Instead they committed a double murder and led Sheriff Doc Standley on the longest posse chase in Western history.

It all started when John F. Wheeler (26) and John Billings (29) robbed a stage in Oregon and both were sentenced to San Quentin. Wheeler learned dentistry in prison. When he got out he moved to the lawless boomtown of Bodie. There Wheeler soon was in trouble again for shooting a Mexican man and wounding his friends. Two weeks after that, he shot another man in an argument over a town lot. Wisely, Wheeler left town and set up a dental practice in Mendocino in August 1879. Wheeler was an intelligent, nice looking, married man, about 6' tall with a fair complexion, hazel eyes and light brown hair. He thrived in Mendocino and was known as 'Doc the Dentist'.[192]

Wheeler had met Hal E Brown (31) at San Quentin. Brown and friends Al Courtwright (44) and John Billings were all released in January and February of 1877.[193] Courtwright returned to Mendocino where he worked a claim in the woods. He was delighted to discover his friend, Doc Wheeler, in town. Upon his release, Hal Brown came to visit Doc in Mendocino and, looking for a new target, they decided to rob the Sheriff of the county tax receipts. Wheeler sent a letter to John Billings who was back in Bodie, telling him about the plan. "I have here in Mendocino a claim worth about $15,000. It can be worked in about two weeks if I have good men. The claim is the Sheriff of Mendocino. I have one good man with me. Come yourself and bring any one you know and can depend on."

Billings arrived in Mendocino from Bodie on September 10, 1879 and brought with him Sam Carr (43), another San Quentin inmate, and a young man named George Gaunce, son of a good family in Oakland who had not previously been in trouble.

Before the attempted robbery Brown, Billings, Carr and Gaunce all left town to avoid suspicion. Brown told folks he was going to Elk to take charge of property he had been left by a relative there. The other 3 men left with him.

All 4 of them actually went to Courtwright's small cabin in the woods, where they hunkered down for the next 3 weeks. The cabin was about 20 miles from Mendocino, east of Westport. Doc Wheeler bought guns, ammunition and provisions in town and met Courtwright in the woods giving him the equipment to take to his cabin.

Wheeler had told the men about the recent Vigilante killing of Elijah Frost and his two friends. They had been lynched the month before in Willets for stealing a saddle. He warned the men to never surrender. Planning seemed to be going well until he outlaws made a mistake by killing a steer belonging to Mendocino Lumber Company, to dry the meat to take on the run. Hs they shot a deer, they would not have been caught.

Constable Host accidentally discovered the buried guts of the butchered steer. He returned to town and reported it to Thomas Dollard and William Wright, employees of the Mendocino Lumber Company who owned the steer. The next day Holt, Dollard and Wright went to investigate. They followed the smell of smoke and soon came upon four men eating breakfast in a small camp. The stolen meat was hung to cure and their rifles were stacked by a tree. Their white hands and high-heeled boots showed they were not woodsmen. Host had no warrant and knew his small party wasn't strong enough to take the men, so the Constable said they were looking for a place to locate a tie camp, had a nice conversation and left.

The men returned to town, swore out a warrant and gathered a posse of seven men, again including Dollard and Wright. They returned the next day but found the camp deserted

Murders in Mendocino

Dollard and Wright – 1879

The group then followed the ridge for about a mile from the abandoned camp. They saw below them, in a rough ravine, the remains of another campfire. Wright and Yell slid down the steep hill and felt the still warm ashes. Wright had just yelled, "They must have stopped here last night!" when suddenly a volley of shots was fired. Wright immediately fell. Dollard was struck in the upper part of the thigh, but fired a shot in return. The outlaws fired rapidly, hitting Dollard twice more. He rolled down to the bottom of the ravine and crawled under a log in the creek.

Galbraith and the wounded Nichols jumped on their horses and galloped back to town for reinforcements. The other men were pinned down until rescue came. When another posse and a wagon team arrived at the ambush site, Dollard was dead and Wright dying. They all returned to town, giving up further pursuit for the day.

A public meeting was held and a 21 man Committee of Safety was organized. The respectable Doc Wheeler was appointed to the Committee. He warned it would be too dangerous to chase the outlaws themselves and they should wait for reinforcements. The Governor posted a $300 reward. Sheriff Donohoe arrived in town that evening with a posse. Unluckily for Wheeler, a posse men recognized the former convict and the Sheriff began to quietly investigate him.

Two separate posse groups left Mendocino on Wednesday evening. On Thursday evening a message was received that three outlaws had been seen on the prairie, back of Little River and had gotten breakfast and supper at the house of a settler that day.

Early the next week, Doc Wheeler was arrested in Mendocino. The clue that led to his arrest was a tin cup and frying-pan found at the outlaw's camp, identified as the same ones that Wheeler had bought. Tracks of a horse with a broken shoe, found near the camp, also matched a horse that he had rented from the local livery stable.[194]

Henry De Haven – 1879

In addition to the murders of Dollard and Wright, Doc Wheeler was implicated in the disappearance and death of Harry De Haven, another ex-con friend. In 1876, Doc and Henry De Haven had filed a patent on a new and improved Baggage Check. Both were in prison for robbery and were obviously intelligent. De Haven also looked Wheeler up when he was free.

De Haven and his gang, based near Gualala, committed many stage robberies on the lower coast. De Haven occasionally stayed at Courtwright's cabin with his San Quentin friends. One day, he stopped coming and someone remarked to Wheeler that De Haven hadn't been around for a while. Wheeler replied that they had 'probably seen the last of him, as he could not be relied upon.' The others believed that Wheeler had killed De Haven. It was almost certain that Wheeler was connected with De Haven's gang and he had probably killed De Haven in an argument over profits.[195] Many years later, a skull and a bag of jewelry were found near where Gaunce testified that Wheeler and De Haven had been seen together. De Haven was never seen again.

Doc Standley was invited to join the hunt. No one knew it would become the longest manhunt ever made by a California lawman. "Doc Standley found Carr cooking breakfast in Courtwright's cabin on 22 October and held him at rifle-point until the others bound him".[196] Carr was sick and without a weapon. He had been abandoned by his partners and, in revenge for this betrayal, he testified against them at their trials.

The three remaining outlaws were spotted near Dutch Charley's, between Cahto and Ten-mile River. Doc Standley and his posse rushed to the area and set up an ambush at Uncle Tommy Damien's cabin, waiting in vain for the outlaws to show up.

Murders in Mendocino

Al Courtwright

Al Courtwright, who owned the cabin in the woods where the men stayed, was also arrested. He gave full descriptions of the men and told what he knew in exchange for having his charges dropped. He was shot and killed by the Constable in Big River while his cohort, Brown, was on trial.

At Rattlesnake Creek, where it empties into the Eel River, Doc Standley found the tracks of 3 men heading downriver. The posse had followed these tracks a short distance when they heard a noise. Looking over the edge of a bluff, they saw three men on the riverbank deep below pick up their guns and run, leaving behind all their food, blankets, clothes and ammunition. When they got to the camp, Doc put on a pair of pants and a coat since his clothes had been badly torn.

Wanting the reward, Wylackie John and his gang formed a posse in Covelo. They cornered the outlaws in a deep gulch as it was getting dark. Wylackie John left part of the posse above the camp and the rest below, planning to close the trap at dawn. The clever outlaws escaped, creeping very close to the posse without being seen or heard.

Doc Standley and Sheriff Moore joined the Covelo Posse, and for 6 days tracked the men through the roughest country in California. They all climbed over Yolla Bolly Mountain in sleet and snow. By now the Covelo posse and their horses were near starvation so Standley and Moore sent them back, keeping Wylackie John and 4 other men. Sheriff Donohoe met them in the Yolla Bolly with fresh horses and food.

They tracked the outlaws over the 7000 foot high mountains to Petit John's Place, in Tehama County. Petit John knew the outlaws were likely to come by as his was the only place around. He too wanted the reward and had asked a neighbor to come help capture them. Unfortunately, the outlaws arrived before his neighbor did. John's wife made breakfast for the men, placing their plates all in a row on one side of the table. The outlaws came in and sat down, leaving their rifles sitting just outside the door. Petit John's wife then went to the barn, thinking John would kill them or be killed trying. The old man was willing but 1 against 3 was bad odds. He wisely didn't attempt to capture them alone and they left just ahead of the posse. Doc tracked them to an abandoned cabin. Unknown to the posse, the men were hidden just up the canyon. As Doc led a pack mule towards the canyon, Billings took aim but, before he could shoot, the mule balked and Standley turned back. The outlaws again slipped past the posse. On the 8th of November the outlaws were at Last Chance Hollow, west of Red Bluff. On the 10th, over 35 miles away, they crossed the Sacramento River above Red Bluff on a railroad bridge where the posse again lost their tracks. By then, broke and out of provisions, the posse returned to Ukiah. Mendocino County had spent a lot of money on this chase and the town believed the outlaws were long gone so the County Board decided not to spend any more money.

Doc Standley would not give up and found another $200 from the strained county funds. Donohoe went to Nevada for information. Standley went to San Quentin to see what he could learn from prison officials and Moore went to Oakland to see what he could learn about Gaunce. They learned that Brown had a brother-in-law, Fred Striker, living in the mountains at Nimshew, 15 miles northeast of Chico.

Standley and Moore took a stage to Helltown and walked 7 miles into Nimshew, arriving late on Dec 3. They heard that 3 strangers had been seen in town and that Fred Striker had recently bought a Winchester rifle. That night a man said he had seen Striker's son, riding towards McClellan's old cabin, about a mile from town, carrying a sack.

By the morning of December 5th, Standley and Moore were frustrated. Despite the reward, no one would join their posse. Finally, a stage driver named Messer agreed to join them and loaned them a Winchester rifle and a shotgun. Clarence A. White, in town from Mendocino, also agreed to help. He was well respected and a crack shot. These 4 men surrounded the cabin in the dark and waited through the freezing night.

John Billings – 1879

Shortly after dawn, John Billings came out of the cabin with a gun and an ax to chop wood for a breakfast fire. When he got about seven feet from the cabin, Standley shouted to throw down his gun. Instead, he ran back towards the cabin. Standley fired, hitting him in the shoulder. Gaunce and Brown dashed out the back door of the cabin and into the brush. Clarence White fired four shots at them as they ran. He then saw Billings aiming at him so he fired, striking Billings in the knee. Billings stumbled to the ground and fired again at White who shot him twice more, killing him.

A Coroner held an inquest on site and Sheriff Moore left to take Billing's body back to Ukiah.

George Gaunce

Night had fallen by now but Doc Standley and Clarence White followed the footprints of the 2 escaped outlaws by the light of a lantern. About 100 yards from the cabin, the tracks divided. One set of footprints, Gaunce's, went south-west down the creek, and the other went up the creek. They soon realized the person going up-creek was lame and slower so they went back and followed the faster man down Butte Creek almost into town where they lost the trail.

Doc and Clarence had now gone over twenty-four hours without sleep or food and it was 2 in the morning so they went to the hotel for the night. At breakfast, Doc heard that a local man had lost a buggy robe during the night. They searched the vacant cabin beside the buggy shed and found Gaunce. Cold, hungry and exhausted, he gave up.

Standley took Gaunce and caught up with Sheriff Moore near Chico where he gave him custody of Gaunce before returning to Nimshew.

George Gaunce was from a prominent family in Oakland and had never been in trouble before. He too was tried, convicted and sentenced to death. His appeal trial in Sonoma also found him guilty, but gave him life in prison. When he entered San Quentin in 1880 he was 29 years old. On 5 Dec 1890 the Governor shortened his term from life to 16 years. The appeal petition was signed by the 12 jurors who tried the original case, a number of members of the City Council of Oakland, James Tunstead the ex-Sheriff of Marin County, E.A. Shoemaker the superintendent of the North Pacific Coast Railroad, M.H. DeYoung, R.W. Hearst, and many other prominent citizens of Alameda, Marin and San Francisco.

There was a great outcry in Mendocino when, on 8 Dec 1890, Gaunce was pardoned and released from San Quentin.[197] George Gaunce went to live with his younger brother, Edwin and his family in Alameda, CA for several years. He worked as a door molder at Cal Door Company from the time of his release until his death. He later moved to his own place at 1700 10th St in Alameda. Then in 1911 he moved again to 1196 Peralta St., which is where he was living when he died. He apparently never married. George L Gaunce died at the age of 63 in 1915 in Alameda, CA.

Hal E Brown

Hal Brown was still running. Now Doc and White set off on 2 fresh horses. They spent the next 4 days tracking Brown, walking the horses through deep snow. Brown, on foot, had gone up Butte Creek into Concow valley where he walked due east, up the slope of the Sierras to the snow line. There he stayed the night with an Indian. He forded the north fork of the Feather River, staying at Last Chance and crossed French Creek to the Mountain House Hotel. He walked the main road to Bidwell's Bar then traveled cross country to Wyandotte before turning towards Rice's crossing, on the Yuba River and back to Bidwell's Bar again.

On the evening of the 10th, Doc Standley and Clarence White arrived at Bidwell's Bar and warned everybody to watch for Brown. Rather anticlimactically, later that day Clarence and Doc saw two men, George Thatcher and Thomas Moran, loading the exhausted, freezing outlaw into their wagon. The usually dapper Brown was wrapped in an old quilt and looked like a common tramp. Doc rode up to the wagon and said cheerily, *"Hello Hal"*. The outlaw replied, "God Damn you Standley, don't you ever quit? And give me back my coat – I'm freezing!"

Standley returned to Ukiah with Brown on December 14th where he was met by 300 cheering citizens. This ended one of the greatest man-hunting expeditions known. It had lasted more than 8 weeks, over 1000 freezing, snowy, mountainous miles, mostly on foot, with little food or sleep. Doc became quite a legend for this feat.

Hal Brown, was born in Missouri about 1830. He was an affable fellow and certainly had stamina. He had led Doc on the longest hunt known. At his trial on March 2, 1880 he was also convicted of murder and sentenced to hang. He appealed and while in jail waiting for his appeal trial in Sonoma, he saved the life of the Sheriff during an attempted jailbreak. He was again convicted and sentenced to death. But his death sentence was commuted to life in prison instead of death.[198]

He was released from San Quentin in 1910 at the age of 71 after serving 28 years. His relatives made an urgent plea that he should spend his remaining years in Texas, where he would seek relief from a '*dreaded malady*', probably tuberculosis. He went to live with a nephew, J.T. Brown in Chico, Texas.[199] J.T. Brown had moved from Chico, CA to Chico, TX about 1875 and opened a general store.

Brown presumably died there. His son worked as a blacksmith in Calistoga.

Doc John F. Wheeler – 1880

Meanwhile, Doc Wheeler was held in Ukiah for trial. On November 30th, a few days before Sheriff Doc Standley returned with Hal Brown, John Wheeler and James Anthony, who was in jail for the murder of Andy Shrum, escaped from jail. They went to a livery stable, stole two horses and fled, but were soon captured near Calpella.

Doc Wheeler's jury took only 2 hours to convict him of murder. At his sentencing hearing, Wheeler made an eloquent statement to the Judge, claiming that he had lived the life of a good citizen, been blackmailed by ex-cons who threatened him and his wife and that he had paid them off to keep them from revealing his past. He said that he would go to the gallows an innocent man. The Judge told him that, had he made his statement to the jury, it might have had some weight, but it was now too late. He was returned to jail to await hanging.

The next morning, Saturday morning May 15th, the city of Ukiah exploded with excitement when word went out that dentist Doc John Wheeler, the ringleader of the Mendocino Outlaws, had committed suicide. At about a quarter to ten, his wife went to see him. He was found unconscious and was taken to the Sheriff's office where 3 doctors tried to resuscitate him, even pumping his stomach. Despite their efforts, at 6:50 that night he died. He had been visited twice by his wife. On both occasions she showed great affection for him and appeared completely broken down with grief. In his cell, the Sheriff found two packages of letters, two bottles of chloral hydrate, a small satchel and a photograph of his wife. On the back of his wife's photograph were the words, "Whose little duckie is this?" His wife was not prosecuted despite the widely held belief that she had brought him the poison. Doc had dressed with great care and requested that he be buried just as found, with the picture of his wife upon his breast. His last wish was honored. So Doc Wheeler, leader of the Mendocino Outlaws, escaped the gallows. His wife, beloved "little ducky" remained unknown.

Chapter 12 - Framed

James Cox – 1884

On Wednesday the 15th of October, 1884 gossip was flying around Kibesilla that Jim Cox had abandoned his 2nd wife and children! This was not unexpected as Jim had abandoned 1st wife Lizzie and 4 children, leaving her for his pregnant mistress, Annie Kell, whom he married shortly before their child was born. Jim and Annie lived near the mouth of Ten-Mile River on Schemmerhorn Johnson's logging claim. Cox worked as a logger for Johnson, while Annie kept the house they all shared.

The day before his disappearance, Jim Cox went to the Company Store to collect $2 pay. The store didn't have change so the clerk, told him to come back the next day. He never returned. Several days later Annie came in and was asked about him. She said Jim had sold his team and wagon to Johnson and left her and 5 children destitute. No one doubted that Annie would swap men and it was easily believed that the unreliable Cox would shift the responsibility for his children to another man. This story held until, a week later, Annie got drunk and told her friend Emma Hitchens a secret. She claimed Johnson had killed Cox and she helped drag his body into the woods to hide it. When Emma sobered up, she told the story to the Sheriff, and Annie and Johnson were arrested. Annie showed the Sheriff where Cox's body was hidden. If she had not made her drunken boasts, they would never have been suspected.[200]

Jim and Lizzie (Frost) Cox

James Caspar Cox was the son of Rev. John Toliver Cox and his wife Mary Power, born in Texas about 1844. He had married Elizabeth A 'Lizzie' Frost in Sonoma in 1868 when she was 16 and he was 24. She was a member of the notorious Frost family of the Little Lake Shootout. They lived with Lizzie's father, Elijah Frost Sr. in Mendocino. Their first child was Florence born about 1870.

Framed

In 1872, several years after their marriage, Lizzie had a child named Clara, the result of an affair with Alonzo Luke Kingsbury, an older married man. Surprisingly, Cox agreed to adopt Clara, possibly after a pay-off from Kingsbury. Clara later married James Evans in 1889 and raised a family. She died in Mendocino in 1935.

Lizzie and Jim had 3 more children: William (1874), Elijah (1876) and Charles (1878). Lizzie and Jim's divorce was final in 1879 and Jim immediately married his pregnant girlfriend, Annie Elizabeth (Parks) Kell.[201] Lizzie married Claudius E. Ramey in 1881 but they quickly divorced because she was fooling around with her cousin Ben Frost who was killed in 1882. In 1883, she married again to Samuel Burgess. At the time of Jim's murder in 1884 at least three of Lizzie Cox's children were living with Jim and Annie instead of their mother. Not surprisingly, parentage of the Cox children soon became an issue.

Jim Cox was 35 when he was killed. The court prepared probate papers named only two sons as his heirs: William Henry Cox (9) staying with his uncle, William J. Cox, in Cahto, and Charles Archibald Cox (7), living at the home of Elijah Frost Sr. his grandfather in Willets. Florence (11) the oldest daughter and Elijah (8) were not named in the court papers. Clara was known as Kingsbury's daughter so was not included.

Annie Cox then claimed she was the only legal heir. Her mark on the document was witnessed by Sheriff Doc Standley, presumably because she was in jail for Jim's murder. Her petition listed only herself and her son, James Tolliver Cox (2) and named James' brothers John, William and Calvin Cox as his heirs. She omitted all his other children, implying that none were Jim's.

Despite this, the Cox children certainly believed that Florence was their sister. William's 1952 obituary noted that he was survived by Mrs. Florence Brown, a sister, of Santa Rose and a half-brother James Cox of Garberville. He named his daughter Florence.

Elijah died in 1947 in Washington State. His obit also noted he was survived by a sister Florence Stamer. He too named his daughter Florence.

Schemmerhorn Johnson

John Butler, known as 'Schemmerhorn' Johnson, was an older logger, reputed to work until he earned $400-$500 and then go on a bender. He was infatuated with young Annie Cox.

Annie and Johnson were tried separately. Annie testified against Johnson and was released without charges. She claimed Johnson had offered Cox $100 to clear out and leave Annie, the children and the team to him. Cox refused. She testified that Johnson was in the cabin while Cox was sitting outside, with his back to the door, when Johnson shot him in the back. As Cox lay dying, Johnson reloaded his gun and put another bullet in his brain. She admitted they then pulled the body into the woods and hastily concealed it under brush, making no attempt to bury it. She claimed she was afraid Johnson would kill her too.

Johnson, in his defense, claimed that Annie planned the whole crime because she wanted to live with another man, not him, and said that Annie had fired the actual shots that killed her husband. The jury believed Annie and Johnson were sentenced to hang in January 1885.[202] Annie immediately took up with another man and jumped his claim.

Johnson kept insisting he was innocent but had no money and few friends until Mrs. John S. Reed (Anna M. Morrison), wife of a wealthy man in Ukiah and cousin of Chief Justice Morrison, took an interest in his case. This well-known writer became convinced that Annie had killed Cox, set up the drunken confession so she could testify to get rid of her husband and be released without charges. She could not be re-tried because of double jeopardy. Mrs. Reed's reprieve petition had signatures of 6 of the original jurors, the prosecuting attorney, Sheriff Standley and about 300 other citizens. She presented her petition to Governor Stoneman,[203] who commuted Johnson's sentence to life in prison on the grounds that he had been "the tool of another person" in committing the crime. Johnson was by then a broken down man of 60 with a short time left to live.[204] He died in prison.

Framed

Elizabeth Ann (Parks) Kell Cox Breedon

When Cox left Lizzie Frost to marry Annie, they went to live with Schemmerhorn Johnson. They brought her daughter Alice Kell and soon had a baby, James Tolliver Cox in March 1881. They apparently were also caring for Cox's 3 youngest boys as Annie said she was left with 5 children and she only had 2 of her own.

Many people came to believe that Annie had killed Cox and set Johnson up. They said she had pretended to get drunk and talked about the murder on purpose, to get Johnson arrested, knowing she would be freed for giving evidence against him. Having gotten rid of her husband, this would put Johnson in prison so she could jump his claim and be free of both men. Who was this woman that people would believe such things about her?

Annie Parks married Charles M. Kell in March 1876 in Mendocino. Their daughter Alice Francis Kell was born in 1877 and the Kells filed for divorce in 1879. Three months after her divorce became final the pregnant Annie married James Cox in June 1880, bringing 4 year old Alice to live with her new husband. Annie soon had his son, James Tolliver Cox.

She did in fact move in with another man and jump Schemmerhorn Johnson's claim when he went to prison. Two years after Johnson was sentenced to death for killing her husband, Elizabeth Ann (Parks) Kell Cox (28) married William W. Breeden (29) in 1886 in Mendocino.

She died in Mendocino at the age of 37 on May 16, 1895. Her burial location is unknown.

Their son, James Tolliver Cox, died in 1958 and is buried in Garberville Cemetery, Humboldt, CA.

Chapter 13 - Vigilantes

Mr. and Mrs. Riche – 1890

The Campers Retreat, a roadside saloon owned by the Riche's, was having a quiet evening. Everyone in the area, including the law, had gone to Middletown for a "gala candidate's ball" that October 10th. Middletown was a stage stop and main town for several nearby quicksilver mines like the Bradford, the Bullion and the Great Western. There were only 3 people at the tavern that night, J.W. Riche and his wife and their bartender-bouncer, Fred Bennett. Mrs. Riche and Bennett were playing cards and Riche was watching when, about 9 pm, the door suddenly slammed open and a masked man entered, followed by 5-6 others, armed with shotguns, rifles and drawn pistols. Riche at first thought it was a robbery but then, recognizing one of the men and thinking it was a prank, laughingly slapped the man and said "You can't scare me!" The bullet that barely missed his head convinced him this was no prank.

Mrs. Riche ran to the man and grabbed his arm to keep him from shooting her husband. She ripped off his mask and he shot her in the side. She managed to pick up her husband's Winchester 44 but someone grabbed the rifle from her. The White Caps Vigilantes fired a last volley as they backed out of the saloon, hitting both Riches. Riche carried his wife to the bedroom as Fred Bennett raced for a doctor and raised the alarm in Middletown. Dr. Hartley immediately left the ball, followed by many others. During the assault, the ringleader, McGuire, was shot in the back by his own men and Doc Hartley found him dead on the Riche's porch.[205]

Mrs. Riche had been shot 5 times in the chest and side. She suffered for 4 days before dying on 15 Oct 1890 but was able to identify Henry Arcaro as one of the raiders.[206] Steven Riche had been shot in the side. He also made statements to the coroner's jury. There was great public sympathy for the Riche's and her funeral was the largest ever in Middletown.[207] Stephen Riche appeared to be recovering before he suddenly died of "apoplexy of the brain" before the trials began.

Vigilantes

J.W. Riche was also known as Stephen Thompson per probate records in Lake County and marriage records in England. He and his wife had married in Croydon, Surrey, England in 1878. They had become debtors and emigrated rather than face jail.[208] They had been in California since 1887 but by 1890 were barely eking out a living in Lake County at their saloon, Campers Retreat.[209] Mrs. Helen Matilda (Sherrington) Thompson/Riche (36) and her husband are buried in Lake County, CA. Mr. Rocca, Superintendent of the Great Western Mine was appointed executor of their estate and worked to settle their debts.[210]

Fred Bennett

Fred Bennett, the intended victim of the mob, was in Mendocino in 1894 and after that his life is unknown.

White Caps

The Lake County White Caps were part of a larger movement attempting to regulate manners and morals that had spread from Indiana to California.[211] All these members were well known in Middletown.

Arcaro, named by Mrs. Riche, confessed and implicated Thomas Martin, Charles Evens, Gus Lund, B. F. Staley, John Archer, C. E. Blackburn, Robert Cradwick, C. W. Osgood and a Frenchman named Bichard.[212] Most were employees at the Bradford Mines although Charles Osgood worked for Great Western.

The leaders of the White Caps were actually using the group to settle personal grudges. Fred Bennett had thrashed several of the men when they got rowdy at the Riche's bar. Blackburn had a conflict with Bennett over a mining claim and McGuire was mad at the Riches over their cows wandering into his pasture. Their personal grudges led to the plan for the White Cap Vigilantes to tar and feather Fred Bennet.

Ten men were arrested for the Riche's murders, and it was estimated that their trials would cost the county $15,000-$20,000, a huge sum in those days. The White Caps would figure in later episodes of the Range Wars.

Murders in Mendocino

Charles E. Blackburn

Charles Blackburn, a Civil War veteran, was the first to be tried. He was sentenced to 25 years in San Quentin. Almost immediately a petition was circulated to obtain his release by Dr. Corbett. Corbett approached an old friend, General Diamond, a well-respected Civil War Veteran who at first believed Corbett's story about the case. Upon learning more however, General Diamond had the Governor strike his name from the petition. Blackburn's fellow Civil War soldiers all considered him a disgrace to the uniform and refused to endorse the petition. Most people felt that Blackburn had been given a fair trial and should be thankful he was not given the death penalty.

In 1895 his 25 year sentence was commuted to 10 years and he was released.[213] When he was released, the prosecuting attorney wrote to the San Francisco Examiner expressing his outrage under the heading of 'Misplaced Mercy' writing: "Having prosecuted these, and knowing whereof I speak, I want to say that the murder of Mrs. Helen Riche by eleven Whitecaps at the Campers Retreat, was without exception, the most atrocious cowardly and unprovoked murder I have ever investigated in a practice of over 20 years. It is erroneous to state the crime was committed because the house conducted there by Riche and his wife was not approved of. The trouble arose from a chastisement which Blackburn received at the hands of one Bennett...."

After his release, Blackburn became construction manager for a factory built by The Women's Sewing Company in San Francisco. They were a charitable organization who provided employment to women who had families dependent upon them, offering fair wages to combat prevalent sweatshop conditions. He apparently completed the factory building successfully.

In 1914 Blackburn, then living in San Lorenzo, called a gathering of old Civil War veterans and all indicated their desire to re-enlist for service in Mexico. Nothing further was found of him.

Vigilantes

Charles Walter Osgood

Charles Osgood pled guilty and was sentenced to 12 years in 1891. He was a 30 year old mine engineer when he was incarcerated, married with 3 small children. He was released on 26 Nov 1898. After his release, he returned to mine engineering in Shoshone, Idaho in 1900. Sadly, his wife Melinda Annette (Farmer) Osgood died in childbirth 1906. Charles lived until 1946 and died in Seattle, WA at the age of 87.[214]

Robert Cradwick

Robert Cradwick pled guilty and was sentenced to 20 years. He was born in England about 1848 and was a 30 year old miner when he went to San Quentin. He was paroled on 27 Jan 1902.

B. F. Staley

B. F. Staley was the 4th and last sentenced and he also received 20 years.[215] He had originally come from New York and was a 37 year old miner. He was released on 20 July 1903.

Evans, Bichard, Archer and Arcaro

The cases against Evans, Bichard, Archer and Arcaro were dismissed for turning states evidence.

Martin and Lund

The cases against Thomas Martin and August Lund were dismissed on the grounds that they had only a slight part in the tragedy.

Most people felt these dismissals were actually given because the preceding trials had already cost the county too much money.

Chapter 14 - Stage Robberies

Murders in Mendocino

Buck Montgomery – 1892

A stage robbery took the life of Amos Buchanan 'Buck' Montgomery as he rode shotgun for Wells Fargo. Buck came to Ukiah with his family as a child. He had a dairy business near Ukiah and purchased the Elite Restaurant in Ukiah in 1891. He was an official shotgun messenger for Wells Fargo on the Weaverville-Redding Stage and became part owner of the stage line.

That day in May, 1892 the slow moving stage had just reached the top of a long grade when a man suddenly stepped from the trees wearing a red bandana mask. He ordered John Boyce to stop and ordered passenger, George Suhr, up top with the driver, to throw out the Wells Fargo boxes. Buck Montgomery, riding inside, fired at the bandit. The robber reflexively fired his shotgun full of buckshot at the stage, wounding the driver and Suhr. As Buck shot the first robber, two shots rang out from behind the stage where another robber was hidden. The horses, startled by the shots, took off running. Suhr, wounded in the legs, was able to catch the reins. Boyce, incapacitated but able to work the brakes, helped and the two wounded men were able to stop the runaway horses before the stage careened over a steep drop, as the robbers made off with the booty.

17 - Buck Montgomery

Dr. Stevenson and his wife came upon the stage and Dr. Stevenson tended to the wounded men while Mrs. Stevenson raced for help. Doc drove the stage to Middle Creek Hotel where Buck's wife and 2 sons arrived just as he died. His funeral procession was the longest ever seen in Ukiah. He was buried in Ukiah Cemetery. Jennie Montgomery moved to San Francisco to raise her boys. She died in 1928 never having remarried. Oldest son Orrie became a Dr. in San Francisco. Grover became a well-known merchant in Gilroy

Stage Robberies

Charley Ruggles

Wild estimates of the stolen loot ranged from $20,000 to $50,000 in gold bullion. It was later determined to be only $3375.[216] The wounded robber was found, less than a mile from the scene. He had been hit with 10 pellets from Buck's shotgun. He said that he had been left to die by his older brother John, who took the loot and ran. Charley was brought to the Redding jail and treated for his wounds.[217] The brothers were sons of Lyman B. Ruggles, a wealthy farmer in Tulare County, a former Chairman of the Board of Supervisors in Yolo County and a highly respected man.

John D. Ruggles

John D. Ruggles had been in trouble before. He was sent to San Quentin for 7 years for robbery but, due to his father's influence, was pardoned after 2 years. He was a widower with no children. While n te lam, he was seen entering the Opera Restaurant. The Sheriff was told and several officers walked in and sat at his table as other diners quickly left. When they told him to put up his hands, he reached for his gun. Deputy Wycoff fired, striking Ruggles in the neck. He had managed to elude capture until June 20th. Told his wound was likely to be fatal, John produced a long confession of how he planned the robbery and claimed he thought that Charley was dead when he left him.

As the handsome young brothers recovered from their gunshots, town ladies brought flowers, candy and novels. Several confessed they were in love with them and would do anything to assist them. Then a newspaper story noted that John planned to claim at his trial that Buck Montgomery was *'in on the robbery'* and had betrayed the Ruggles by firing on them and been killed in revenge. This proposed defense infuriated the community. It was the final straw for local men who soon formed a lynch mob of 40 well-armed men.[218] They took the jailer prisoner and spent over 90 minutes drilling a hole in the Sheriff's safe to get the keys. The noise and light of their torches were clearly heard and seen outside, but no one intervened.

Murders in Mendocino

The brothers were handcuffed and marched through a large silent crowd to a blacksmith shop several blocks away where a large crossbeam was suspended from two pine trees. They were given a chance to make a statement before they were hung.

John pled for his brother's life. He also denied his involvement in the murder of a young girl during a Cazadero stage robbery or the murder of a drover in Siskiyou County, two other crimes he was charged with. He offered to tell them where the stolen gold was if they would spare his brother's life but the vigilantes would not agree and both were hung. Their bodies remained on the beam until cut down about 9 am the following morning. [219] The gold was never recovered.

18 - John D. Ruggles

Stage Robberies

Sheriff Doc Standley - 1896

After yet another stage robbery, several suspicious newcomers were seen on the summit of the Hot Springs grade. Doc Standley was sent to the remote woodsmen camp to talk to them. These cabins could only be reached by a difficult trail, broken by river ravines. Nothing was found to incriminate the occupants of the first two cabins, but the man in the third cabin suddenly disappeared. Deputy Johnson, an expert tracker, followed him to Rattlesnake Canyon but gave up when darkness fell.

19 – Sheriff Doc Standley

The next morning, Doc Standley heard the robbers were close to town at Camp Bethel. He went out first and Deputies Johnson and Alex Burke followed in the afternoon. They were about to end for the day when they saw a man with light reddish hair and a fair complexion. He didn't match the description of the stage coach robber, so Standley rode up to speak to him. The man suddenly pulled his gun and shot Standley and before Standley could pull his rifle, he was shot again. The bandit was a medium sized, heavyset man, weighing about 155 pounds, round faced, with prominent nose and about two weeks' of beard. He was dressed in a dark suit of clothes and wore a sack coat.

Standley was brought to town by the wife of Deputy Ford, who lived nearby. The bullet that broke his arm struck midway between the shoulder and elbow and he had suffered a flesh wound in the right leg, above the knee. Everyone with a rifle was soon on their way to the site of the shooting. The shooter was sighted twice and the posse trailed him east to the Russian River and down the river as far as Bailey's Bridge, where the trail appeared to cross the river. Doc believed that the robber was still near Camp Bethel and encouraged the men to keep looking in that area. Officers soon discovered a cabin where the suspect had stayed.

Murders in Mendocino

Sheriff Johnson and the posse followed tracks from the cabin to Roeder's Lane where they saw a man walking towards them reading a newspaper. The sheriff asked the man innocuous questions then the suspicious posse rode up the road around a curve, jumped off their horses and quietly surrounded the man. They called to him to raise his hands which he did, dropping the paper. They arrested him and put him on a horse to return to town, confiscating his 2 pistols. The man claimed he could not ride well and rolled about in the saddle, a ruse to grab a pistol. He was quickly subdued. He denied any connection to the stage robbery but did remark that he was sorry he had not killed Doc Standley.[220]

Doc Standley was Sheriff of Mendocino from 1864-1866. He then worked as a teacher in Ukiah before he was appointed deputy in 1872. When budget cuts eliminated his position, he worked his sheep ranch from 1874-1882 and volunteered as a deputy. It was during this time that he tracked the murderers of Dollard and Wright in the longest manhunt. His exploits helped him be re-elected as Sheriff again from 1882 to 1892. After recovering from his gunshots, he moved to Nome, Alaska for the Klondike gold rush, in 1897 where he mined, ran a freighting business and worked as a deputy sheriff. The family briefly returned to Ukiah in 1902, returning to Alaska in 1904 with daughter Jessie. Sadly, Doc fell down a staircase in 1908, badly injuring his spine, which caused paralysis and blindness. He passed away in Portland as his wife and daughter were bringing him home to Ukiah. He died July 8, 1908 at the age of 63 and is buried in Ukiah.

His obituary noted him as "one of the best men this country had ever produced". He was greatly admired for his 30 years of service and is honored among the greatest lawmen of the Old West. He was survived by his wife, Sarah (Clay) and children Minnie Jamison, William H., Nell F. Gibson and Jessie Hildreth.

Stage Robberies

John Riley Barnett – 1897

The Los Angeles Herald of Sept 29th reported that the Ukiah-Booneville Stage had been robbed again by 2 masked men and that J. R. Barnett had been shot and killed. The robbery occurred near the site where G. W. Hilton and 'Deacon' Oldham had robbed the same stage 3 years earlier. As the stage was passing through a heavily wooded section of road, six miles from Ukiah on a Tuesday afternoon, a man stepped into the road and called for the stage to stop and throw down the express boxes. James Rose, the driver, immediately complied. J.R. Barnett (owner of the stage line) and F.D. Berryhill were passengers on the 2 o'clock coast-bound stage. Barnett heard the robber's order and reached his hand into his pocket to throw his purse under the front seat. The robber, thinking he was pulling a gun, fired his shotgun hitting Barnett in the neck, killing him instantly. They grabbed the 3 express boxes and ordered the driver to drive on as fast as possible, which he did until reaching the Elledge Ranch about a mile away. Elisha Finney drove up in a wagon just then, and brought the body to town. Berryhill got a saddle horse from the Stipp farm and rode to town to give the alarm. This all happened about 3 pm and the sheriff was notified by 5 pm.

A posse, consisting of Under-Sheriff Handy, Nebon McClure and Virgil and J. L. Johnson left for the scene of the tragedy as soon as they were notified, but the robbers had three hours start and it was dark before the posse reached the scene. There they waited for the return stage to get Rose's description of the robbers and find the exact location where it happened. Rose arrived later that night, but could give no particular description of the bandits, other than that they were both short and heavy. A bloodhound led the posse to the bandit's camp but it the weather was so cold he refused to track further so the posse returned to Ukiah.

On Wednesday, Deputies Virgil and J. L. Johnson returned with the three empty boxes, broken open with a rusty ax and an iron wedge.

Murders in Mendocino

A large reward was offered, search parties were formed, and the local woods were patrolled by armed citizens.[221] Several people described suspicious characters they had seen. Robert Donohue and another man named Crow were approached by a tramp who inquired when the stage was due. As they talked, another man came out of the brush and Donohoe asked if the other man was the tramp's partner. The tramp claimed he had never seen the other man before. Donohue thought this was suspicious behavior and a posse was sent out but failed to find a trace of the men. Another man named Dunn saw 2 men in the woods with a shotgun but was not aware of the crime at the time so thought nothing of it. The posse tracked the killers to Hopland Road where another man, Roeder, said he had seen 2 men the night of the murder. The same men were also seen by Mrs. Patton.

The murdered man, John Riley Barnett was born in Illinois and had arrived in California in 1874. He owned a feed and livery business in Cloverdale for 3 years before moving to Willits where he bought into the stage business. He won the contract to carry mail on the Ukiah-Humboldt line and moved to Ukiah in 1891 becoming the best known stage contractor in the State. He was also a founder of the Savings Bank of Mendocino County. He left a wife, Louisa Jane (Bowers) Barnett and large family.[222] Louisa Barnett died at the age of 60 in 1903 after an illness of 3 weeks. They had 9 children of whom 6 survived her. She is buried with her husband in the Odd Fellows Cemetery in Ukiah.

At the time of her death, no one had ever been charged with the murder of her husband.[223]

Charles Meyers

The first suspect arrested was Charles Meyers. He was brought up from San Francisco by Sheriff Johnson. He was identified by John Crow who had been with Donohoe when they met the tramp. Sheriff Johnson held Meyers until further identification could be made.[224] Myers was employed on a farm near Geyserville at the time of the robbery and was able to provide a perfect alibi. He was released on 13 Oct.[225] He promptly sued the sheriff for $10,000 for false arrest and defamation.

Stage Robberies

John Neely

In November a 2nd suspect was arrested in San Francisco named J.T. Brown, aka John Neely by Sheriff Johnson.[226]. Shortly after the robbery, Donohoe said he was 'almost sure' that Neely was with the men.[227] After his arrest Neely was cleared when Donohoe decided he was too old to have been one of the men he had seen on the road.

Frank Barrington

Then in late January, a 3rd suspect, Frank Barrington of Alexander Valley, was arrested. He was almost 6' tall with light hair and wore a light thin mustache. Barrington protested that he had an alibi for the time of the murder but 'Lish' Finney claimed he was one of the suspicious characters he saw near Ukiah the day of the tragedy. Finney, a teamster, claimed that about an hour before the stage was due, 2 men came out to the road and asked how long it would be before the stage would pass. He identified Barrington as one of those men.[228] Fortunately for Barrington, he was able to establish an alibi. The man he was working for on the day of the robbery confirmed he had been present at a winery on the Morgan place and he too was released.

P. Barrett

In early February former Sheriff Doc Standley arrested a 4th man named P. Barrett at Keswick. This man had a wife and children living at Iron Mountain and was a train engineer. He had led a quiet and industrious life and his acquaintances did not believe he was involved.[229] He too was discharged for lack of evidence.

Billy Rose

The driver of the stage, James William Rose, died in 1940. He was a member of the first settler families in Anderson Valley.

No one was ever prosecuted for the Barnett murder.

Chapter 15 – Fraud

Abner McNeill – 1875

Two young friends, Abner McNeil and Bob Darr were drinking heavily at a dance one night. The very drunk Darr scraped a line on the dirt floor with his shoe and threatened to shoot the first man who stepped over it.

Abner crossed his arms and said "You wouldn't' shoot me – I'm your friend" and stepped over the line. It was a fatal miscalculation. Darr shot him in the stomach and he died several days later.

Darr was convicted of manslaughter in July of 1875 and sent to San Quentin for 5 years. He was released in Feb 1877 after serving only 18 months.[230] He returned to Mendocino and, by 1880, owned a saloon in Ten-mile River. Local sentiment was that he got off too easily.

Philip Gibney – 1881

A few years later, Darr was involved in another murder. Philip Gibney, a frequent patron of Darr's Saloon, worked at the 10 Mile River Mill of Stewart and Hunter. One evening, Gibney was sitting on the porch of the saloon when he was killed by a shot in the back.[231]

Robert Darr was arrested.[232] Despite his protest of innocence, he was quickly convicted of Gibney's murder and sentenced to life.[233] But new information came out after the trial that provided another suspect for the murder.

Gibney had shot at a man named Martin in a jealous rage and there was good reason to believe Martin, not Darr, had killed him. Hundreds of neighbors and friends then presented a petition for Darr's release, signed by all of the Associate Justices of the Supreme Court and the entire jury who had convicted him, the District Attorney who had prosecuted him, and a large number of prominent citizens.[234]

Darr finally received a full pardon on 22 Dec 1890 after serving almost 10 years for a crime he did not commit.

Fraud

Robert Darr

Robert M. Darr was born in Virginia in 1834 and married Jerusha Adams in 1862 in Colusa, CA. In 1868 the Darrs and Jerusha's parents, James and Maria Louise (Graham) Adams, moved to Mendocino, settling in Point Arena. Bob and Jerusha had a daughter, Lena (who married Guy W. Ledger) and 2 sons, William Wirt and Jesse Darr. Jerusha filed for divorce shortly after Bob Darr was convicted of Gibney's murder and sent to prison for the 2nd time. She married Albert W. Schiller in February 1882. Jerusha died in 1917 in Greenwood-Elk and is buried there.

After his 2nd pardon in 1891, 58 year old Bob Darr again returned to Mendocino. He had lost his saloon so worked as a farmer in the Manchester area.

In 1897, Bob (63) married Nancy Heldt (47) whose first husband, Dutch Fred Heldt, had left her a very wealthy widow. But in 1902 he suffered permanent injury in an accident.[235]

Then, in 1904 Bob and Jerusha's son, Wirt Darr, was charged with the rape of 13 year old Estelle Skiffington.[236] After 2 hung jury trials, he was finally convicted at his 3rd trial in 1905 and sent to San Quentin.[237] He was paroled in 1908. Wirt died working on a state highway gang in 1921.

In 1905, Bob's other son, Jesse, was arrested for selling liquor to Indians and spent 30 days in jail.[238] Jesse died on 19 Feb 1912 at Fort Bragg. He was only 39.[239]

In 1910 Bob, then 76, filed for divorce from 60 year old Nancy, alleging that she had beaten him, threatened to kill him with a butcher knife and scalded him with hot water.[240] He petitioned the court, to appoint a guardian for his wife, stating that she was incompetent due to alcoholism.[241] The incompetency petition was dismissed, but the divorce was granted.

Robert M. Darr died on April 5, 1914 in San Joaquin, CA.[242]

Murders in Mendocino

'Dutch' Fred Heldt – 1892

Frederich Heldt came to California with his brothers, Daniel and George, from Alsace, Germany around 1855. They all prospered. Fred and his partner Silas Osborne opened the first saloon in Mendocino City, a 3 story bar and hotel, around 1860 on West Main Street. Neither able to read or write, they kept a glass for each client under the counter putting a bean in for each drink. Fred used his profits to buy several buildings in Mendocino and Fort Bragg and a store in Ukiah, and soon had enough to purchase the large Bald Hill Ranch north of Fort Bragg. By 1873 he was one of the richest men in the area.

Fred Heldt married Nancy, a full blooded Pitt River Indian, on 13 September 1879. Nancy was a handsome woman about 25 years younger and by all appearances they had a happy marriage until Fred suddenly died on 15 Dec 1892, at the age of 59.

Fred was eating soup with Edgar Martin in the Ukiah saloon Martin owned with Hugh Donohoe. Fred owned the building and was a regular customer. That day, Fred suddenly became violently ill. Fearing he was dying, he sent Martin to get his brother so he could make a will. Instead of getting Fred's brother, Martin brought Fred's wife, Nancy, who could neither read nor write. Fred died about 8 hours later without having seen his brother or, apparently, made a will. Fred and Nancy had no children. In an indication of the racial prejudice of the time, Fred's obituary noted that he was survived by 2 brothers on the coast and one brother in New York City. His wife of 12 years, Nancy, was not mentioned.[243] Fred was buried on his Bald Hill Ranch.

About 10 days after Fred's death, Ed Martin the saloon owner, filed a will with the Mendocino County Probate Court with Fred Heldt's signature on it. The will, in Martin's handwriting, was signed the day of Fred's death. Martin also forwarded a copy of the will to a prominent San Francisco attorney and telegraphed him to be in readiness to attend to the urgent matter. This will made Martin the sole executor of Heldt's large estate. It was witnessed by Martin's partner, Hugh Donohoe and his wife. The will stipulated that Fred's 3 brothers and one sister were each to receive $2000. His eight nephews were to get $500 each. Nancy was to have the Bald Hill Ranch property then worth almost $100,000 and it named Ed Martin sole executor without posting the usual financial bonds.

Nancy immediately became suspicious. Martin had only been in Mendocino for 4 months and Fred had known him for only a month. Fred, though illiterate, was a shrewd businessman who didn't trust easily. It was entirely out of character for him to appoint a man he barely knew to be executor of his estate. The will had been drawn up in the saloon and witnessed only by the saloon keeper and his wife. Nancy had been with him until he died and had seen him sign no documents. Nancy filed a criminal complaint charging Martin with poisoning her husband. Heldt's body was exhumed and his stomach sent to San Francisco for testing. Unfortunately, the murder charge had to be dropped because the test results were inconclusive. So Edgar Martin was held only on forgery charges. However Martin's problems were soon to get worse.

Martin was re-arrested when Mrs. Donohue confessed that she and Hugh had signed the will after Heldt's death when Martin offered them $1000 each to sign it, and had threatened them if they did not. William Heeser, Secretary of the Bank of Mendocino and Mendocino Discount Bank and a notary, employed for many years by Heldt to draw up his legal instruments, was positive the signature was a forgery. Sam Wheeler, cashier at the Bank of Ukiah, also declared the signature a forgery.

Martin was found guilty of forgery and fraud and sentenced to 14 years in Folsom Prison. The judge, noting there were serious questions concerning the death of Fred Heldt, but not enough evidence to prove he was murdered, sentenced Martin to 14 years, the maximum allowable under the forgery charge.[244]

Murders in Mendocino

Edgar A. Martin

After being sentenced to 14 years on the forgery charge, Martin tried to escape through the attic above his 2nd floor cell but his plans were frustrated when he was moved back to a first floor cell the night before his transport to Folsom Prison. In frustration, he shared his plan with another inmate who, rather than escaping, told the authorities where to find the evidence.[245]

Shortly after his sentencing, news articles revealed more about Martin's long life of crime[246]. Martin was soon discovered to be none other than E. A. McDuffie, who had previously been charged with multiple forgery offenses. He was also known by the aliases Morton, Arthur and McMartin. His wife was the former Carrie (Dryfus) Heinzenberger of San Leandro, a widow who married Martin in 1884 after the sudden death of her wealthy husband.[247]

According to Detective Russell, who investigated him, E. A. McDuffie, aka E. A. Morton, had first appeared in San Francisco in 1858 as a young man. He drifted to San Jose and Marysville working as a peddler and horse trader, "the other man invariably being swindled". When he became too well known, he moved south to a San Bernardino mining camp called Calico in 1882 with a "rather handsome woman" who passed as his wife. Their peddling of tin-ware and dry goods was successful enough to open a store in Calico. McDuffie left his 'wife' in charge of the store and went into partnership in the freighting business between the Borax mines and Daggett with a man named Quinn. Quinn conveniently died soon afterward, leaving McDuffie owner of several six-mule teams and freight wagons.

He then traded half interest in his freight business to Seymour Elf for a half interest in Elf's Parumph Ranch. He gave Elf notes for $3000. Not only did he not pay a dollar on those notes, within 3 months the freight business was attached for McDuffie's private debts. Elf paid off $2800 I debt in exchange for a bill of sale from McDuffie for full ownership of the freight business. A few weeks later, McDuffie presented a forged agreement between himself and Elf, claiming Elf

Fraud

owed him $2200 for 50% interest in the freight business he had just purchased. This document was witnessed by A. E. Morton (McDuffie's alias). Poor Elf fought this case through the courts but was ultimately defeated and declared bankruptcy to avoid paying the forged claim.

McDuffie and his 'wife' then became friends with a shopkeeper named Delaney but soon had a falling out. Delaney complained to everyone in Dagget about them, banning them from his store. Not long after this, the previously healthy Delaney suddenly died. McDuffie then presented a will (later shown to be a forgery) to Delaney's estate in which Mrs. McDuffie was to receive $3000. Despite Delaney's heirs contesting this, she was awarded the money.

McDuffie then bought a share in the Alvord mine owned by a man named Dent. Shortly after this partnership agreement, Dent too died in suspicious circumstances which were never fully investigated. Of course, McDuffie inherited the mine.

20 - Edgar A. Martin

His next partner was Isaac C. Weaver who caught McDuffie and his wife attempting to swindle him with a forged bill of sale and forced them into court. They were finally so discredited that they were forced to leave Dagget.

McDuffie next appeared in 1866 in Victor in San Bernardino County, with his brother, as owners in a marble quarry. The LA Herald wrote up their find of a *"new ledge of fine marble"* trying to entice partners to invest. The marble didn't exist. The McDuffie Brothers Real Exchange ran another swindle, selling land claims. They owned 160 acres of land which they showed prospective buyers who would pay them a $50 fee to secure filings on this land, only to find the McDuffie's didn't own the land they had promised them. They eventually defrauded so many people that they were forced to leave San Bernardino County.

Edgar then moved to San Diego and opened a real estate office there, but spent most of his time making the acquaintance of prominent men. He also spent hours at the courthouse using small strips of tracing paper to trace their signatures. He was ready in the spring of 1890 when E. H. Darrah was 'accidentally' shot while hunting in Oregon. McDuffie was coincidentally gone from San Francisco at the same time. His absence didn't arouse suspicion until later when, in July, another well-known wealthy man, John Heerander, also died suddenly, supposedly of heart failure. A few weeks later, McDuffie presented a note against both estates, payable to E. A. Morton (an alias), containing the purported signatures of both deceased men. The signatures appeared genuine but Heerander always had his attorney endorse all such documents. Since this note did not have the attorney's endorsement, it immediately raised suspicion and Heerander's attorneys hired Detective Russell to investigate. Russell then found out about the Delaney will in Daggett where Mrs. McDuffie had gotten $3000. This will contained the names of E. A. McDuffie, E. A. Morton and E. A. Martin. Faced with evidence that the Heerander-Darrah note was forged, McDuffie surrendered the note and left San Diego empty-handed.

He next appeared in Fresno, trying to collect on a forged note for $6000 against the estate of Warren E. Burt. This signature also was deemed to be a forgery. It had been copied from a hotel register, ironically the only time Burt had used that form of his signature. An accomplice turned against McDuffie when, instead of paying him $500 in cash, he actually issued him a note for $500. This man later swore he saw a stack of 20 forged wills for wealthy men who were still living.

Edgar A. Martin, as he was known in Mendocino, was finally arrested and tried for forgery in the Heldt case in 1892, but many believed that he was also a murderer given the sudden deaths of so many former partners. Mrs. Martin disappeared when he was arrested.[248] Upon his release from Folsom on April 15, 1901, he went to Los Angeles and San Diego under the alias of Duffy leaving more swindles behind in each location before he again dropped out of sight.

Then in July of 1904 he was arrested in Hazen, Nevada where he had become the postmaster, using the name Henry C. Lawrence. This time he was caught attempting to murder J. D. Garrison. He owed Garrison money but they were still on good terms when Garrison accompanied him to measure a parcel of land. Garrison was walking away from Lawrence to pace off a boundary when he was shot twice. When Lawrence/Martin saw him moving he came back and shot Garrison again, leaving him for dead in the desert. Garrison managed to drag himself back to town where he pressed charges. Lawrence/Martin escaped from jail before his trial but was recaptured 12 hours later.

In August, the sheriff found out that Lawrence was actually Edgar A. Martin/Morton/McDuffie/Duffy. Lawrence, of course, claimed he was not, saying he had a fiancée in San Francisco who could prove he had not been in the penitentiary during the years Martin was incarcerated. He would not give the lady's name or address but claimed she would clear him *"when the time came."* That time never came. Nevada authorities took great care to compare descriptions and photographs. A careful investigation of his body was made. Every mark known to be on Martin was located on Lawrence, even the scars left on his wrists from a faked suicide attempt.[249]

He was also suspected of murdering Jim Eagle in Hazen whose black slouch hat was found with a bullet hole in it. Eagle was carrying several hundred dollars when he was last seen alive with Lawrence/Martin, riding out to inspect government land that Lawrence was trying to sell him. Eagle's body was never located so Lawrence/Martin could not be charged with his murder.

He was convicted of Garrison's attempted murder and sentenced to 14 years in prison in Carson, Nevada in December 1904.[250] After his arrival there, he feigned insanity and appealed his case to the Supreme Court, which refused to grant him a new trial. He was still at the State Prison at Carson, Nevada in 1910. He probably changed his name again upon release as he disappeared after that date.

Murders in Mendocino

Nancy Heldt Darr

Nancy was a Pitt River Native American woman, raised by John B. Hargrave of Navarro Ridge. Nancy was an Indian 'servant', not part of the Hargrave family. When Fred Heldt's estate was finally probated, Nancy inherited ½ of the estate including the entire Bald Hill Ranch, about 2 miles north of Fort Bragg with about 800 acres, 400 head of cattle, 17 horses, hogs, wagons, saddles and bridles, 120 head of sheep and a gold watch and chain. The other Heldt heirs (siblings and nephews) got the other ½ of his estate, consisting of other properties.

Nancy married Robert Darr in 1897, five years after Fred's untimely death. They divorced, due to her alcoholism, in 1910. By 1914 Nancy was described as a "well-known local character" for frequently coming to town with her 2 dogs, getting drunk and passing out in the street. Nancy was arrested in Nov 1915 on a charge of arson for setting fire to her property at Bald Hill Ranch.[251] Nancy died in 1917 of pneumonia at the age of 62.

She left all her property to a nephew, Tom Moore, but he had predeceased her.[252] Fred Heldt, a relation of her first husband, and a woman named Sallie Haynes, a Covelo Native American woman who claimed to be a cousin of Nancy's, initiated a long court fight over her estate which took until the end of 1920 to resolve. Sallie Haynes was finally given 100 acres south of the main ranch and the other heirs were given the remainder of the Bald Hill property and assumed the mortgage of $8700 on the property.

Fraud

Armstrong McCabe – 1892

Armstrong McCabe, a 60 year old saloon keeper in Hopland, was standing alone at one end of his empty bar late one evening when 3 shots rang out, fired through the window, killing him instantly.

He had come to Hopland two years earlier and opened a saloon across from the stage depot. The year after his arrival, he married Mrs. Mary Maxima (Ynitia) Bolton Willard. She was a full blood Miwok Indian woman, 18 years younger than McCabe, and, like Nancy Heldt Darr, had been left quite wealthy when her husband died in 1888. The Willard children distrusted McCabe but were unable to dissuade their mother from marrying him. Their worst fears were confirmed when, shortly after the marriage, McCabe obtained rights to the large landholdings of the Willard estate.

Things began to fall apart for McCabe when the postmaster in Sanel got a letter from a woman in San Francisco asking if he knew the whereabouts of McCabe. The letter claimed she was his wife and had not heard from him in months. Of course, this news created great gossip in town and the Willard boys eagerly investigated. Frank Willard went to San Francisco to meet with the letter writer, Sabrina (Cafferty) McCabe. She produced papers proving that McCabe had married her in San Francisco on 18 Oct 1890. They had never been divorced, despite his many threats to kill her if she wouldn't sign divorce papers, and she was still legally his wife.[253]

Frank Willard was furious at the insult to his mother and that McCabe had taken fraudulent possession of the Willards' large inheritance. He returned to Sanel and told everyone, including his mother and McCabe, what he had found out. They had an argument at the dinner table over the matter. It was shortly after that altercation that McCabe was killed.

Frank was arrested, tried and found not guilty as there was no proof, but folks generally believed that Frank Willard had shot him.[254]

Murders in Mendocino

Sabrina (Cafferty) McCabe

After McCabe's death, the jilted Sabrina gave an interview with the San Francisco Chronicle and claimed "he was the biggest liar on the face of the earth!" and she wouldn't believe he was dead "until she was able to view the body" because he had tried to pull that stunt on her before. Sabrina explained that shortly after he married her, McCabe began talking about property he was to inherit from the estate of his first wife in Mexico. He borrowed money from her to go to Mexico to 'settle the matter' promising that when he returned she would be "a queen loaded with money". McCabe did leave with Sabrina's money, but instead of going to Mexico, he opened the saloon in Hopland and found a bigger mark in Mary Willard.

He then pulled an elaborate ruse to try to get Sabrina to sign divorce papers. He returned to San Francisco in April 1891 with a Mexican man that McCabe claimed was an attorney with papers in Spanish that McCabe wanted Sabrina to sign. When she refused to sign until she could get them translated, McCabe threatened to kill her. He then offered her $1000 to sign papers for a divorce. When she would not do this either, he stormed out. Several days later, the daughter of the house where he was staying came to tell Sabrina he had committed suicide. The girl asked what they should do with his body and Sabrina advised them to call the police. McCabe made a miraculous recovery and furiously came to Sabrina's house and threatened her again, trying to force her to sign divorce papers. Despite these unsuccessful divorce attempts, McCabe returned to Sanel and bigamously married Mary Willard anyway.

Fraud

Chief Camilo Ynitia-1856

Mary Maxima (Ynitia) Bennet Willard McCabe was a Native American woman, born in 1841 to Chief Camilo Ynitia, a well-known full blooded Miwok Indian, in Marin County.

Chief Camilo of the Miwok and Chief Solano of the Suisunes had signed peace treaties with Mexico under Vallejo in 1836. General Vallejo always treated Chief Camilo and Chief Solano with great consideration because it was their treaties that allowed Vallejo to control the Indian tribes without bloodshed.[255] There was far less Indian killing in Marin than farther north. These were the only 2 Native Americans ever to receive land grants from the Mexican Government.

In 1843, Camilo, the last Huipu of the Miwok Tribe was granted the Olompali Rancho in Marin County, over 8,878 acres. He was known as a shrewd businessman and traveled frequently to San Francisco to purchase and sell stock. He owned 600 head of cattle and was a notable breeder of fine horses. In 1852, after annexation of California, perhaps fearing the high cost of proving his claim through the US courts, Camilo sold 8245 acres of Rancho Olompali to James Black, the largest landowner in Marin County, the coroner and the tax assessor. Black paid Camilo $4290 in gold coins and $910 remained due. This was about $.63 per acre. Camilo kept 632 acres which he called Rancho Apalacocha.

Camilo Ynitia married 4 times. He had no children with his first 2 wives. His 3rd wife, Cayetana bore him 3 children, son Juan Pablo (1839), and 2 daughters Mary Maxima (1841) and Maria Antonia (1845) Both girls had very prominent godparents.

Mary Maxima's godfather was Gregorio Briones, wealthy and well known owner of the 8911 acre Rancho Bolinas. His father Marco Briones had accompanied Serra in 1769 and married Maria Ramona Garcia. Gregorio served as Alcalde of San Jose in 1830, Pinole (1832-1837) and San Mateo (1837-1839) and San Francisco (1839-1840). He built one of the earliest haciendas in Marin County. Rancho Bolinas was the center of the beef and lumber industry.

Murders in Mendocino

Maria Antonia's godparents were William A. Richardson and his prominent wife Maria Antonio Martinez. Richardson arrived in San Francisco in 1822 from England. He married the eldest daughter of the Commandante of the Presidio of San Francisco. He helped to lay out the first town lots and built la Casa Grande, the first adobe house in San Francisco. He was granted Rancho Sausalito in Marin County. These godparents were from well-known and very prominent families.

After Cayetana died, Camilo married his 4th wife, 14 year old Susanna Maria Onorio in 1852, with whom he had no children. In 1851, Camilo became friends with his neighbor, Dr. Reuben Knox, who leased the adjacent Rancho Novato. Knox had brought his sons Joseph and Henry, nephew Reuben, and 6 black slaves with him but, shortly after signing a lease with first purchase rights to Rancho Novato, Dr. Knox died. His boat, loaded with heavy machinery, capsized in San Pablo Bay, killing Knox, his 27 year old nephew Reuben, and Camilo's 21 year old son, Juan Pablo.

His son, Joseph Knox, remained at Rancho Novato but could not afford to buy it. It was sold in 1852 for $28,500 over $4/acre. Camilo's ranch had gotten only 63 cents per acre a few months earlier so it would appear he was cheated. Joseph Knox stayed as a tenant of the new owner and employed Henry Willard as his ranch foreman while he practiced law and became a local judge.

Camilo made his will on Sept. 28, 1855 with Joseph Knox as his attorney. It stipulated that Rancho Apalacocha go to his oldest daughter Mary Maxima and her husband Henry Holden Bennet. The property could not be sold without her approval. She and Henry were to care for her younger sister, Maria Antonia, until she became of age or married and they were to care for his aged sister, Valina. He left his young wife Suzanna "$910 still owed by James Black, 3 oxen, 2 horses, and some pigs". He left the rest of his livestock to both daughters, his wife and to Valina's son Besidini. Joseph Knox was to be executor of Camilo's estate.

Fraud

Camilo's Strange Death

When Camilo suddenly died in 1856, his death was shrouded in mystery. The exact date and cause of death is still not known. It happened between April 2, when Camilo conveyed land to Henry Bennet and July 28, 1856 when Joseph Knox responded to a petition, filed in the Probate court by a court appointed attorney for 10 year old Maria Antonia, which claimed that "Maria Antonia objects to proof of the will of the said deceased on the ground that the will was not executed according to law and the deceased was not of sound mind." Joseph Knox, who had written the will and was executor of the estate, responded that Camilo was of sound mind. The first public notice of Camilo's death was an announcement in the newspapers for creditors to present claims to his executor, Joseph Knox, dated 9 Aug 1856.

Despite the fact that Camilo was a well-known almost legendary figure, no inquest was ever done as no file is missing from sequentially numbered inquests. Other Native American inquests were done that year so this was not a racial issue.

No news of his death was published, despite the fact that contemporary death notices referenced far less important Native Americans and 'Chinamen' by name. This was highly unusual for such a well-known local man whose good friends and godparents to his children included such prominent wealthy rancho owners.

And, despite having been paid $4290 in gold coins for having sold Rancho Olompali to Black, no money was found.

On Sept 17, 1856, Knox petitioned to sell Camilo's personal property to pay off debts. An auction disposing of 4 horses, 2 colts an ox cart and a gun raised about $911 but, after paying off all the creditors, Camilo's 17 year old widow, Susanna, was left $453.45 plus the money still due from Black.[256]

Knox, the executor, was then released and Mary Maxima's husband, Henry Bennet, became owner of Rancho Apalacocha.

Henry Holden Bennet - 1856

Mary Maxima Ynitia had been married at 13 in 1854 to 34 year old Henry Holden Bennett, a lumberman. Shortly after Camilo's probate was concluded, Bennett leased out Rancho Apalacocha for 6 years at the unusually low sum of $100/year and agreed to pay the lessee for any improvements made, a suspiciously odd and unfavorable agreement for the Bennets.

Within months of her father's death, her husband, Henry Bennet, also died at the young age of 37. This death too had a news blackout. There was no record of his death with the Marin County Coroner's office, no inquest was done, no obit appeared, despite the fact that his death should have raised concerns given his young age and following so soon after the death of his famous father-in-law.

Further adding some suspicion to this situation, within 3 months of his sudden death, his 16 year old widow, Mary Maxima, was married again, this time to 31 year old Henry Willard, the Novato Ranch foreman.

They promptly moved north to Ukiah.

21 - Mary Maxima and Maria Antonia Ynitia

Fraud

Henry Harper Willard

Henry Willard, was born in Otsego County, NY in 1828 and came around Cape Horn with the Stevenson regiment, arriving in San Francisco in 1847. He worked gold mines in Placer County before returning to Marin to become ranch manager for Mrs. John Reed at Corte Madera del Presidio. He was a constable in Novato from 1854-1856 then became ranch foreman for Joseph Knox at Rancho Novato.

After his hasty marriage to 16 year old Mary Maxima Bennet, the Willards suddenly moved north in 1856, settling about 3 miles below Ukiah. The following year, Joseph Knight, Willard's former employer, also moved to Sanel with Mary's sister, 13 year old Maria Antonia Ynitia.

In 1857, Mary Maxima and Maria Antonia tried to foreclose on the Rancho Apalacocha lease and learned of the obligation to reimburse the lessee for the buildings. The sisters, claiming "to have no money whatsoever to spend on law nor even for our own maintenance, as also the land being about 500 acres of nearly all mountain land and not of much value, empowered John Knight to act as their attorney, borrow money and purchase the improvements of the lessee." Knight borrowed $1000 at 1¾ percent interest and paid the tenant $912 for the buildings. Knight then leased out the property for $350/year.

That year, when most claims were quarter sections of 160 acres, Willard purchased 11 claims totaling 1790 acres in Sanel. Willard made about $40 a month as ranch foreman. He was so broke that he had to borrow money to foreclose on Rancho Apalacocha, yet he suddenly had enough money to purchase almost 1800 acres of land. He continued acquiring land until his natural death in August, 1888. When he died, he left 47 year old Mary a wealthy widow, with 22,000 acres and an estate worth $65,000.

Armstrong McCabe, the con man, saw the illiterate Indian widow as an easy mark. After McCabe's murder she never married again. Mary Maxima (Ynitia) Bolton Willard died on 9 February 1901 at the age of 60 and is buried beside Henry Willard in Hopland. [257] When she died, the Willard Rancho was worth about $35,000.[258]

Murders in Mendocino

The Willards

After Mary Maxima (Ynitia)(Bennet)(Willard) McCabe died in 1901, her sons inherited the Willard Ranch. It was auctioned off for only $15,500. The attorney representing the heirs contested this low sale price, proving the land to be worth at least $28,000. Finally Mr. Burns, the high bidder, raised his offer to $20,000 and the heirs agreed to accept that.[259] Family trouble continued.

Joseph Willard – 1903

In 1903, Joe Willard was killed in an accidental shooting while he was hunting. It was surmised that he had pulled his gun after him while crossing a fence and it accidentally discharged. A nearby rancher heard the shot, but thought nothing of it. Joe's dog remained with him all night long, and was barking to keep a herd of horses away from the body, when the horses' owner found him. Joe's body was still warm, indicating that he had lived through most of the night.[260] He left a wife and 2 children. Foul play was not suspected.

Sheriff J. Henry Smith – 1905

The headline read, "Frank Willard, a drink-crazed man who was about to be committed for insanity, shot and killed Sheriff Henry Smith in Judge White's chambers a few minutes before 10 am this morning."[261]

22 - Frank Willard

Like many Native Americans, Frank could not tolerate alcohol and had been committed to the insane asylum twice before, and been released each time.[262] When Frank came to town that Thursday he was clearly not in his right mind. He was asking for help to restrain men "throwing x-rays on him". He was under the delusion that he was suppressing a 'tough

Fraud

element' in town for Governor Pardee. After hearing of his odd behavior, Sheriff Smith took him into custody.[263] Unfortunately, Frank wasn't searched, and no one realized he wass armed. Dr. Dickinson and Dr. Bond had filled out commitment papers to send Frank to the State Hospital again and everyone had left the chambers except Judge White, Sheriff Smith and Undersheriff Gibson and Frank.

Sheriff Smith was trying to talk a very drunk Frank into giving up his money. Willard gave part of the money to Smith but complained that, "it was pretty hard to take a man's money from him when he was to be committed to the asylum." The telephone suddenly rang and Sheriff Smith stepped over to answer it, telling Gibson to get the remaining money from Frank. Willard suddenly stood up, pulled a pistol from his pocket, and ran for the door. Sheriff Smith dropped the phone and rushed Willard who turned and shot the Sheriff then shot wildly at Judge White, before running out the door. Gibson chased Frank out the door. Judge White slammed the door behind them and locked it before turning to Smith, who was still standing. Smith suddenly collapsed on the couch and died without making a sound.

Frank ran, followed by angry armed citizens. Three men in a wagon finally caught him. As the wagon entered town, it was met by a large lynch mob. The Sheriff was able to disperse the crowd and later that night, Frank Willard was quietly driven to the insane asylum.

He was declared sane at his trial, despite having been confined on 3 separate occasions in the State Hospital for the Insane.[264] He was sentenced to be hung at San Quentin. The jury took only 33 minutes to deliberate before declaring him guilty. News during the trial showed the prejudice of the times: "Frank Willard a degenerate? Shall he be so termed? Yes, let it so be. There he sat his straight hair – his high cheekbones, his retreating forehead all proclaimed that Indian blood ran through his veins; and again there were those small black eyes set deep in the head, the crafty cunning eye that is constantly shifting – the eyes to distrust, that shows the deep seated devil that is stored away in the heart." Other descriptions included "snake like eyes hidden under beetling brows", "stolid Indian features with no expression", "madness of spirit had come down through the ages of his Castilian and Indian blood ancestors". He was actually told by his attorneys not to speak to them in court as they believed this would prejudice the jury! The Supreme Court confirmed his sentence.

Then the Federal Government became involved, because Frank Willard was a "half-breed" Indian and a 'ward' of the government. His case was brought to the attention of the Attorney General by a school teacher on the reservation, who was of the opinion that Willard's conviction was due to the great popularity of the murdered official, and prejudice against his 'half breed' slayer.[265] Frank Willard was tried again by a jury to determine his sanity. They were out only 5 minutes before again judging him sane and reinstating his death penalty. He received 2 separate last minute reprieves but was finally hung on 14 June 1907 at San Quentin. He was 44 and had never married.[266]

Henry Willard

Henry Harper Willard, noted in the news accounts as "the brother of Frank Willard, the half breed who has been condemned to death", was shot three times and seriously injured by James Meyers on the sidewalk in front of Meyers and Cantrell's saloon in the presence of 8 or 10 people. Henry had been drinking heavily since Frank was sentenced to hang and he had threatened to kill DA Duncan, Judge White and others. That Monday evening, Henry was drinking at Jim Meyer's saloon and, violently drunk, called Myers every vile name he could think of until Meyers ordered him to leave. Henry returned about an hour later as Meyers and others were talking on the sidewalk in front of the saloon. The inebriated Henry began yelling again at Meyers who told him he wanted no trouble. Henry called him a coward and started towards him saying he would "lick you anyhow", armed with a rubber hose full of buckshot. Meyers pulled his revolver and emptied it at Willard. Three shots hit his neck, shoulder and arm. Surprisingly, Henry survived.

Fraud

Henry Willard had a reputation as a "bad man". It was widely believed that he and his brother Frank had killed their mother's husband, Armstrong McCabe. Henry had married Mary Louise (Wheeler) in 1891 and had 3 children but had threatened to kill several men for *"alienating his wife's affections"*.[267] He continued drinking and disturbing the peace until he was banished from the county in 1906.[268] He later returned and died in 1948 at 88 years old in Willets and is buried in Willets Cemetery. His children survived him.

The rest of Mary Maxima (Ynita)(Bennet)(Willard) McCabe's family lived more peaceful lives, perhaps because most of them identified as, and could pass for white.

Mary Cayetana married Antonio Prairie. In 1930 she was living with her sister Annie and brother Henry. She was widowed and all were listed as white. She died in Sanel in 1938 at the age of 80. She is buried at Hopland Cemetery.

Ellen married Thomas Babcock. They had 4 boys and 2 girls. She died 22 Feb 1901 in Hopland and is buried in Hopland Cemetery.

Charley moved to Oregon and married Jessie Moore and had 2 sons and a daughter. They all identified as white. He died 1933 in Klamath Falls, OR at 67 and is buried at Mt. Calvary Cemetery there.

Robert died in 1890 at the age of 22 of typhoid fever. He is buried in Hopland Cemetery.

Anna married Frank Tindall. They had no children and always identified as white. She died at the age of 94 in Ukiah in June 1964.

Sarah married Byron Redden and died in childbirth in 1894 at 18. Her daughter Matilda survived. She is buried in Hopland cemetery.

John was widowed, living in Oregon in 1910. In 1913 he married Elsie. They adopted a daughter and had 2 sons. He died after 1942 probably in Oregon.

Clara married George Burns and had 3 children. After his death she married Thomas McKenzie. Clara died in 1920.

Murders in Mendocino

Joseph Knox

Joseph Knox was born in the South and raised in Missouri. He graduated from Yale in 1850 and immediately became Justice of the Peace in Marin. When his father, slave owning Dr. Rueben Knox, died in the boating accident, Joseph could not afford to purchase Rancho Novato, but leased it and practiced law, hiring Henry Willard as ranch foreman. Knox became Marin County's first elected judge and Associate Justice of the Court of Sessions. In 1855, he wrote Camilo's will. Camilo died between April and July in 1856 and Henry Bennet died several months later, both suddenly and both kept oddly quiet, probably through Knox's influence. Sixteen year old Mary Maxima was hastily re-married to Knox's ranch foreman, Henry Willard, and moved to Mendocino near Ukiah.

A few months later, in 1857, the 27 year old Yale educated attorney, Joseph Knox, suddenly resigned his judgeship in Marin, freed his slaves and moved to Sanel, Mendocino where Willard and Knox purchased large adjoining tracts of land. This was done despite a letter to his mother in May 1856 indicating his intention to remain at Rancho Novato for another 5 years.

23 - Joseph Knox

He also claimed to have married Camilo's 12 year old illiterate Indian daughter, highly unlikely at a time when white men who married Indian women were disparaged and called 'squaw men'. One hardly expected this Yale educated, slave owning, southern Judge to do so. But were they really married?

A few years later, in November, 1860, Knox and Willard decided to sell Camilo's old Rancho Apalacocha to John Knight. Knox wrote strange sales contract, stating that both girls were of legal age and that he was the husband of Maria Antonia. It noted that she had a child over 1 year old, implying that Knox had married her in 1858 when she was 13. No record of an 1858 Knox marriage exists. A later 'copy' of a marriage record was dated 1888, long after this sales document was prepared. A publication of biographical sketches done by Alley, Bowen and Co for the 1880 <u>History of Mendocino County</u> goes into great detail about Knox. Despite personally interviewing Knox for the publication, it does not mention Knox as married or having children.

Despite the 1860 sales contract stipulating both girls were of legal age, buyer attorney John Knight was concerned that Maria Antonia was not yet 15, legal age to agree to the contract. He went to San Rafael Mission where he found birth records showing she was still only 14, nullifying the contract. But Knox had planned for that possibility. The contract also stated that, if a Judge believed that Maria Antonia was not of legal age, the Judge should appoint Joseph Knox as her legal guardian and order him to sell her interest to pay her debts and return the surplus for her maintenance. This was a most unusual request! If they were legally married as he claimed, her husband would automatically be her legal guardian. She was probably his common law wife at this point, especially since there had been no adult to agree to her underage marriage. The Judge did, in fact, appoint Knox as her guardian and uphold the sale. Both girls were still unable to read or write and their names were signed with X and witnessed by Henry Willard.

And what of Camilo's missing treasure? It was widely known that Camilo had received $4290 in gold coins from James Black for the sale the Olompali Rancho in 1852. The legend of his "lost treasure" claimed that he decided to bury the gold. Because he was drunk, he took 6 year old Maria Antonia with him to help him find the hiding place later. So, it is quite incriminating that in 1857, Joseph Knox, who could not afford to purchase Rancho Novato, purchased 2400 acres of ranch land in Sanel. His former employee, Henry Willard, too broke to foreclose on Rancho Olompali, also bought 1790 acres at the same time in the same location. Given the odd circumstances around Camilo's death, Henry Bennet's death, the fast marriages to otherwise 'inappropriate' spouses, and the large land purchases, it seems probable that Maria Antonia was 'persuaded' to show Knox where the treasure was buried and that Knox dug it up. Willard was part of the plan and they used Camillo's gold to purchase their land in Sanel in 1857.[269]

Henry Willard had arrived in Sanel with Mary Maxima in 1856 and Joseph Knox and Maria Antonia arrived in 1857. After purchasing their large tracts of land, they started a saloon together and founded Hopland. The 1870 census shows Joseph Knox with children Louisa (10) and Maria (8). His wife Maria Antonia was not shown although she did appear in the 1880 census. Knox was active in politics and was VP of the Democrat Club in Hopland in 1900, Deputy Assessor in 1904-1905. In 1900 Joseph and Maria Knox were caring for an 8 year old grandson, Joe M. The last mention of Knox was in 1907 when he sold property in Hopland. He died leaving Maria land rich but cash poor.

In 1913 Maria, Mrs. J.A. Knox, was granted an allowance from the county of $6 per month. In 1919 she was granted $10 per month at H.H. Gibson's store, which was reduced to $8 in 1924. Maria Antonia Knox died in 1925 at the age of 80. Her daughters each received half ownership in the remaining Knox property.

John Knight

Attorney John Knight also came to California in Stevenson's NY regiment during the Mexican War so he and Willard had served together. He first settled in Marin and became friends with Fernando Feliz, the original grantee of Rancho Novato. When Feliz received Rancho Sanel and sold Rancho Novato, Knight relocated, becoming the first Anglo settler in Sanel in 1852. He was given the 1000 acre Knight's Valley as payment for his legal work proving the Rancho Sanel land grant through the US courts. In 1861, Knight purchased the 500 mountainous acres of Rancho Apalacocha in Marin for $3693 (about $7/acre) and so the last of the original land grant of Marin's Rancho Olompali passed from Native American into white ownership.

John Knight married Sarah Teresa Te-Yees Joaquin, a young Indian woman in 1858, and had 4 sons and a daughter with her. In 1870 he was a 40 year old attorney and Knights Valley was worth $10,000. He sold much of his property in the late 1870's to the Crawford family.

Then, in 1880, gold and quicksilver were discovered on his remaining property and he sold that off as well.

He was well known for his hospitality and kindness but, after he sold his land, he descended into alcoholism. He was noted as "Sick – Drink" on the 1880 census. His and his wife, Sarah Teresa, separated and she moved to the Round Valley reservation where she worked as a basket maker. She died in 1914. Their children included John Knight (1859-1920), Thomas Lincoln Knight (1865-1928), James Knight (1872-1944), William Knight (1877-?), Mary Wylackie Knight (1878-1930) and Steven Knight (1878-1961).

He lost his law practice and was reduced to living on the County Poor Farm. On Christmas Eve 1892, John came to town and spent the day celebrating at Asbill's Saloon. He was too drunk to return home so the Marshall took him to the damp and freezing jail. Passed out without a blanket, he died there the next day of exposure. His death led to severe censure of the Marshall and belated improvements to the disgraceful jail.

At his death, news articles noted that 'Old' John Knight, once counted among the richest men in northern California, died at the age of 62. The Ukiah Daily Journal carried a tribute: "His faults and errors made him the greatest sufferer, and as for his virtues, he fed the hungry and clothed the poor in those days when fortune gave him her smiles, and his good deeds should not soon be forgotten. Few of the old residents of Mendocino County but can relate to his generosity and hospitality. Many remember these attributes of his nature with gratitude. His many friends in Sanel most earnestly exclaim "peace be unto his ashes" and his gifts to the community here are a lasting tribute to his memory."[270]

Chapter 16 – Gunslinger

George W. Parker – 1893

On June 19th, 1893, George William Parker (44) was shot to death at 1:35 am at Niepp's saloon by James D. Sherman, who had been a good friend of his for several years, and was with 7 other men in the saloon at the time.[271] Sherman was manager of Marks and Newfield's large sheep ranch near Ukiah.

George W. Parker was born in Buffalo, New York, and lived many years in San Rafael before moving to Ukiah where he owned a jewelry store. He had been a jeweler in Ukiah for 9 years and had become a city trustee and a well-respected man in town. He was noted as the finest workman in the county in May of 1893. He was, however, known to become belligerent and uncontrollable when drunk.

Earlier that evening, a man named Lick Simmons came into Stump's saloon and announced that Parker was drunk outside and he was going to try to take him home. Scott Howard offered to help him but after two hours of trying they could not persuade Parker to go home so they left him near his house. He followed them back to town and they all wound up at Niepp's saloon where Parker grew progressively more drunk and belligerent. Sherman came in a bit later and, when told of the problem with Parker, he said he was a good friend and would see that Parker got home. They all continued drinking but a petty argument soon broke out between Sherman and Parker over who was a better shot. They began to scuffle and were separated by friends. Sherman told Parker to leave him alone, then bought 3 successive rounds of drinks to settle 3 more arguments Parker started.

Unable to goad Sherman into a fight, Parker got out a small penknife and threatened to *"cut Sherman in two"*. Sherman said *"Stop George, I don't want no trouble."* Howard took the penknife away from Parker and tried to calm him down. Meanwhile Sherman moved his gun from the right pocket of his overalls to his coat pocket. Parker, ignored the attempts to calm him, drew his gun and began to advance on Sherman saying *"God damn you"*. Sherman finally pulled his gun and shot

Parker 4 times, killing him. He immediately gave himself up. George Parker was 44 when he died and left a wife and 4 children.

Jim Sherman was first exonerated by the Coroner's Jury as it appeared a clear case of self-defense. Then evidence was submitted that Sherman had made threats against Parker. So he was arrested again on June 9th and tried for Parker's murder. The jury deliberated only 1 hour before finding him guilty of murder in the 2nd degree. He was sentenced to 6 years in San Quentin on 15 Dec 1893.[272] He was held in Ukiah pending his appeal trial. In April the Sheriff was able to prevent a lunch mob from killing him. At his Supreme Court appeal trial, the earlier ruling was reversed and Sherman was acquitted on the basis of self-defense and released in September 1894.

James D. Sherman

Sherman got off lucky that time, because James Daniel Sherman was actually a notorious outlaw. He was also known as James Talbot, aka James Daniels, and was the black sheep of a well-respected family from Ohio that included John and William Tecumseh Sherman, his first cousins.

James married Allie Williams in San Antonio, Texas in 1876. Shortly after his marriage, he became an outlaw for murdering 2 black men. He began working with a gang who killed two shopkeepers while robbing their store and escaped as drovers on a cattle drive. On their return to Kansas, the gang stole a herd of cattle, killing the owners, two men and a woman. During this time he used the name Jim Daniels and was indicted under that name in 1881 for horse stealing in Hill County, Texas. He and his gang then joined a rough outfit at the Millet Ranch, in Baylor, Texas. After a shootout there with law officers he joined another cattle drive which stopped in Caldwell, Kansas. James was then using the name Jim Talbot. After recognizing Mike Meagher who was the Mayor in Caldwell, he decided to stay to settle an old score. Jim sent for Allie and their children, a boy of about 3 named Jimmie and a daughter about 1, named Sarah.

Murders in Mendocino

Mike Meagher - 1881

Caldwell, Kansas was the roughest town on the border. Mike Meagher former town Marshall in Wichita, Kansas was now mayor. While he was Marshall in Wichita, Mike shot Jim Talbot's first cousin. When Jim realized Meagher was Mayor of Caldwell, he vowed revenge.

Jim Talbot and his gang drank, whored and raised hell. One day the gang toasted dawn with a volley of shots. It was the final straw. Marshall John Wilson, a noted desperado in his own right, appointed Mayor Mike Meagher as a special deputy and they went out to arrest the troublemakers, every man in town with a gun backing them up. Jim Talbot refused to run. He stood in the middle of the street shooting at the two Marshalls. He killed Meagher before jumping on a horse and racing out of town.

The wild shootout in the middle of town and the murder of the well-known Mayor Meagher made national news. With the help of Jim's friends, Allie and the children joined him and they moved west to Mendocino where Jim Talbot became Jim Sherman again. He went straight and became the well-respected manager of the Marks and Newfield Ranch. He was elected constable and had been deputy sheriff there for over 10 years. No one knew he was a notorious outlaw.

But, while he was held for Parker's death, someone notified Mendocino Sheriff J. R. Johnson that the man he knew as Jim Sherman was actually Jim Talbot, wanted in Kansas, and there was a large reward for his arrest. Only a few people knew this secret. One was his wife, Allie, the other was Meagher's brother, John, who could have tracked Sherman to California. Neither took credit or ever collected the reward.

The Sheriff followed up and Sherman was arrested for Meagher's murder immediately after his acquittal in Parker's death. He was returned to Kansas for trial. At his first trial there was a hung jury, 11 for guilty and one for acquittal. At his 2nd trial, he was acquitted again after only 4 hours of deliberation.

John Lambert Vallely

After his release in Kansas, Sherman returned to Covelo in 1895, expecting to find Allie waiting for him. Allie, expecting he would be convicted, had moved in with 29 year old John Vallely in Round Valley. Vallely knew Sherman and was in Niepp's saloon the night of the Parker killing.

Sherman was enraged when he found Allie and Vallely living together and it was incorrectly reported that he had stabbed Vallely to death. As with many news stories, this death report was premature.

John Lambert Vallely was the son of an Irishman named John Vallely who had also arrived in California with Stevenson's Regiment. He moved to Mendocino and married Mary Elizabeth Lambert in 1862 when she was only 12. Their only child, John Lambert Vallely, was born in 1866 when she was just 16. The Vallelys separated and Mary Elizabeth married William J Shields in 1868, remained in Mendocino and had 8 more children.

After surviving the fight with Sherman over Allie, John L was arrested in 1897 in Ukiah for petty larceny for stealing a suit of clothes from Police Chief Redwine at Ell's livery stable near the depot and was sentenced to 3 years in San Quentin. He was released in 1899 and returned home to Mendocino where he married Eva (Brown) Garfield in 1912.

Eva was a 23 year old full-blood Little Lakes-Redwood Indian, daughter of James Brown and Peggy Anthony. Eva had a daughter Ellen Moore in 1907 and son Russell Garfield in 1909 and sold her allotment to the Concow Cemetery Association in 1909.

After their marriage, the John and Eva Vallely had 3 more children, John Jr., Frances, and Lloyd.

John Lambert Vallely died in 1929 at the age of 63.

Murders in Mendocino

John D. Sherman - 1896

Allie was forced to return to Jim Sherman but it was not a happy relationship and she was often heard to say that she was only with him because he threatened to kill her if she left. J.D. Sherman worked in a blacksmith shop and the family was living on The Handy ranch, 2 miles from Covelo. One night Sherman started for home on a mule about 8:30 in the evening and was nearing his front gate when a shot rang out. Sherman had been shot with a 38 or 40 caliber rifle by someone directly in front and slightly to his right. The bullet had passed through his neck severing the spinal cord. John Bishop, manager of the Handy ranch came home from town soon afterward and found his body in the road. He was buried in Covelo.

There was no lack of suspects. John Vallely had been badly beaten and shot over Allie and was the prime suspect. Allie herself might have done it. She was suspected of having turned Jim in to the law in the first place. A local man named Rogers had a grudge against Sherman and John Meagher might have killed him in revenge for his brother's murder. Sherman had also been doing detective work for the family of Joe Gregory, accused of lynching Jack Littlefield and was also investigating the murder of Charles Felton. Any of them could have been responsible.

Allie and her children moved to Ukiah within days of Sherman's death. Allie must have soon died because in 1900, the youngest daughter, 11 year old Dell, was in an orphanage in Sacramento. She married Fred Gyselaar and had a daughter named Freddie, later divorced and lived in San Francisco until she died in 1982.

Lucinda, the middle child went to Washington in 1900 and married in 1908 to William Anderstrom. Her sister Dell was a witness at her wedding.

James, the oldest at 23 was in Wyoming in 1900 working as a cowboy. He married and had a family there and died in 1957 in Tacoma, WA.

Chapter 17 – Round Valley Range War

Murders in Mendocino

Round Valley Range War

As we noted in the first chapter, land ownership issues in Round Valley festered for years and finally erupted into the Round Valley Range War. Ranchers illegally grazed their herds on reservation land, tore down the fences protecting Indian crops, and eventually claimed the land, supported in their efforts by Indian Supt. Henley. Round Valley became notorious for murders. The wealthy George White was king of the valley and held it with a strong grip. Sheriffs were paid to look the other way. Honest men were framed and sent to jail, harassed, threatened, burned out and killed for their land and no one was punished.

George E. White

George E. White was born to a well-known West Virginia family in 1832, a distant cousin of Stonewall Jackson. In May of 1854, George and his brothers, James and Calvin White, George Hudspeth, Dr. Atkinson, and Charles Bourne, on a trip to the gold fields, entered Round Valley, shortly behind the Asbill party. George claimed 1600 acres in the Valley and Charley Bourne agreed to remain to manage his claim, receiving 600 acres in exchange for his services. Charley Bourne built the first cabin in the valley and bought a herd of cattle. His herd became the 1st stock in the valley not owned by the Reservation. White's herd, driven up from Los Angeles, arrived soon after and White built the 2nd house. The 3rd house was built by Devinna and Craft on what later became the Melendy Ranch. The 4th house was built by Lawson and Arthur who brought the first hogs to the valley. This settlement became the town of Covelo.

During that same summer, Sanders Hornbrook, Martin Corbett, Lawson, Old John B. Owens (whose son JB was killed by Burke), James H. Thomas, T. D. Laycock, C. H. Eberley and a Mr. King also arrived. There were 19 white men in the valley in 1857-58 and two white women.[273] These were the men who began harassing Catherine Angle.

White was determined to own the entire Yolla Bolly range, far larger than just Round Valley, by any means. One day, his men found a body on the beach that had been thrown overboard after dying of

Round Valley Range War

smallpox. They dragged the infected body to a Rancheria watering hole and threw it in. All the Indians died except 4 who were sent to the Reservation, and White appropriated their land. This plan worked well so White repeated the process. Typically he paid his men to file claims on the only water sources. Once the claims were proven up, they transferred the land to White. He ranged his stock over government lands for free and controlled the only water.

Wylackie John Wathen was White's ranch foreman and partner in crime. As settlers attempted to move into Round Valley, White and Wylackie John and his gang of buckaroos forced them out, unless they agreed prove up their claims and turn their land and herds over to White. Those who wouldn't cooperate were forced out. White's favorite move was to get his men to file fraudulent charges of rustling to put settlers in prison with perjured testimony or bankrupt them with legal fees. Those who survived these efforts and persisted were killed and the murderers got off on 'self-defense' with White's paid-off judges. His men patrolled White's 150,000 acres and were forced to commit murder on his orders or be killed themselves. They were frequently promised rewards but rarely lived long enough to collect them. By the 1880's White and his men were feared, not only in Mendocino County but in Lake, Trinity and Humboldt Counties as well. Riding high, the Cattle King decided to marry in 1859.

24 - Geoge E. White

Murders in Mendocino

Hannah Elizabeth Welling

Hannah Elizabeth Welling was born in New York about 1840 to John Walstein and Mary Ann (Wisner) Welling. Her father left the family and moved to San Francisco after a bankruptcy in 1850. Hannah and her mother came to San Francisco to join him after 1855. Her father, a tailor, owned a grocery in San Francisco, possibly how Hannah met George. She was 19 when they married in 1859 and she moved to the White Ranch in Covelo. They had a daughter, Georgina Emma White, the following year. Then, in 1861, White suddenly put Hannah and the baby on a horse with a little money and a saddlebag of clothes and sent them to her parents in San Francisco, promising to join them shortly. He never arrived.

In 1862, shortly after her mother died, Hannah filed for divorce. White paid men to commit perjury, claiming she had been unfaithful to him so he would not have to pay her alimony, and even questioned the paternity of his daughter Georgia. Despite White being one of the richest men in California, Hannah was forced to settle for only $600, most of which she paid her lawyers.[274] Her father was listed as a speculator in 1862, living at 82 Jesse Street and it is not clear what income he had or if he helped to support Hannah and Georgia.

25 - Hannah Welling White Lee

In May 27, 1869, 29 year old Hannah married William S. Lee in Alameda, CA.[275] William was originally from Pennsylvania. Sadly, she was widowed just two years later when her 41 year old husband died of consumption. They had no children together. After William Lee died, Hannah never remarried. He left her a farm on Bay Island in San Francisco Bay. In 1875 Hannah sold 6 acres of the farm to CS Metzger for $1600. She sold another parcel in 1876 to B Benedict and in 1877 additional property to Metzger. She was living on Bay Farm Island in 1878 and 1879. Her father was also listed there as a fruit peddler.

In 1880, Hannah (40) and her daughter Georgina Emma (19) were apparently struggling. They lived on Rausch Street in San Francisco off Howard near 7th St. Hannah was a servant and Georgie was a dressmaker. But the Bay Island land was appreciating fast and by 1882 it was worth about $262 per acre. By 1885, Hannah had bought lot 50 and ½ of lot 51, block 28 in the Veitch tract in Alameda. Alameda Island and Bay Farm Island made up the City of Alameda, the prestigious "Garden of California" and well known resort area until after the depression. She held her father's funeral from her home on Bay Farm Island in 1887.

Hannah finally got her revenge on George E. White. She testified for his 3rd wife, Frankie, against George at their divorce trial in 1888. He had paid men to commit perjury claiming she was unfaithful. Hannah testified he had used the same men and story against her in their divorce. Hannah died at the home of her daughter Georgina Crozer at 1425 High Street, in Alameda, CA on May 26, 1899 at the age of 59.

Georgina married Enoch L. Crozer and had children Hannah (1885), Miriam (1887), Enoch (1889) and Ruth (1895). In 1904 she sued her uncle, William Pitt White and John S Rohrbough for a right to the homestead property of George White. She lost.

Elizabeth Alice Fetty

In March 1868, immediately after his divorce from Hannah Welling was final, George White went home to Lewis County, West Virginia and two months later, on May 7, 1868 36 year old George White married 18 year old Elizabeth Alice Fetty. Oddly they were married in Athens, Ohio, not at either family home. They did not appear to have any relatives in Athens. There was also no wedding announcement despite their prominent families. Perhaps they eloped.

She was the daughter of Esaias and Margaret (Carmack) Fetty of Lewis, West Virginia. Her older sister Mary Catherine married George's brother, Alexander Perry White. A younger sister, Adelaide, married his cousin Wilson White. A niece married John Rohrbough son of George's sister Marilla. Her brother William Newton Fetty came to California with her and worked for George E White for many years.

Murders in Mendocino

George was 37 and very wealthy. Unfortunately, this marriage did not go well ether. Alice complained of his infidelities and George decided to get rid of her. She sought divorce. He may have had other ideas. Suddenly this 23 year old apparently healthy woman died of consumption in San Francisco on 27 July 1873. Given George's other behaviors, it may be speculated that she was given small amounts of poison until she died.

Alice was originally buried in St. Mary's Cemetery in Oakland, CA. Her body was later moved to the Fetty family's plot in Waldeck Cemetery, Waldeck, West Virginia.[276]

While White was acquiring his wealth, marrying and pretending to be fine upstanding citizen, he and Wylcakie John were terrorizing three counties. He was bribing and paying off sheriffs District Attorneys and Judges. He owned the newspapers who only printed positive articles about him. There were over 16 murders in Yolla Bolly area widely attributed to the White gang who would terrorize anyone he ordered them to, as it was worth their life to refuse. This soon became a war by White on anyone who tried to settle in Round Valley. Among the earliest murders ordered by White was the killing of Owen Cunningham by Elisha Cain on the evening of November 21, 1869.

Owen Cunningham – 1869

Owen Cunningham, a 45 year old Irishman had been sharing a cabin with Elisha Cain (one of White's buckaroos) and Benjamin Doyle. On the night of November 21, 1869 they all went out drinking. Cunningham went back to the cabin to get something to eat. Cain followed and they got into an argument. Cunningham threw Cain to the floor but no serious harm was done and Cunningham resumed cooking. Cain, who was sitting on the bed, picked up a maul hidden under the bed and struck Cunningham in the back of his head paralyzing him. Cunningham lived several hours before dying. Cain was tried and the found guilty. An appeal was filed the next day. Defense attorneys paid for by White persuaded the jury he was "Not Guilty".[277] To pay back this debt, Cain killed Jack Littlefield for White several years later.

Elisha Cain

Cain was born in Missouri about 1835 and had been in Mendocino since 1866 and remained loyal to White. He and 3 men were arrested when they failed to show up for trial in the Littlefield lynching case in 1899 and were transported to Weaverville for the trial.[278] Cain moved to Caution, Trinity County for several years before moving back to Mendocino when he was about 72. He died on 1 August 1910 in Mendocino at the age of 79. He appears to have never married.[279]

In 1874 a secret investigation by the Interior Department against the Round Valley settlers indicted a group including the Henley brothers, George E. White, William Pitt White and William N. Fetty for a pattern of filing claims and selling land that they didn't legally own.. Charges against all were finally dropped in 1883.

In 1875 a special order was sent to White ordering him to remove his stock from reservation lands. He ignored the order and the US Attorney in San Francisco refused to bring suit.

Murders in Mendocino

Augustus Daniel Packwood – 1877

The Packwood Brothers from Missouri were the next to feel White's wrath. Wylackie John ordered them to scare off a settler named Johnson. The Packwoods intimidated Johnson into leaving by threatening to burn down his house with him and his family in it. Johnson and his family wisely left. Wylackie John then took over the Johnson spread but paid the Packwoods only $70. Gus insisted they had been promised more so White decided to have Gus Packwood killed as an example to the others. The unsuspecting Gus and a group of White's men rode out one day to 'get his money'. At noon, they all sat on the ground to rest. As Gus half dozed in the shade, George Kindred, another of Wylackie John's men, knelt behind a fallen log and shot Gus Packwood in the back.

Two weeks after the murder, Wylackie John turned himself in to the Justice of the Peace in Weaverville claiming he had fired in self-defense, despite not having been anywhere near the place. Kindred and the other 4 men testified in Wylackie John's defense, insisting the killing was self-defense, despite the fact that Gus was shot in the back.

The prosecution presented two investigators, Robert Grieves and Paul Hereford, who found Packwood's gun and testified that that the gun had not been primed or fired. This should have demolished the fabricated 'self-defense' story. But Justice Thomas determined that there was "insufficient evidence to warrant the belief that a conviction could be obtained" and ordered the prisoners discharged.[280]

Their prosecution testimony of course made Grieves and Hereford new targets of the White gang.

By 1878 George White, now known as the Cattle King of California, had built a mansion in Covelo, more elegant than anything north of San Francisco. The large white house nestled among green lawns and shady trees, with running water and gas in every room.[281] His grand white barns held fine horses and fruit orchards lay nearby. His wealth allowed White to control the elections for Sheriffs and Judges.

Round Valley Range War

Robert Grieves – 1878

White decided Robert Grieves had to be punished for testifying for the prosecution against Wylackie John in the Gus Packwood murder trial and decided to make an example out of it.

Robert was a popular and honest young man and had just married Katie Frost on July 31st, 1878 in Mendocino. He made a new will that day, leaving his 160 acres and all his personal property, to Katie. He was shot the next day on Aug 1st, 1878[282] while out with his friend Wilson Lloyd. The man who shot him was White's 2nd cousin, John P. White, who made sure to do it in Trinity County because the Trinity County Judge could be bought. John P. White, father of George's future wife Frankie, was arrested in Mendocino and transferred to Trinity County for trial because White 'owned' the law in Trinity.

Wilson Lloyd, the eye witness to the shooting, was told by Wylackie John to take $1000 and leave the county. Lloyd 'accepted' this 'offer'. He was apparently followed and killed but, despite extensive searches by the Masons, of which he was a member, his body was never found.

The prosecution presented a strong case of premeditated murder against John P. White. The defense attorneys, paid for by George White, claimed it was an accidental shooting. They again produced perjured witnesses who swore that Grieves was the aggressor. They had disposed of the only witness, Wilson Lloyd. Despite the fact that Grieves was a newly-wed man with a reputation as a peaceable, quiet and inoffensive man, who was probably unarmed, John P. White was acquitted. [283]

It was obvious to everyone that George E. White could not be stopped and that there would be no 'justice' from the law. White had publicly paid men to lie under oath. He paid off attorneys and judges to obtain the results he wanted. Everyone knew it but nothing could be done.

Murders in Mendocino

Weck and Martha McPherson – 1879

Wylackie John Wathen was the director of the next act in this tragedy. Martha Jane Hagler was married at 14 to Thomas 'Weck' McPherson, 21, in Healdsburg, Sonoma County. Their first child was stillborn when Martha was only 15. Her 2nd child, Hattie Elizabeth, was born 11 months later in 1866. Martha's third child was Charles Walter born in 1869 and she was 8 months pregnant with Bertha when her oldest child, Hattie, then 4 years old, suddenly died. Bertha was born on 28 Aug 1870. Martha was overwhelmed taking care of toddler Charley and her newborn Bertha and grieving the loss of her beloved 4 year old Hattie. She was at her most vulnerable when their friend, Wylackie John Wathen, visited Martha at their isolated ranch.

John used his considerable charm to start an affair with Martha and over time urged her unsuspecting husband, Weck, to invest $5000 in a sheep ranch and move his young family to Round Valley. It sounded like a good plan to Weck and Covelo was not as isolated as their current ranch so they moved there in 1874 with their 2 children.

Weck was elected as a Justice of the Peace in Covelo. Wylackie John and Martha's affair continued for over 5 years but by 1878, Wylackie John was getting restless. He wanted to marry Ellen Anthony of Mendocino, and was sure that Martha, still in love with him, would make that difficult. Martha was then 29 with a 10 ½ year old son and 9 year old daughter. So Wylackie John began to spread rumors about Martha, implying that she was unfaithful and that Brady Tuttle was the 'other man'. These rumors soon came to the attention of her husband. Of course Martha denied it, but Weck had sensed that there was someone else and these rumors created so much tension in their marriage that Weck took the children and moved in with his brother near Geyserville.[284] Wylackie John Wathen, pretending to still be in love with her, convinced the unsuspecting and desperate Martha to give him a bill of sale and deed to the McPherson's Oak Ranch as a means of 'saving it from McPherson' in the pending divorce. Martha's father had just died, her husband had taken her children and she was a being called a loose woman by the good folks in Covelo. With no one else to turn to for advice, Martha did, in fact, deed their Oak Ranch on Long Ridge in Trinity County to Wylackie John Wathen. This was what Wathen had been waiting for and he now made sure the rumors escalated until they reached Weck in Geyserville.

Weck McPherson rode to his former home, Oak Ranch, now called the Wathen Place to see Wylackie John on the night of the 2nd of October. He went to Duncan Camp where he stayed the night and talked to Wylackie John who convinced him that Brady Tuttle had been living as man and wife with Martha, making him a laughingstock in the county. Martha was actually staying at the Lightfoot Ranch with Paul Hereford and his family and had nothing to do with Tuttle.

The next day, Weck rode to the Lightfoot Ranch. Jim Neafus, sent by Wylackie John, had arrived there just ahead of Weck. When Weck arrived and asked for Martha, Mrs. Hereford told him that she was out hunting. Weck then asked to see a saddle Martha had won at a fair and, told it was in her room, Weck went down the hall. Suddenly Neafus and Mrs. Hereford heard Martha yell she would shoot him if he attempted to enter her room. There was a brief scuffle and a shot was heard. They both ran down the hall and saw the couple struggling over a rifle. Martha had it by the still smoking muzzle, while Weck held the stock. He pulled the gun from her hands and shot Martha 3 times, killing her instantly.

Weck then ordered Neafus and Mrs. Hereford to carry Martha's body out of the house, but Mrs. Hereford refused to touch the corpse. Neafus could not do it alone so Weck set down the rifle to help. When Weck turned to ask Mrs. Hereford to get a handkerchief to tie around Martha's shattered lower jaw, Neafus ran. Weck caught him and brought him back. After helping Weck to move the body, Neafus begged for his life and convinced Weck to go. McPherson rode off leaving Neafus and Mrs. Hereford alive with Martha's body. He told them he intended to kill Tuttle and then kill himself.

Murders in Mendocino

On the 9 mile ride back to his former home, Weck stopped and wrote a letter to his brother, Lycurgus 'Kirk', explaining how he had killed Martha and planned to kill Brady Tuttle and then himself and why. When he arrived at the Wathen place, he stood his gun against the house and chatted with Julia, Wylackie John's half Indian daughter while McDaniel, went to find Tuttle to tell him Weck wanted to see him.

Meanwhile Neafus had quietly arrived at the ranch and warned the men that Weck had just killed Martha and planned to kill Tuttle. The shearers formed a group to arrest him. They confiscated Weck's rifle and told him to put up his hands. Instead, he ran, and they fired 8 shots into him including 3 in the breast, one in the groin, 3 in the back and one in the knee. Sheriff Philbrook arrived and arrested Spanish Louie, W. C. Sherwood, James Moore and C. C. Sorenson and took them to Weaverville, accompanied by Edward Jones and Jim Neafus who had witnessed both killings. The arrested men were discharged when the case was ruled "justifiable homicide".[285]

Poor Martha was buried at the Hereford's Lightfoot Ranch where she had been shot. McPherson was buried at the Oak Ranch he had built with such high hopes.

In his letter-will to his brother, Weck asked Kirk to take care of his children and noted that George E. White in Covelo owed him $275. He left his horse and 2 colts at his old ranch, now Wathen's place, and 2 horses belonging to his wife. He instructed that his wife's watch and rings, and her saddle were to go to his daughter Birdy (Bertha), while his watch and saddle were for his son Charley.[286] Kirk McPherson raised the orphaned children who lived with his family in Healdsburg, Sonoma County. Charley later married Nancy Etta Hale and had 2 children. Bertha married John Harry Sierck in 1891 and also had children.

Wylackie John Wathen promptly married Ellen Anthony of Mendocino and moved her to Weck's Oak Farm.

Round Valley Range War

Frankie White

Meanwhile George E. White was looking for his 3rd wife. Although he had no lack of available local women, another distant cousin caught his eye. She was the daughter of John Powers White who had moved from West Virginia to California with his wife Christiana Helmick and his younger brothers Samuel and Adam for the gold rush. In 1850 they were all in El Dorado County where John and his 19 year old wife Christiana ran a boarding house. Sam and Adam were miners. John and Christina went to Iowa in 1856 and were in Illinois in 1859. Adam White remained a miner in the gold fields.

John and Christiana returned to Shasta County in 1860 but

26 - Frankie White

Christiana had been growing more mentally ill. She was committed to Stockton Mental Hospital on 17 Aug 1869, after physically attacking her husband. She died there in 1887 of organic brain disease. John and the children, Evaline (16), Virginia Belle (14), Emma (12), Frankie (10) and Clarence (8) were in Oregon in 1870 but John was having financial trouble so reached out to his wealthy cousin George E. who agreed to give him a job. They were all in Round Valley by 1875 and it was Frankie's father who shot Robert Grieves, the newlywed, in 1878. In return, George E agreed to pay for the younger children's schooling. He also decided to marry Frankie.

The 1880 the census showed George E White, a widower, (47), Frankie a single cousin (21), John Rohrbough, a single nephew (20) and Carter Rohrbough, a single nephew (26) all living at the house in Covelo. Her father John P White and her older sister Eveline (White) Simpson, a widow with a 6 year old daughter, Eva, lived nearby on Long Ridge in Trinity County near the Wathens, Asbills and Neafus families. That year George shipped 40 tons of wool valued at $24,000, a lot of money in those days.

Murders in Mendocino

Frankie and George White married in 1881. He was about 48 and Frankie was 22. The honeymoon didn't last long. First she discovered he was unfaithful. Then she found out that George was dealing in counterfeit money. When she confronted him, he threatened to kill her to keep her quiet. The final blow was when Frankie's widowed 26 year old sister, Evaline (White) Simpson, came for a visit and George began a flagrant affair with her.

He took Evaline to Santa Cruz and San Francisco where they registered as man and wife. He put her in charge of a saloon and inn he owned on the road between Round Valley and Ukiah, so he could openly visit her. He then bought a house on Claremont Avenue in Berkeley which she occupied as his 'housekeeper'.[287] Having heard the rumors, the disbelieving Frankie knocked on the door in Berkeley one evening in 1883 and found them there together. Wylackie John refused her entry and threatened her again. That was the last straw. Knowing White's penchant for murder, Frankie never returned to Covelo, moving instead into the Russ House, the finest hotel in San Francisco.

George immediately sued Frankie for divorce claiming desertion and adultery and she counter-sued, citing his infidelity. This started the longest and most sensational divorce in California. It hard to overstate the courage it took for Frankie to stand up to him. By 1883, White owned over 150,000 acres in 3 counties and was considered the richest rancher in Northern California. He owned 2500 acres on his homestead in Covelo in Round Valley plus 3 other large sheep ranches in Mendocino County totaling 35,000 acres. He also owned a huge property in Trinity County called Long Ridge which was 40 miles long and 6 miles wide divided into 5 ranches and another tract of over 30,000 acres in Trinity. He ran over 30,000 sheep, large herds of cattle and over 300 horses. He had tremendous influence in 3 counties. He fattened his cattle for the market on Indian preserves and defied the US Government and the Army who tried to remove him. Everyone knew he had ordered men framed, jailed and killed. Everyone also knew he controlled the law and judges in these counties.

But the outraged young Frankie was no pushover and she filed for divorce in San Francisco. George had mistreated her and threatened her. He was very publicly dallying with her own sister and he had the nerve to sue her for divorce! She requested $500 per month alimony and a division of their assets. George of course fought back, and this started the longest divorce in California history. The newspapers had a field day.

Meanwhile George and his gang continued their predations.

Staggs Poisoning - 1885

Staggs had rented a quarter-section from George E. White at Alderpoint Range in Humboldt County where he ran 1200 sheep. He prospered and had no known enemies, until one day he was found dead in his bed. All his property and money was missing. It was soon determined that he had been poisoned by strychnine. Strychnine was a favorite method of ridding an area of bears – and apparently inconvenient men.

Several of the White Gang members openly bragged of poisoning him. No one was ever arrested for Stagg's murder. His sheep were branded as part of the White herd.[288]

Newt Irwin – 1885

Newt Irwin was next. White offered him $500 to poison Billy Nowlin. He certainly tried. One day Irwin gave Billy a quarter of beef. On his way home, Billy Nowlin gave a piece of the meat to his dog and watched in horror as it died. Nowlin then realized the White gang was after him and became so afraid of being poisoned that he began taking gradually increasing doses of poison for the rest of his life. He never again ate food without first giving some to his dogs.

Billy Nowlin wouldn't be intimidated and started rebuilding so White decided to kill him. In 1885, White again sent Newt Irwin to do the job. He had tried to drive sheep onto Nowlin's land in earlier confrontations. That day, Irwin rode up to Nowlin and tried to draw his gun. It became caught in the lining of his coat and Nowlin, a faster draw, shot Irwin, killing him. He then rode 60 miles to Weaverville to turn himself in.

No gun was found on Irwin's body (because White's men had picked it up) so Nowlin was held for trial on murder charges. White's men again committed perjury and the jury sentenced Nowlin to 8 years in San Quentin in 1885.

William Nowlin

William 'Billy' Spencer Nowlin was born in Missouri and came to California at the age of 23 and settled in Trinity County. Nowlin was soon 'invited' by Wylackie John to participate in an attack on Joseph Le Van and his brother. Nowlin refused to get involved in the dirty work, which made him an enemy of Wylackie John and White.

Nowlin and his partner H. C. Hembree had bought a claim in Trinity County, patented in 1877, land on which White had been grazing his sheep for free. When White's men attempted to drive their sheep onto Nowlin and Hembree's land, they were ordered off by the armed new owners. White pressed charges against them for assault with deadly weapons. After they were held in jail for months, both were tried and, despite perjury by the White gang, were acquitted. They returned home to find their house and fences burned to the ground and their sheep branded as White's.

After Nowlin was found guilty of killing Newt Irwin in 1885, his case was appealed to the Supreme Court. At the Supreme Court trial, several years later, Alexander 'Brick' McPherson, no relation to Weck McPherson, testified that George White and Wylackie John had admitted to him that they had sent Irwin to kill Nowlin and bragged about sending men to remove the gun from Irwin's body so it would appear that Nowlin had killed an unarmed man. McPherson also testified that they had told him of several witnesses who had committed perjury at Nowlin's first trial and that White "owned the judge up there and he would do as they wanted."[289]

Nowlin was finally released and stubbornly returned to his land. He married Annie M. Atkinson in Mendocino in 1894 and worked as a blacksmith in Spruce Grove, Humboldt County. Bill and Annie separated 1912 and divorced in 1915. Billy Nowlin died in Mendocino at the age of 92 on 17 Feb 1939.[290] He is buried in Ukiah Cemetery. Billy Nowlin stood up to George E. White and lived to tell about it.

His neighbor was not so lucky.

Murders in Mendocino

George Erickson – 1886

George Erickson was a wealthy cattleman from Norway called "the Swede", who arrived when Trinity County was a wilderness. He was widely known as a good woodsman, honest, fearless and a dead shot. He had acquired quite a bit of property on Long Ridge, a large area touching Mendocino, Trinity and Humboldt counties and refused to be driven off by White. He wouldn't start a fight but he wouldn't avoid one either. Wylackie John, Tom Haydon and John Vinton, all cronies of White, lived nearby. They ran off Erickson's stock and tore down his fences. They had him arrested for stealing stock on several occasions. Although he was acquitted each time, the legal fees and jail time almost ruined him. Intimidation wasn't working so White decided to kill him. He sent a man named Schappe who shot at Erickson but missed. Erickson shot 17 bullets over Schappe's head, deliberately not hitting him. White then ordered Schappe to file charges for attempted murder. The DA, afraid to defy White, delayed filing the necessary paperwork, so Erickson was freed and again returned to his ranch. It was a short reprieve. On Sept 9, 1886, shots were heard and Erickson's rider-less horse was found. They found the body of the un-armed 38 year old Erickson shot in the back. Erickson was married to Dina (Burnsen) Erickson who was 26 and they had 2 sons. A daughter was born 4 months after he was killed. Dina later married Hans Nelson when she was 33 and they moved to Nevada.

Ericson was well liked and had friends in the world outside of Round Valley. They hired Detective Lawson of San Francisco to investigate his murder and bring the killer to justice. There had been 9 murders in 15 years and only Billy Nowlin had been (wrongly) convicted for any of them. Det. Lawson found evidence of a conspiracy to kill Erickson for White. Sheriff George H. Kunz, John Norris, George F. Trogdon and Ben Arthur had each agreed to put up $125 to pay $500 to the man who would kill Ericson. George Orr had drawn the short straw.

Round Valley Range War

George Orr

Orr had been in Humboldt and Trinity Counties about 4 years before the murder. He was born in California about 1858 and had married Daisy Barnwell in Humboldt in 1882 and moved to Trinity County where he went to work on Sheriff Kunz' ranch. Kunz involved Orr in the plot to kill Erickson just a few weeks after Orr began working for him. Kunz promised he would "get off" whoever got arrested for it. George was troubled and told Daisy about the offer and the big money but she begged him not to get involved. So George went back and told Sheriff Kunz that he didn't want to do the killing. But he did tell Kunz that Erickson had gone up the Mad River. Orr and Kunz followed him.

Kunz, planning to frame Orr for the murder, changed boots with Orr, who apparently didn't find this odd enough to object. He also took a handful of Orr's rifle shells which he scattered around the area where he shot Erickson and told Orr to keep working on a brush fence. Kunz followed Erickson and shot him in the back as he rode by, firing 4 shots to deflect suspicion since he known as a crack shot. He then went back and changed boots with Orr again. The two then drove a band of sheep over his trail to cover the tracks.

With assistance from Det. Lawler, George Orr was soon arrested. He confessed to the entire plot and implicated John Norris, Kunz and the others. With Orr's confession, for which charges against him were dropped, the community was up in arms.[291]

John Norris

John Norris also confessed and testified that in June 1883 a group met at Trogden's house to decide how to get rid of Erickson. Norris's first plan, filing false charges to get Erickson arrested on stealing cattle from Ben Arthur, failed when Erickson was released for the legal delay. After his confession and testimony against the others, Norris too was released.

John Norris was born in Ohio about 1844. He was married and had a son named George in 1876. He remained in Trinity County after the Erickson killing, later moving to Sacramento where he died.

Murders in Mendocino

Ben Arthur

After Erickson was released when the DA delayed filing charges, Ben Arthur had suggested killing him. The wealthy Ben Arthur stood trial for Erickson's murder but, despite the testimony of Norris and Orr, the jury found him "not guilty" and he was released in February.[292] He then filed a claim and was actually paid from George Erickson's estate for the 300 head of sheep that he falsely claimed Erickson had stolen.

Ben was born in Ohio and arrived about 1856 with a drove of hogs. He bought land from J.Q. Duncan and established a ranch near the Eel River, east of the Humboldt county line about 1871. By 1877 he had 3,000 acres in various parcels. He married Elizabeth Murphy with whom he had 5 children at the time of this incident. His ranches were foreclosed upon after he took out mortgages to pay attorneys for his trial. He moved to Trinity Mines to live with his brother and his family moved in with the Billy Nowlin family. Ben died in 1911 in Eureka, Humboldt County.

Sheriff George Kunz

Sheriff Kunz was fully implicated in the murder and was well-known to be White's man. Norris testified that Sheriff Kunz told him he had hired Orr to kill Erickson for $500, put up by the others. Another motive, suggested at his trial, was that Sheriff Kunz had involved Orr in the plot and framed him so Kunz could have a relationship with Orr's wife, Daisy, who had previously spurned his advances.

Sheriff Kunz was found guilty and sentenced to hang on January 23rd, 1887. The jury was out only 45 minutes before pronouncing his verdict. He appealed to the Supreme Court and at his appeal trial, he was found "not guilty". George Henry Kunz was 49 at the time of his trial, a single man from Germany. After his release Kunz moved to Sacramento where he died in 1916.

So, in the end, despite the most expensive criminal trial in the history of Trinity County, no one paid for the murder of George Ericson.

Alexander Brick McPherson

White was directing all these murders while fighting Frankie in divorce court. In July 1887 the State Supreme Court in San Francisco decreed that George had to pay Frankie attorney fees and back alimony totaling $3600 while the divorce was pending. George appealed again and, of course, came up with a plan to kill Frankie to end the case.

George and Wylackie John approached Alexander 'Brick' McPherson, a coachman at the Russ House Hotel. Brick was a well-known local con man. He was a good looking man of 40, though only 5" 4" tall, with flaming red hair. White offered to pay Brick a lot of money to "kill her, I don't care how, throw her in the bay, anything so you get rid of her." Wylackie John, the mastermind, suggested Brick take Frankie out for a ride and drive the carriage over an embankment. If she didn't die in the accident, he was to bash her in the head with a rock and claim her death was an accident. White and John would follow and 'assist him' in case he was injured. McPherson rightly assumed he would be killed as well.

He was a con man – not a murderer. He immediately told Frankie and went with her to meet with her attorneys. They asked Brick to play along so they would know what was being planned. Brick happily agreed when they too paid him for his time. So Brick McPherson convinced George White that he had a better idea. He would get Frankie into a compromising position so they could be caught and she would lose the case for her own infidelity. White agreed to pay him for his help. Brick was pleased as he was getting paid from both sides for this con.

Frankie and McPherson went to the Wilson House Hotel one afternoon with another couple named Ostender. They were all followed by White's detective. White and the detective planned to break into Frankie's hotel room at 10 pm so the detective could testify that he had found her in a compromising position.

At the appointed time, George and the detective knocked on Frankie's hotel room door. He could hear voices in the room and when the door was not immediately opened, White, in feigned outrage,

Murders in Mendocino

demanded a hotel clerk bring a key. George was standing on a chair in the hall trying to look through the transom window when suddenly Frankie's door was opened, by her attorneys. The door across the hall also opened revealing Frankie and the Ostenders. Brick was nowhere to be found. They all laughed at George's fury and embarrassment as the bewildered clerk arrived with the key. Not only had the plan failed, the hotel clerk sold his story to the papers and testified to it in court. George was then ordered to pay Frankie an additional $850 for attorney's fees and increase her alimony from $125 to $175 per month. He appealed again but was now the laughingstock of San Francisco and the north coast.[293]

Brick McPherson was no knight in shining armor. He was born in Massachusetts about 1844 and had been in trouble in San Francisco for years. He was sentenced to San Quentin for swindling several people out of money. He served 10 months and was released in March 1892. In 1893 he was leader of a gang that unsuccessfully tried to bribe Customs Officials to ignore Chinese slavers and opium importers. He was having financial difficulties when Wylackie John and White approached him in 1894. He testified for Frankie about this plot in 1895.

He pulled another swindle in 1898, obtaining money from wealthy men to smuggle opium but escaped prosecution. In 1905 he was found guilty on 25 charges of obtaining money under false pretense and sent again to San Quentin for 18 months. He was discharged in March of 1907. He kept a low profile after that. The 1920 census found the 75 year old Brick working as a clerk in a law office. One wonders what scam he was pulling with that position!

Due to the large expense of paying for so many witnesses to travel and be put up at hotels in San Francisco, the Appeals Court judge in San Francisco moved the divorce trial to Covelo. Since George could no longer safely kill her, Wylackie John Wathen decided to go with Brick's idea and prove infidelity. He got 50 of his men to swear they had seen Frankie with John Rohrbough, in compromising situations and agreed to pay them $300 each to commit perjury at the trial.

This new accusation was a huge emotional blow to Frankie. She had seen her husband repeatedly commit perjury, carry on a blatant affair with her sister and plot to have her killed more than once. She now heard her prominent and beloved 'Cousin Johnny' Rohrbough swear in court that he'd had an affair with her. She was devastated at his betrayal.

Of course, all the lurid details were published in the newspapers. And almost every resident in Mendocino and Trinity County was in court to testify for one side or the other. Even White's first wife, Hannah Elizabeth Welling Lee, appeared and testified for Frankie that White had used the same men to commit perjury in their divorce, claiming she was unfaithful, and that he refused to acknowledge their daughter, Georgia. The sensational White divorce was the 'trial of the century', even covered by newspapers back east who sent reporters to Covelo.

In 1888 a woman's reputation would be ruined by far less than these accusations. Frankie already faced public disapproval from many who believed she had married the much older wealthy White for his money and found her claims of his affairs and murder attempts unbelievable. He, supported by his wealthy cronies, and the newspapers in Mendocino , Humboldt and Trinity Counties was publicly insisting that she had been unfaithful. Even these unproven allegations would certainly ruin any chances she had to re-marry or live a normal life. Proving White wrong would never remove the shadow of suspicion around her.

Meanwhile she faced serious financial hardship. Even though the court had repeatedly ruled in her favor, White still refused to pay any of the alimony or legal fees as ordered by the court so Frankie was supported by her father and her brother. Her legal fees kept mounting as did her distress.

Murders in Mendocino

Wylackie John Wathen – 1888

On January 2nd 1888 the Divorce Trial of the Century resumed at the Gibson Hotel in Covelo. Frankie's father, John P. White, and her brother, Clarence, were in court to support her. They were furious to see a woman of poor reputation escorted in during a break, knowing she was getting paid to lie about Frankie. Clarence walked out to see Frankie's lawyers, meeting across the street during the break, to give them suggestions for her cross-examination.

Wylackie John saw Clarence in the entrance hall of the hotel and asked where he was going. Clarence said he was going to speak to Frankie's attorneys about the lying woman. Wathen said, "I'll drop you right here!" and reached for his gun which got caught in his pants pocket. Clarence carried his gun in the front belt of his trousers and got off the first shot, hitting Wylackie John in the left eye and killing him instantly.

27 - Wylackie John Wathen

Everyone was stunned! The Judge yelled "Hooray!" and dismissed court for the day. Wylackie John, the mastermind of the Round Valley gang was dead!

John David Wathen had been captured as a baby and raised among the Indians. He was intelligent and spoke several Native languages. He was nice looking man of medium height, with fair hair and light blue eyes. He dressed well, was polite and soft spoken and didn't drink, smoke or chew tobacco. He was also a sociopath with no conscience.[294]

In 1872, the 39 year old Wathen abandoned his Indian wife and children to marry 15 year old Melissa Mills in Mendocino.[295] They divorced before having any children. After his affair with Martha McPherson, the 47 year old Wathen then married 21 year old Ellen Virginia Anthony in May 1880 in Mendocino.[296]

Clarence White

Clarence White was arrested for killing Wylackie John Wathen. George E. White had his men remove Wathen's gun so they could claim Clarence had shot an unarmed man. Despite this perjury, it took only 8 minutes for the Jury to acquit Clarence on a plea of self-defense. Round Valley quickly hailed Clarence as a hero and he gave newspaper interviews that did not reflect well on George. When he was interviewed by the San Francisco Call (4 Nov 1895) Clarence took the opportunity to rebut White's lies about the shooting. White claimed that Wylackie John's head was turned and he was not looking at his assailant, he also claimed that Wylackie John was not his Foreman and that he himself was innocent of many of the allegations against him. Clarence told of the many times George had offered him money to kill people including D.T. Woodman, Ben Arthur, George Geary and Tom Hayden. Clarence also claimed that White had offered Ves Palmer, Alexander Beggs, George Anthony and Charles Wathen each $1000 to kill Clarence. He strongly suggested that an investigation should be made into the estate of Chris Sorenson after his recent murder in Trinity County, claiming that Wathen and White owed Sorenson money and had killed him to keep him from collecting.

Clarence was born to John P. White and Christiana in Shasta County, CA in 1862. He had lived at the Covelo ranch and worked for White for many years. In May of 1878, Clarence had helped Sheriff Standly catch the Mendocino Outlaws. In 1880 he worked as a detective in Butte County. He worked as a stock raiser most of his life although he also did a little mining and loved racehorses.

Clarence died in Dec 1906 at the young age of 44 of consumption at his home in Covelo. He was survived by his wife, Ethel (Fawcett), and 2 sons, Mervyn (10) and Walter (8). He is buried in Valley View Cemetery in Covelo. His sisters Emma Robinson and Virginia Thomson are buried there as is their father, John Powers White.

Murders in Mendocino

Jim Neafus

Jim Neafus also was among the first settlers in Round Valley, arriving with the Asbill brothers. Neafus was born in Kentucky in 1832 and had first come to California with his father, a trader in 1841. After his father was killed, 11 year old James started back east with an older friend but was captured by Indians in New Mexico. He lived with one tribe for 18 months before he was sold to another tribe. He escaped and made his way to Fort Bennett where he enlisted as a soldier in the Mexican-American War at the age of 16. He became a relentless Indian fighter and helped in the earliest kidnappings of Round Valley Indian women with Pierce Asbill.

He lived with Lydia, a Concow Indian, although no marriage record was found. Given the times, and his reputation as an Indian fighter, she was probably forced into the relationship. They had a daughter and a son.

28 - Jim Neafus

He allied himself with George E. White and witnessed both McPherson murders in 1879. Shortly after that, he become ill and his wife left him and went back to the reservation with his children. He lost his property and needing money, agreed to give false testimony at White's divorce trial in 1886 for $300. After Clarence killed Wylackie John, the perjuries soon became so obvious that the Judge declared it was "without comparison in his experience" and pressed charges against the liars. Instead of the promised $300, White paid him $5, just enough to get out of town before he could be arrested.

When Jim asked for more money, White gave him a rifle and told him to go out and earn the rest by robbing the stage above Blue Rock. Neafus agreed, believing that White would protect him if he got caught. So he and John Asbill, Frank's son from his Indian wife, robbed the stage.

Neafus cleverly shod his horse with mule shoes turned backwards. But, when the horse with backward shoes was found in his stable by Sheriff Standley, Jim Neafus and John Asbill were arrested. Jim was 57 when he was sent to San Quentin for 2 years. In his petition for parole in 1891, Neafus confessed to the perjury and outlined the plot. He also testified that the stage robbery was instigated by White who wanted some papers from the mail.

After his release, Jim moved to Washington County, Idaho where the 67 year old man, now ill, broken and friendless, committed suicide in March of 1897 by shooting himself in the head with his rifle.

Frankie White thought her problems were finally over when she won her divorce on May 8, 1889. The final decree noted that George White's wealth was over $1,000,000 and Frankie was to get between $600,000 - 700,000 of community property, $12,500 in attorney fees plus all the back alimony she was due and her alimony was raised to $250 per month until the estate was settled. The court imposed a bond of $16,000 on White to cover 3 years of payments.

Well aware of George's conniving, Frankie filed a motion for a court receiver to be appointed to prevent him from disposing of his assets, but the court denied her petition.[297] George of course, appealed yet again and still wouldn't pay a penny.

The case had already lasted over 5 years and there was no end in sight. Frankie spent the next 20 years attempting to collect her money and was forced to fight her case all the way to the Supreme Court - three times! She won each time but it did her no good. In 1890, the Supreme Court refused to give George a new trial and re-affirmed her judgement. She was owed $4000 in unpaid alimony and $10,000 in living expenses at that time.[298] By 1893 Frankie had still not received one dollar from George and the fight continued, this time over the value of his property.

Now, 10 years after the suit was filed, Frankie's attorneys stated that George's property was still worth over $600,000. His attorneys, Henley and Wheeler, claimed he was not worth a penny over $250,000 and claimed that most of his wealth was in land, which they insisted was not community property. In August of 1893, a Court appointed Referee ruled that there was no community property to be divided! He determined that the 'real' property was valued at $132,000 and the personal property at $54,725 and that White's income was about $31,404 but that his expenses exceeded his income and he had liabilities of $132,584.[299] George White requested that the alimony, which he had never paid a penny of, be reduced from $200 to $50 per month since he was in debt. Of course, Frankie appealed. White had worked the system. Allowed to conduct his 'regular and normal business', he had taken out loans on his land, then leased or sold all the land and stock to John Rohrbough and others with the understanding that he would buy it back once the divorce was final.

Frankie and her attorneys again requested a receiver for White's affairs. In 1880 White's fortune was counted as well over $1,000,000. In 1886 White had claimed to be worth $300,000 and by 1893 he claimed he was worth only $32,000. White had openly made statements that he would convert all his holdings to cash and spend his last dollar before he would pay Frankie a cent. He kept no books that could be inspected and had deliberately kept the Judges in the dark concerning his real assets.[300] Finally, Judge Seawell did appoint a receiver to take charge of White's remaining property. That receiver determined that White's real property was worth $285,000 and on Feb 2nd, 1895 Frankie was awarded $100,000 for alimony. George White fought Frankie every step of the way, refusing to pay her a single penny, all of which was by now owed to her attorneys. When the court tried to force White to sell property to pay this judgement, a new lease was produced by Rohrbough, again postponing the sale. The court, exasperated at the lies and delays, had White and Rohrbough arrested on contempt. They were slapped with a $500 fine and a week in jail, but released after only 3 days, not much discouragement for avoiding a $100,000 settlement.

In December 1895, much of George E White's land was finally auctioned. Frankie was the only bidder for 20,000 acres owned totally by

White and 20,000 additional acres in which he owned 50% interest which had a $70,000 mortgage on it. She was still owed over $40,000 for alimony.

In 1897 Frankie sold 18,500 of those acres to pay off the mortgage to Sun Insurance Co. Frankie finally received clear title to the land in 1900 after John Rohrbough, claiming 50% ownership, appealed the sale all the way to the Supreme Court and lost. He then had the gall to sue Frankie for his court costs of $63.25!

White had lost Wylackie John, he was spending a fortune on legal fees and had dispersed all his land and stock, but he still controlled Round Valley and the troubles continued.

Murders in Mendocino

Sylvester 'Ves' Palmer

Sylvester 'Ves' Palmer had arrived in Round Valley about 1888 at the height of White's power and refused to be intimidated into leaving. After Wylackie John Wathen was killed, White tried to swindle his widow, Ellen (Anthony) Wathen and children, out of his estate. Ellen asked Ves Palmer for advice since he was the only man in the valley willing to stand up to White. Palmer made sure that she got every penny due. He married her in 1891, 3 years after the death of her husband[301] and they had 2 more children.

In 1894, Joe Gregory, a member of White's gang had almost killed a man named Jack Littlefield. The two fought and Littlefield knocked down the larger man in a fair fight. Littlefield turned to mount his horse when Joe Gregory suddenly jumped on his back, stabbing him repeatedly. The un-armed Ves Palmer jumped into the fight and beat Gregory so badly he almost died. Palmer then carried Littlefield to his place, paid a doctor to stitch him up and nursed him back to health. Palmer and White became the best of friends and Littlefield became his ranch manager.

29 - Ellen and Ves Palmer

Palmer and Littlefield both testified in support of Frankie during her divorce trial making them marked men. Newspapers, controlled by George E. White, noted that Jack Littlefield and Hiram Tuttle, working for Palmer, were charged with stealing cattle on several occasions. Each of these cases were dismissed for lack of evidence. Palmer's land was surrounded by White's ranches so he moved his family to Round Valley for their safety. He and Jack Littlefield remained to operate the ranch.

But Palmer and Littlefield's courage to stand up against White had a terrible cost. On 1 Oct 1895, news reached Ukiah that Alfred 'Jack' Littlefield was dead.

Round Valley Range War

Jack Littlefield – 1895

The gossip was flying in Ukiah! Jack Littlefield had been lynched! John Vinton claimed he had been ambushed and shot by Littlefield Sheriff Van Horn arrested Littlefield and claimed that a group of 25 heavily armed vigilantes had overpowered him, Dep. Crow and Joe Gregory. He said Littlefield jumped off his horse and ran, but was shot by the vigilantes who hung him from a tree. Oddly, none of the officers went to Covelo to report this lynching!

Jack Littlefield was lynched about a mile and a half south of Red Mountain House along the Covelo-Weaverville trail. His murder became front page headlines and the Governor sent his attorney general to investigate, offering a $500 reward for every man arrested for his murder. The San Francisco Call published an expose of White. Frankie was interviewed and told the newspapers that White "ran the whole country but personally was a coward and cold blooded as a lizard".[302] Brady Tuttle and Charlie Felton, part of White's gang, were lynched soon after Littlefield. The perpetrators of this 2nd lynching were never found but it was believed Palmer's men had their revenge.

Trinity Coroner Heath, Sheriff Bergin, Former Sheriff Bowie and Deputy Box dug up Jack's body and reconstructed the crime scene, determining that only 5 men and horses had been there, based on the tracks. There had been no 'mob' of 25 vigilantes, as alleged by Sheriff Van Horn. It was determined at trial that Littlefield had been shot in the neck by Crow and Gregory had fired 2 more shots at his body before they left him hanging in the tree.

Deputy John L. Crow and Sheriff Van Horn, Jim Vinton, Fred Radcliff, Tom Haydon and Joe Gregory were arrested. Dryden 'Buck' Laycock was served with a warrant. They were tried in Weaverville and the trials almost bankrupted Trinity County.

Littlefield was completely exonerated of Vinton's fake shooting during the subsequent trials..

Murders in Mendocino

Sheriff Bayliss Van Horn

At the first trial, it came out that Sheriff Bayless Van Horn and a group of men had gathered at Tom Hayden's and determined to get rid of Littlefield and Palmer. Sheriff Van Horn and Constable Crow had no arrest warrant and were in Humboldt County where they had no legal jurisdiction when they arrested the unresisting Littlefield. Instead of taking him to the closest magistrate in Weaver, they took him through a lonely mountain pass, along a trail that went past the location where Vinton claimed he'd been shot. That is where Littlefield was killed.

No one in the county expected a guilty verdict, most of all the defendants. Bayliss and Crow were found guilty of murder in the 2nd degree!

Sheriff Bayliss Van Horn was born in Colusa, CA. in 1870. He was 26 when he was found guilty of the Littlefield lynching and sentenced to 25 years. He was paroled in 1905 and pardoned in 1910. He married Aileen Rose Bulware about 1915 in Butte County. In 1920 Bayliss (49), Aileen (19) and their daughter Carol (18 months) and Aileen's brothers Verne (18), Darrel (12) and Orlin (10) lived in Marysville, Yuba County.

30 - Sheriff Van Horn

Bayliss became a salesman for an oil company and by 1922 was a manager for the Consumer's Oil Co in Marysville. By 1930 the family had moved to Union, Humboldt County and he worked as a laborer in a woods camp. They had 3 children, Carol, Wesley E, and Marjorie. Bayliss died on 7 July 1954 at the age of 83 and is buried in Ukiah Cemetery.

John Lewis Crow

John Crow, who had been deputized to arrest Littlefield on the fake charge of shooting John Vinton, was surprised when Sheriff Bergin and Constable Box arrested him at Vinton's house in December.

He and Bayliss Van Horn were tried together. Both defendants entered the courtroom jaunty and confident, clearly expecting to be acquitted. John Crow turned pale and collapsed into his chair when the verdict was read. He was sentenced to 25 years and despite repeated appeals both verdicts were upheld. They finally arrived at San Quentin in 1898.

John Crow was born in Illinois about 1846. His family moved to Oregon and he came to Mendocino about 1880 and worked for George E. White. He married Ella Carner in Mendocino in 1894. Ella's sister was Tom Hayden's wife.

He was 51 when he arrived at San Quentin in 1898. He died in San Quentin in 1903 of consumption at the age of 56. He is buried in Pleasant Valley Cemetery, Grants Pass, OR.

Murders in Mendocino

Joseph F. Gregory

Joe Gregory was born in Canada about 1868 and came to California with his family when he was 2 years old. He was in and out of trouble most of his life. In 1892 he was sentenced to San Quentin for a year for assault with a knife on Byron English.

After his release, he married Dora (Powell) and had children Bud, Jesse, and Carlos. He had been arrested and was out on bail for stabbing Jack Littlefield in the back when Littlefield was lynched in Oct. 1895. He was arrested and was the 3rd member of the lynching party to be put on trial.

Frank Doolittle testified that he heard a conversation between Gregory, Vinton, Crow and Hayden in front of Perry's Saloon in Covelo when they discussed taking the law into their own hands and hanging Littlefield. Doolittle confirmed that George E White, Bayliss Van Horn, Buck Laycock and a great number of prominent citizens agreed with the plan.

Dan McDonald testified that he was at Hayden's house when Mrs. Hayden came in and said that young Johnnie Wathen and Jack Littlefield were out on the Wylackie Ranch. Vinton said it was a good time to hang Littlefield and Hayden agreed. Mrs. Hayden asked about Johnnie Wathen and Vinton replied they would hang him too. McDonald refused to participate and the lynching was postponed.

Joe Gregory was convicted of the murder and lynching and sentenced to 25 years in prison. The Supreme Court upheld his conviction on 3 Feb 1898.

In 1899 he was briefly returned to Weaverville to testify at the Tom Hayden trial before he was taken back to San Quentin. His wife Dora divorced him and married Charles H. Goodwin about 1900. In 1906 the Parole Board recommended that he be considered for commutation of his sentence as he was suffering from Tuberculosis. He died in San Quentin on 16 July 1908 and is buried in Valley View Cemetery in Covelo.

Round Valley Range War

Tom Hayden

Tom Hayden was the 4th man tried for the Littlefield lynching and it ended in a hung jury. These trials had financially broken Trinity County. The DA released Hayden because there simply wasn't enough money to pay for another trial. The defendants' tactics had finally worked. They had each called in 20 or more witnesses, summoned to court at county expense, from over 100 miles away and put up at local lodgings for the duration of the trials. The expenses for mileage plus room and board for all these witnesses was just not sustainable for the County. So Haydon was released after his hung jury.

Tom Hayden killed again in 1910.

John Vinton

John M. Vinton was foreman for George E. White after Wylackie John was killed. He concocted the story that got Littlefield arrested. Vinton claimed he saw Jack Littlefield over 100 yards away, a bandana over his face, just before he was shot in the chest. This claim was found false when the shirt Vinton was wearing was found hidden, with powder burns on it, proving he had been shot at close quarters. It was later determined that Vinton had shot himself and made the false claim at the instigation of White. But he got off scot free.

The prosecution had just completed the trials of Van Horn, Crow and Gregory. The county was hemorrhaging money in the middle of the 4th trial for Tom Hayden. It would be difficult and expensive to bring the same witnesses in for a 5th trial, so Vinton was never tried.

Vinton had come west after deserting a ship to escape punishment for a crime on board. He went first to Humboldt County where he was known as Clark Melville. He arrived in Mendocino County about 1887 and resumed the Vinton name. He was a partner with George E. White and John Rohrbough and was trying to fill Wylackie John's shoes.

In 1896, after the Littlefield incident, 45 year old Vinton married the 16 year old Miss Clara 'Lady' Shore in Mendocino. John and Clara and their 9 children lived in Willets where he died in May 1937.

Murders in Mendocino

Ves and Ellen Palmer remained in Round Valley after Littlefield's lynching in 1895, despite open threats to lynch him too. White harassed Palmer with more false accusations resulting in more arrests and lawsuits, trying to bankrupt him. He was acquitted of all these charges but all these legal fights cost money.

Ves's step-daughter, Hattie May Wathen, had not been *'in her right mind'* for some time and went missing one night in 1899. After a long search she was found wandering in the woods several miles from home. She had tried to walk 16 miles to her sister's house in the dark. Ves and Ellen kept her at home as long as possible but she was finally committed to the insane asylum a few years later and died there in 1902 at the age of 21. She is buried with her father Wylackie John Wathen in Valley View Cemetery, Covelo.

In 1901, Ves leased his ranch to Mr. Nicholson and the Palmer family moved to Elk Creek, where he engaged in copper mining for several years. He lost part of his right hand in a blasting accident there in 1905. Despite this, he was still a crack shot at 82 years old when he visited friends in Round Valley to hunt.

The Palmer family then moved to Dixon in Solano County. His stepson, Johnny D. Wathen Jr. and his wife Ethel (Norgard) sold their property to Tom Hayden and joined them in Dixon where they lived on an adjoining property.

Ves died in Dixon on Sept 2nd, 1943 at the age of 86. Ves and Ellen (Anthony) Wathen Palmer who died in 1935 are buried together in Dixon Cemetery.

Back in Round Valley the murders continued.

Round Valley Range War

Billy Williams – 1895

White's Saloon in Covelo was accused of selling liquor to Indians, and White's saloon manager, Alex Perry, was going on trial in Federal Court for this offense. Billy Williams was to be a witness for the prosecution. Since it was harder to buy off Federal judges, White decided it was easier to just kill the witness.

On Aug 20th, a warm night, Billy was sitting on his porch having a smoke while his wife put their children to bed. A voice called to him from the edge of the dark yard. When he went out to see who it was, he was shot. His wife, hearing the shots and the sound of horses running, ran out and stumbled over his dead body in the front yard.[303]

Billy was known as an honest man of mixed parentage living a few miles out of Covelo.[304] His white father had left him about $3000 in property. Billy was survived by his wife, Annie (Pollard) Williams, and daughters Mabel, Mary Frances, and Alice. Annie later married James W. McGetrick.

An investigation into his murder noted that 38-55 musket-balls had been used to fire the fatal shots. There were only 2 such weapons in the entire valley. The horse of the assassin was unshod and tracks were followed from Billy's to the house of Tom Potter, one of two men who owned a 38-55 rifle. He took his horse to the blacksmith to be shod the morning after the murder. Tom Potter was arrested but released as there was "not enough evidence" to hold him.

White still controlled justice in the Valley and no one was ever prosecuted for Billy's murder.

In 1898 Perry and 3 other men were again indicted for selling liquor to the Indians. Charges were dropped again.

Perry died in 1921. He had also been an early settler in Covelo, arriving in 1866.

Murders in Mendocino

Tom Steele – 1897

The next to feel the wrath for defying the gang was Tom Steele. Tom was a half Cherokee man with a small spread at the edge of the Reservation. Henry Peterson, a member of White's crew, *"offered"* $300 to Steel to murder Ed Bizza, an Italian man with a valid claim who was refusing to be intimidated. Steel was furious at this offer/threat and told Henry Peterson he'd kill him if he ever threatened him again. When Peterson reported back to White that Steele had refused his *"offer"*, his fate was sealed. White decided to send him to prison to get rid of him.

For 2 years, an unbranded maverick calf had grazed with Steele's cattle. He had repeatedly put out public inquiries to find out who owned it but White's men insisted it wasn't theirs and advised him to brand it his own. As soon as he did so, White swore out a complaint of cattle stealing. The 23 year old Steele was sentenced to San Quentin for 3 years based on perjured evidence from White's men. When he was released in 1888, all his cattle had been rebranded as White's and he had to start over.

Still refusing to be intimidated, Steele agreed to be a witness for the prosecution in the Littlefield lynching trial in Jan 1896. This new transgression did not go unpunished. In Feb 1897 Tom Steele was shot and killed by Dick Bell. He left a half-Indian wife, daughter of C.L. Nuckolls, and 3 small children.

Apparently there had been bad blood between Deaf Dick Bell a full blood Digger Indian, and Steele, half-Cherokee. Dick came to *"quarrel over a sack of wheat."* The men fought and Steel punched Bell, knocking him down and turned away to walk into his house, when Bell drew a revolver from his pocket and shot him, killing him instantly. Mrs. Steele and her father, a white man who could testify, testified that Steele was walking away when Bell shot him in the back. Despite this, Dick Bell was sentenced to only 18 months for killing Steele. His attorney was paid for by White.

Louise Bogan White

In February 1898, the headlines read, "Gay Old Lothario and Pretty Young Girl for Wife"[305]. George E White had married again! He was a confirmed spiritualist and consulted the famous Mrs. J. J. Whitney on all matters. George was advised to watch the columns of a marriage paper in the city. Pretty Louise Bogan (22) lived at 310 Tehama St and advertised in the paper. She freely admitted to the newspapers that George was an energetic lover and that his blazing diamonds and frequent presents, including a fancy trousseau, certainly made him more attractive. He was 72 but gave his age as 55 on the marriage license.

Their marital bliss came to an abrupt halt when Louise purchased an expensive suite of furniture instigating an argument. George consulted his spiritual advisor who advised him to leave. Louise promptly filed for divorce on grounds of desertion in April 1901. She withdrew her suit but filed again with a new lawyer in March of 1902 on grounds of infidelity, accusing George E. White of improper relations with Mrs. Whitney. Her grounds were pretty convincing since George had been living in Mrs. Whitney's house in San Francisco and expected his young wife to live there as well.

George E. White was still refusing to pay Frankie a penny. To thwart the court orders, he had leased his all his land and stock to others so it could not be attached to pay her. Then, in January 1899, George filed a petition of insolvency in the United States District Court. The value of his assets as given in the statement was $110,000, including all the real estate, which was supposedly mortgaged for $109,000. He still owed Frankie $41,669. White declared to the news media that he had been harassed and pursued by his creditors, meaning Frankie, *"driven almost to distraction"*. He requested his homestead in Mendocino County, consisting of 1500 acres, valued at $5000, together with about $1000 worth of personal property, which he claimed the law allowed him. With this bankruptcy filing, Frankie could not collect another penny.

George White died on 9 June 1902 at Covelo of stomach cancer. News accounts said that J. S. Rohrbough, his favorite nephew, was to get the bulk of his estate estimated at $1,000,000. Frustratingly for Rohrbough, George E. White died without a will. A hearing on Louise's divorce was to be held in Ukiah the morning he died. Since the divorce had not been granted when he died, Louise automatically became his heir and she petitioned the court to be made executor of his estate and to be granted the homestead and mansion in Covelo.

In defense against other claimants, including Rohrbough, Louise dropped a real bombshell. She confirmed to the court that George really had created fraudulent leases with Rohrbough and others to defraud Frankie, finally proving what everyone had believed for years! She became owner of the homestead and Rohrbough had to pay her lease fees.

Louise White then moved to San Francisco where she became briefly notorious again. In 1909 she lived at 236 Diamond Street with her mother when she took a one week position as a stenographer with prominent attorney, James Walter Scott. Louise, a pretty 26 year old, filed a criminal charge against Scott, alleging that he had sexually assaulted her on Thursday evening, between 5 and 6 pm, while they were working late. Despite this apparent outrage, Louise returned to work on Friday and again on Saturday to pick up her check with no sign of distress. After receiving her pay on Saturday, she calmly walked to the police station, where the Captain of Detectives was a relative, and reported the assault of 2 days earlier. Her blackmailing scheme was dismissed when Attorney Robert C. Owen testified to a telephone conversation with Scott from 5:30 to 5:40 and Eugene Davis, a real estate man in the building, testified he met Scott at 5:40 and went to a café with him where they remained until boarding a car for home at 7:45. The office boy, William Rogers, vouched for this timeline as he was also in the office until 5:22 pm. Despite this, Louise was not prosecuted for this false charge.

Louise was listed in the 1916 San Francisco Directory as a stenographer, widow of George E. White, living at 3766 21st St. After that she disappears from records. Perhaps she remarried.

John Rohrbough

John Rohrbough was born about 1859 in West Virginia. He came west about 17 to join his uncle, George E. White, eventually becoming his partner. John married Myrtle Jenny Fetty in Mendocino in 1894.[306] Her father was Perry Evan Fetty, brother of George E. White's 2nd wife, Alice Fetty, who had died suddenly under odd circumstance, while her divorce from George was pending. John and Myrtle (Fetty) Rohrbough had 8 children.

John became a key part of White's gang of thugs and had no qualms about committing perjury or murder. White had mortgaged his properties before declaring bankruptcy and left the cash with Rohrbough. He also held leases for many of George's properties and livestock so the court could not attach them to pay Frankie. He expected to be left the bulk of George's wealth. When George died, and no will was found, his estranged wife, Louise, automatically became his heir. John was exceedingly vexed.

John remained in Covelo and claimed the title of Cattle King after White's death. Using the cash from George's mortgages, he purchased back most of George's properties for pennies on the dollar when they were foreclosed upon. He built Round Valley Flour Mills in 1888, ran herds of cattle and sheep, a stage line and had other business interests. He was always described as a 'prominent citizen'. He was an organizer of, and President and V.P., of the Bank of Covelo started in 1920.

John S. Rohrbough died in a San Francisco hospital Jan 1939. He was about 79 years old and still owned large holdings in Humboldt, Trinity and Mendocino Counties. When he died his obituary was exceedingly complimentary about his honesty and how respected he had been for fair dealing. He is buried in Covelo with his wife Myrtle (Fetty) Rohrbough, who lived in Round Valley until her death the following year.

Murders in Mendocino

Frankie White

Frankie had filed her suit for divorce in 1883. Many of the Round Valley murder victims were men who had taken her side against George E White. White was never charged but the Round Valley community knew he was getting vengeance for those daring to take the part of a wife who had repudiated him. Her life was not easy. In 1887 Frankie's mother died in an asylum. In 1888 her brother shot Wylackie John. In 1889 Frankie testified that the perjuring witness, George W Morrison, had lied and emphatically denied any infidelity. In Aug 1889 the divorce was granted and George E was ordered to pay $200/mo. and give a $16,000 bond. In 1890 the Supreme Court again ordered George to pay. He did not. In 1894 the court again ordered George to pay her. He claimed he was bankrupt and she asked the court to declare him incompetent. The court denied his bankruptcy petition and appointed a receiver over his affairs. In 1895 the Court granted her a $100,000 judgement and Frankie agreed to this final settlement. George appealed again to the Supreme Court and lost so his property was auctioned. Frankie bid at the auction and was awarded 40,000 acres encumbered by a loan. By 1896 she finally had clear title but had to sell 18,750 acres to pay off the loan. George had the cash from this and other loans and leases he had taken out on his property and stock and was living very well as she struggled to pay her attorneys and cover her living expenses. In 1898 Frankie was still trying to get the remaining money she was owed and sued Costigan and White for fraudulent leases. While all this is going on George married Louise Bogan. George declared Bankruptcy again and this time it was approved. George died in 1902.

Frankie was still attempting to collect the remaining money she was owed in 1905. She was living on a ranch 12 miles east of Willits on the Eel River. She occasionally traveled to San Francisco and purchased additional parcels of land including 1320 acres in 1905. Her father died in 1907 in Stockton.

In 1909 she was noted as returning to Traveler's Home after a visit to San Francisco. She attended the funeral of her brother Clarence in 1910. Frankie had run out of money to pursue the remaining cases. In 1913 Frankie donated 60 acres to Round Valley land Company.

Frankie was mentioned in the obit of her sister, Mrs. Emma Robinson, who died in 1915 in Covelo. Emma left a lot in Covelo to her sister Virginia B Garrett.

And Frankie was mentioned in a Dec 17, 1916 news article about the Round Valley, where she was noted as still alive, in her mid-fifties, but living in greatly reduced circumstances and in poor health.

It is not known when Frankie died. She never remarried. This beautiful, brave young woman who defied the millionaire bully Cattle King White, and survived several murder attempts and nationwide scandal, poverty and over 20 years of legal suits trying to get what she felt was right, died childless, and alone having outlived her entire family. She is probably buried in the Covelo Cemetery with her father and 2 sisters but no headstone survives.

Chapter 18 – Last Range War

Murders in Mendocino

The Norgaard Family

Originally, two Norgaard brothers, both named Chris, migrated to CA from Denmark. They were born in the 1860s and arrived in 1884. Both worked in the lumber industry and were called Big Chris and Little Chris. They were rough but generally acknowledged as honest and had many friends. After Little Chris became quite successful in Trinity and Mendocino County, he sent back to Denmark for a bride. Unfortunately, Cecelia's arrival caused trouble and Big Chris apparently shot his brother in the stomach and moved to Trinity County. He married a woman there named Annie.

Cecelia, nursed Little Chris back to health and they kept the incident quiet. Rather than enter into the range wars, Little Chris Norgaard moved his family to Ruth, opened a general merchandise store and began gathering mortgages while his neighbors killed each other. After Wylackie John Wathen was killed in 1886, and with George E. White in San Francisco attending almost continuous divorce proceedings, White's hold on Round Valley loosened and Little Chris Norgaard felt it was safe to begin a stock raising business in Round Valley again so he began to fence in his land. In 1907, Chris Norgaard's oldest daughter Ethel married Johnny D. Wathen, Wylackie John and Ellen (Anthony) Wathen's son, over her father's strong objections. When she married, her father disowned her.

The White/Wathen Gang, including Tom Hayden, had always been at odds with the other ranchers among whom the Norgaards were prominent. Each side accused the other of stealing cattle and tearing out fences. Johnny and his father-in-law had many verbal arguments before Johnny and Ethel decided to move to Dixon to join his mother Ellen (Anthony) (Wathen) Palmer and his step-father, Ves Palmer. Johnny planned to sell the Wathen Ranch to Tom Hayden.

Hayden and the Norgaard family had been enemies for years. Hayden's Ranch adjoined the Norgaards on one side and the Wathen range on another. Hayden had been released by a hung jury at his trial for lynching Jack Littlefield. Trouble was coming and everyone knew it.

Last Range War

Morris H Norgaard – 1910

One day in December 1919, 15 year old Morris and his 13 year old brother, Cervera Norgaard, were out rounding up cattle and found a herd of Tom Hayden's horses on their range. The Norgaard boys began driving the horses back towards Hayden's ranch when they were suddenly shot from ambush without warning.

Tom Hayden had been staying at John and Ethel (Norgaard) Wathen's house. After shooting the 2 boys, Hayden left his horses on Norgaard's ranch and went back to the Wathen house. He never looked at the bodies, believing he had killed them both. When he arrived at the Wathen house, he handed Ethel, sister of the murdered boys, her husband's still warm gun. He didn't say a word to her about shooting her brothers. He walked out to the barn and told Johnny he had killed the boys "in self-defense."

Hayden had killed 15 year old Morris Norgaard and left his 13 year old brother Cervera for dead in almost the same location as the Littlefield lynching. Johnny Wathen sent for the Sheriff who found Cervera Norgaard badly wounded but still alive. Ceverra told the story of the ambush and murder to the Sheriff the next morning and Hayden was arrested. The Constable who brought Hayden in testified that Hayden told him: "Why Milton McKnight, you know I had a right to kill that boy. He was running my stock."

Hayden's trial was described as "the last range war" because the whole valley took sides. On one side, Hayden's faction and the old White gang cattlemen fought to keep open ranges and graze cattle on government land. On the other side were the Norgaards, farmers and stock raisers who proved up their land and fenced it.

Murders in Mendocino

Tom Hayden

Tom Hayden's 2nd murder trial lasted 5 weeks in Weaverville. He pled 'not guilty' claiming self-defense. As was common for the White gang, perjured testimony was given, including by John S Rohrbough. Hayden's defense attorneys introduced into evidence 4 shells, purported to be from Milton Norgaard's gun. These witnesses claimed the shells had been found at the shooting site. This was proven false since they had been found 52 days after a very thorough search by the coroner's jury which had found no such evidence.

The prosecution presented Charles Brewer who testified that Hayden was a leader of the White Caps, Vigilantes of the Mad River Stock Association. The group had a long standing conspiracy to kill the Norgaard family. Charley Brewer had already stood trial for shooting at the Norgaard boys and been acquitted. This time he testified that Hayden's group had paid him to shoot at 2 of the Norgaard boys and had contributed to a fund to defend him at his 1909 trial. Charley testified that a new fund had been raised by the group for this killing.

31 - Tom Hayden

Tom Hayden testified that the Norgaard's had been trying to drive him out of the county and attempted to prove the "bad character" of Morris Norgard. John Rohrbough, who had inherited George E White's title as Cattle King of Round Valley, testified in Hayden's defense that Morris was "a threat." The prosecution showed that Morris Norgaard had studied in Oakland at a business college there and was not considered a troublemaker by anyone.

Using a ploy that had worked before, Hayden called over 20 unnecessary witnesses to court, driving up the county bills, and it was widely expected that he would again escape justice. Sheriff Johnnie Boyce actually let Hayden have the run of the town and declared himself in sympathy with the defendant. One character witness even sent word to the prosecutor that "for $800 he could swing the jury".

But Little Chris Norgaard wanted justice for his son's murder and was willing to pay for it. He paid the county's costs for the prosecution and retained DA Robert Duncan of Mendocino and Attorney Henry Rogers of San Francisco to assist DA Horace Given of Trinity County in the case. When Tom Hayden was actually convicted of 2nd degree murder on June 14th, 1911, the entire community was shocked! The White faction had gotten away with murder for so long that no one had expected a conviction.

Tom Hayden was sentenced to 20 years in San Quentin. He appealed all the way to the Supreme Court and was out on bail while the appeals were pending, but his sentence was upheld. He was ill before he finally entered prison in 1912 and was pardoned after serving only one year of his sentence. The prosecution attorneys were not notified of his pardon and were furious when they learned of his release. Chris Norgaard attempted to have Hayden arrested again on the charge of attempted murder for trying to kill Cervera in the same ambush but the DA would not issue a warrant. Hayden was fatally ill and was sent to San Francisco for an unsuccessful operation. He died at home in Covelo on 6 June 1913 at the age of 60. He is buried in Valley View Cemetery in Covelo.

Frank Hayden

After his father's conviction, his son Frank Hayden was arrested on attempted murder charges for trying to kill another of the Norgaard boys. The Norgaard-Hayden Feud finally ended with an agreement that the Haydens would buy out the Norgaards at an agreed upon price and the Norgaards would leave the area and agree not to engage in the cattle business in Southern Trinity or Northern Mendocino within 10 miles of Trinity County. As part of the agreement, charges were dropped against Frank Hayden for the attempted murder.

The Norgaards moved to the Ukiah area. But the trouble still wasn't over.

Murders in Mendocino

Elmer Norgard

In early August of 1912, Elmer Norgaard, another of Little Chris's sons, and his friend Ernest Tyree were arrested near Everett, Washington and charged with cattle rustling in Round Valley. A man named Engblom was pressing charges against the boys, claiming they had stolen his cattle. The boys maintained they had purchased the cattle and had a bill of sale to prove it. Both pled not guilty and had separate trials.

It soon became apparent that Engblom was not in his right mind and was scared to death of the White Gang. During Tyree's trial, Engblom attempted to hang himself. Engblom then hired an attorney from Ferndale, 90 miles from his home, to avoid word getting back to the Round Valley Gang, in fear for his life. He told the attorney to contact the DA and dismiss charges against the boys. He confirmed that Tyree had, in fact, paid for the cattle. He swore that Pitt White and Lampley had coerced him into having the boys arrested. Despite this, Tyree was convicted on the basis of Engblom's testimony.

In early December of 1912, Engblom shot himself in the neck but again survived. He finally killed himself on the 23rd of December in 1912. Engblom had lived in the area for 14 years and Ukiah authorities knew he was insane for years before the trial, yet his testimony was believed over that of the boys. Tyree even provided a bill of sale for the cattle but despite this proof and the confession of coercion by Engblom, Tyree was convicted and sentenced to 5 years in San Quentin. Luckily, the jury recommended parole. At Elmer Norgaard's trial there was a hung jury and was discharged. His retrial was cancelled when Engblom blew out his brains.

That was not the end of Elmer's troubles however. In Feb. 1913, 21 year old Elmer was charged with stealing a calf worth $25 from the Indian herd 5 years earlier, one of the White Gang's favorite ploys. It cost $20,000 to bring him to trial in 1915. He was acquitted without the jury even leaving their seats. His troubles continued though. In 1921, Elmer Norgaard's wife Ruby was declared insane.

Last Range War

Little Chris Norgard

Life improved after the family moved to Ukiah but there were still problems. In Sept 1913, Annie, Big Chris's wife, died at a Eureka hospital. She had been accidentally shot by her son while he was cleaning his gun.

In 1916 Little Chris purchased 45 acres of the Hildreth Ranch, planted alfalfa and prunes and was quite successful. In 1924 he purchased the Hotel Grand, the largest building in Eureka and made many improvements to it. He built several buildings in Ukiah in 1927 including a large garage on State and Stephenson St that was occupied by Ukiah Auto Top Shop and CC Stark.

In 1934 his daughter Emma (Norgaard) Erickson, was killed in a car accident and his wife, Cecelia, was badly injured. Emma had married the son of the murdered George Erickson. His wife Cecelia died 2 weeks after the accident, never regaining consciousness. Chris's son, who was not seriously injured, was the driver. The grief from the loss of his wife and daughter seemed to break Chris's health.

Then, Cervera, who had finally recovered from being shot by Tom Hayden, suddenly died on 1 Sept 1938 following a hernia operation. He was survived by a wife and 7 year old son in Stockton.

Little Chris Norgaard, who had been seriously ill for some time, suffered a relapse upon hearing this news, and died on 5 Sept 1938 leaving his family considerable wealth in property including land in Ukiah, the Sterling Hotel in Eureka, a ranch on the Redwood Highway south of Ukiah and other property. He was survived by sons Elmer, Farris, Sterling, and Chris Jr. and was buried beside his wife, Cecelia.

He was also survived by his daughter Ethel but he had left her nothing in his will.

After his death, Ethel (Norgaard) (Wathen) Beck of Dixon contested her father Chris's will, claiming that she was entitled to part of his estate.

Ethel (Norgaard) (Wathen) Beck

Ethel Norgard married Johnny D. Wathen Jr., son of Wylackie John Wathen, against her father's wishes in 1910. As a result, her father, Little Chris, disowned her. Tom Hayden, who bought the Wathen Ranch, had murdered her brother Morris and wounded Cervera with her husband's gun. She was not welcome in the Norgaard family.

John D. Wathen Jr., Ethel and their 2 children moved to Dixon, Solano County shortly after Tom Hayden murdered her brother. They remained together until the 1930 census, possibly longer, before divorcing. Ethel married Henry C. Beck before 1939.

In his will, Ethel's father, Chris Norgard, left her $1.00 as "one of the distributees of Cecelia Norgaard" and the rest of his estate was left to his 5 sons. Ethel contested his will and claimed that her father was under the insane delusion that he was not her father and that she was out to do him harm. Her brothers protested that her claims on the estate were not legitimate and that Little Chris had been of sound mind when he disowned her and said she was not part of the family. But, in Oct. 1940, a jury determined that she was entitled to a share of the estate. They found that Little Chris had been of unsound mind when he had made his last will in 1938. So she got part of the estate but also earned the undying enmity of her brothers.

John D. Wathen died in Dixon in 1956. He is buried near his father 'Wylackie John' and a sister Hattie May (1881-1902) and his daughter Ellen in Dixon Cemetery in Dixon, Solano, CA.

Ethel (Norgaard) Wathen Beck died in Dixon in 1973. Her son, John D. Wathen III was executor of her estate.

The End

And so the history of white settlers in Mendocino began with the Asbill brothers and Jim Neafus kidnapping and selling into slavery young Native American women. As more settlers arrived they waged a war of extermination, led by men who controlled the law, owned the news and convinced the settlers they had to kill or be killed. These massacres and atrocities destroyed the Indian way of life and were later determined to be genocide, but settlers prospered.

The deadly Coates-Frost family feud started over abolition and lasted decades. Range wars soon followed, led by a small group of men determined to become massively rich by any means necessary. Their efforts to control huge areas of land through false accusations, perjured testimony in court cases and murder soon made Mendocino County notorious for its lawlessness and crooked lawmen. Many of the most ruthless men were eulogized as fine upstanding citizens when they died.

For 75 years most people were too frightened to fight this corruption but the few brave ones included several exceptional women who would not be bullied and stood up for their rights like Catherine Angle, Kathleen Strong, Evelyn Anthony Wathen and Frankie White.

With the conviction of Tom Hayden, the White gang lost its stranglehold. The murderous range wars stopped and the blood soaked land of Mendocino finally found a measure of peace. Fraud, lawsuits and intimidation continued but much less openly. The Native Americans are still struggling to recover a small fraction of the land that was stolen

Murders in Mendocino

End Notes

End Notes

[1] https://en.wikipedia.org/wiki/Manifest_destiny

[2] <u>Early California Laws and Policies Related to California Indians</u> by Kimberly Johnson-Dodds, 2002:
<u>https://www.library.ca.gov/crb/02/14/02-014.pdf</u>

[3] <u>Early California Laws and Policies Related to California Indians</u> by Kimberly Johnson-Dodds, 2002:
<u>https://www.library.ca.gov/crb/02/14/02-014.pdf</u>

[4] Wikipedia: Peter Hardeman Burnett

[5] <u>Aboriginal Population of North Coast of California</u>, S F Cook, 1956, University of CA Press

[6] <u>www.manataka.org</u>: Manataka American Indian Council, Bloody Island Massacre by Gordon Kooshdakaa

[7] <u>www.manataka.org</u>: Manataka American Indian Council, Bloody Island Massacre by Gordon Kooshdakaa

[8] www.manataka.org: Manataka American Indian Council, Bloody Island Massacre by Gordon Kooshdakaa

[9] <u>www.manataka.org</u>: Manataka American Indian Council, Bloody Island Massacre by Gordon Kooshdakaa

[10] <u>The Kelsey Brothers: A California Disaster</u>, 2012, John Parker, <u>http://www.wolfcreekarcheology.com/KelseyTalk.pdf</u>

[11] <u>The Kelsey Brothers: A California Disaster</u>, John Parker, Ph.D. 2012
https://www.academia.edu/5539505/The_Kelsey_Brothers_A_California_Disaster

End Notes

[12] The Searcher: Oct 1988, pg. 192-198: Deaths and Burials of Men Associated with the Bear Flag Revolt.

[13] Putah and Cache: Bloody Island by Pete and Scott Richerson: http://bioregion.ucdavis.edu/book/10_Clear_Lake/10_17_circ_cl_bloodyi.html

[14] www.manataka.org: Manataka American Indian Council, Bloody Island Massacre by Gordon Kooshdakaa

[15] Ancestral Ties of the Scotts Valley Band of Pomo Indians to the San Francisco Bay area. Heather A Howard, PhD and James M McClurken, PhD, 27 March 2007

[16] San Francisco Bulletin, Sept 1, 1856.

[17] San Francisco Bulletin, 13 Sept 1856, quoting the California American

[18] Indian War Files:

[19] Wikipedia – Mendocino War

[20] Indian War files: quoted in http://www.counterpunch.org/2007/02/05/the-genocidal-namesake-of-the-hasting-school-of-law/

[21] Journals of the Legislature of the State of CA. Vol. 1 page 33.

[22] San Francisco Bulletin, 28 Jan 1860

[23] Bitter Memories at Round Valley: - http://www.roundvalleyschools.org/pages/uploaded_files/Bitter%20Memories%20in%20Round%20Valley.pdf

End Notes

[24] https://www.nps.gov/parkhistory/online_books/5views/5views1c.htm

[25] California Legislature, Majority and Minority Reports of the Special Joint Committee on the Mendocino Wars (Sacramento 1860) http://delnortetah.wikispaces.com/file/view/California's+Yuki+Indians+Defining+Genocide+in+Native+American+History.pdf

[26] Genocidal Namesake of the Hastings School of Law, Bruce Anderson, Feb. 5, 2007, http://www.counterpunch.org/2007/02/05/the-genocidal-namesake-of-the-hasting-school-of-law/

[27] Lawrence H Orricer and Samuel H Williamson, Purchasing Power of Money in the US from 1774 to 2008, http://www.measuringworth.com/ppowerus/

[28] Killing for Land in Early California, Frank H Baumgardner, 2005

[29] Agricultural Labor, Race and Indian Policy on the Round Valley Reservation, 1850-1941, Dissertation of William J. Bauer, Jr. 2003

[30] http://www.militarymuseum.org/FtWright.html

[31] We Were All Like Migrant Workers Here, William J. Bauer, 2009, page 55.

[32] http://www.csuchico.edu/lbib/spc/bleyhl/Bleyhl_700-874.pdf: page 203-204

[33] Killing for Land in Early California, Frank H Baumgardner, 2005

[34] https://lynette707.wordpress.com/2010/06/10/a-good-white-man/#more-1650

End Notes

[35] Killing for Land in Early California, Frank H Baumgardner, 2005

[36] Freedom's Frontier: California and the Struggle over Unfree Labor, Stacey L. Smith, 2013

[37] Ibid – page 232

[38] William E Coffer, Genocide Among the California Indians, http://delnortetah.wikispaces.com/file/view/California's+Yuki+Indians+Defining+Genocide+in+Native+American+History.pdf

[39] History of Mendocino and Lake Counties, Carpenter and Millberry, 1914, page 100

[40] Mendocino County Index: Marriages

[41] History of Mendocino County California, Lyman Palmer, 1880

[42] 1860 US Census, Little Lake Township, Ancestry.com

[43] Santa Cruz Weekly Sentinel, 17 Oct 1868, page 1

[44] California Military History, Fort Hunter Liggett

[45] Ukiah Daily Journal, 13 March 1891, page 3

[46] Ukiah Daily Journal, 20 March 1891, page 3

[47] Ukiah Daily Journal, 23 Oct 1891, page 2

[48] Ukiah Daily Journal, 15 Dec 1893, page 3

[49] Laytonville Rancheria Cemetery, Willits, CA. - http://files.usgwarchives.net/ca/mendocino/cemeteries/layton.txt

End Notes

[50] Chicago Sunday Tribune, 15 April 1894, page 25

[51] Ukiah Daily Journal, 28 July 1950, page 1

[52] Mendocino County Index: Cemetery Index

[53] Ukiah Daily Journal, 25 Jan 2004, page 3

[54] Ukiah Daily Journal, 3 July 1891: Angle-Drew marriage notice.

[55] Ukiah Daily Journal, 20 Aug 1982, page 6, "90 years ago"

[56] Chicago Daily Tribune, 15 April 1894, page 2: Kakan Angle's Life

[57] Ukiah Daily Journal, 30 November 1894, page 3

[58] Mendocino County Indexes: Marriages

[59] Ukiah Dispatch Democrat, 18 June, 1926, page 5

[60] History of Mendocino County California, Lyman Palmer, 1880 page 324

[61] Letter from Sheriff William Heeser to the Daily Alta California, 28 Jan 1862

[62] Our Hargrave Family by Jeanne Hargrave: https://jeannehargrave.wordpress.com/2013/03/27/our-hargrave-family-migrations-the-years-1866-1869/

[63] History of Mendocino County California, Lyman Palmer, 1880

[64] Fort Bragg Advocate, 26 Sept 1894

End Notes

[65] Our Hargrave Family by Jeanne Hargrave: https://jeannehargrave.wordpress.com/2013/03/27/our-hargrave-family-migrations-the-years-1866-1869/

[66] History of Mendocino County California, Lyman Palmer, 1880 and FAG # 111115264.

[67] Sacramento Daily Union, Vol 30, #4595, 13 Dec 1865

[68] Ukiah Daily Journal, 22 Jan, 1865

[69] History of Mendocino County California, Lyman Palmer, 1880

[70] A History of California and an Extended History of its Southern Coast Counties, James Miller Guinn, 1907

[71] San Diego Union, 26 Oct 1914, page 5

[72] Los Angeles Herald, 15 April 1894, page 2

[74] Dictionary of Early Shasta County History, Dottie Smith, Redding Record Searchlight, 10 Aug 2012

[75] California Wills and Probate Records, 1782-1999. George W Knight

[76] San Francisco Chronicle, 22 May 1873, Page 3

[77] Ukiah Daily Journal, 21 August 1896

[78] San Francisco Bulletin, 22 May 1873, Vol XXXVI, Issue 39, Page 1

[79] San Francisco Bulletin, 19 May 1873, Vol XXXVI, Issue 36, Page 1

[80] San Francisco Bulletin, 28 Oct 1867, Vol XXV, Issue 18, page 3

End Notes

[81] <u>Vengeance, Vendettas and Violence</u> by William B Secrest, 2004

[82] San Francisco Bulletin, 2 Nov 1867, Vol. XXV, Issue 23, page 1

[83] Ukiah Daily Journal, 12 Oct 2003

[84] Ukiah Republican Press, 3 Feb 1905

[85] San Francisco Bulletin, 8 Feb 1872, Vol XXXIII, issue 103, page 2

[86] California Prison and Correctional Records, 1851-1950, Couts, p202

[87] Olympia Daily Recorder, 23 June 1922, Vol XXI, Issue 40, page 1

[88] San Francisco Bulletin, 4 Sept 1879, Col XLVII, Issue 130, page 2

[89] <u>History of Mendocino County California</u>, Lyman Palmer, 1880

[90] <u>Badge and Buckshot</u> by John Boessenecker, 1988

[91] Daily Alta Californian, San Francisco, CA 27 Jan 1886

[92] Anderson Valley Advertiser, 27 Sept, 2015 by Malcolm McDonald

[93] Mendocino Beacon, 5 Jan 1885

[94] Ibid

[95] <u>California Feuds: Vengeance, Vendettas & Violence on the Old West Coast</u>, William B Secrest, page 139

[96] <u>Vengeance, Vendettas and Violence</u> by William B Secrest, 2004

[97] Daily Alta Californian, San Francisco, CA 27 Jan 1886

End Notes

[98] Willets News, 17 May 1928

[99] Sacramento Daily Union, Vol 33, #5027, 8 May 1867

[100] 1860 US Federal Census, Big River Tnshp, page 55, family 478

[101] History of Mendocino County California, Lyman Palmer, 1880

[102] Ukiah Republican Press, 30 Nov 1938, Page 1

[103] Ibid

[104] Ukiah Republican Press, 11 June 1909

[105] San Luis Obispo Tribune, 5 April 1879, page 1

[106] San Luis Obispo Tribune, 12 April 1879.

[107] Cerfancestry.blogspot.com/2012 – A Murder in Ukiah (there are some wonderful photographs in this blog and it is well researched).

[108] Los Angeles Herald, 19 April 1879, page 4

[109] Find A Grave – Elias B Marks

[110] Ukiah Daily Journal, 3 Jan 1890, page 3

[111] Los Angeles Herald, 22 April 1890, page 1

[112] Mendocino Index: marriages

[113] San Francisco Call, 24 Feb 1904, page 11

[114] San Francisco Chronicle, 10 Feb 1904, page 7

End Notes

[115] Ukiah Dispatch Democrat, 26 Feb 1926, page 3

[116] Mendocino Index – Marriage record 6/288

[117] Find A Grave #28765293, Willits Cemetery

[118] California Wills and Probate Records, 1782-1999, Garrett Fitzgerald, Ancestry.com

[119] Mendocino Index: Marriage record #10/493

[120] Mendocino Index: Newspaper Vitals, Fort Bragg Advocate, April 7, 1926

[121] Ukiah Daily Journal, 25 July 1890, page 1

[122] California Prison and Correctional Records, 1851-1950, Ancestry.com

[123] San Francisco Chronicle, 23 Dec 1872

[124] San Francisco Bulletin, 16 Dec 1870, page 3

[125] California Voter Register 1866-1898: 1873, William R Edgington

[126] FindAGrave Memorial #108399757

[127] Mendocino Democrat, 6 March 1873, page 3

[128] Mendocino Democrat, 26 Dec 1872, page 3

[129] San Francisco Bulletin, 1 August 1874, [age 2

[130] Mendocino Index: Marriage record 2/458

End Notes

[131] George W. Cleveland: azclevelands.net/history/histGW.htm

[132] <u>Pacific States Reports</u>: Book 17 Extra Annotated (1850-1883) by California Supreme Court. Page 135

[133] Mendocino Index: Marriage record 2/436

[134] Mendocino Index: marriage record 2/30

[135] San Francisco Chronicle, March 13, 1873, page 1

[136] San Francisco Chronicle, 13 March 1873, page 1

[137] San Francisco Bulletin, 19 July 1873, page 1

[138] San Francisco Bulletin, 3 March 1873, page 1

[139] San Francisco Chronicle, 13 March 1873, page 1

[140] San Francisco Chronicle, 11 May 1874, page 2

[141] San Francisco Call, 9 Aug 1896, page 5

[142] <u>History of Mendocino County California</u>, Lyman Palmer, 1880

[143] Arizona Sentinel, 5 June 1875, Page 2

[144] San Francisco Call, 20 March 1898, page 17

[145] San Francisco Chronicle, 2 Sept 1874, page 3

[146] Mendocino Index: Marriage record 2/318

[147] California Select Marriages, 1850-1945

End Notes

[148] Mendocino Index: Marriage record 4/41

[149] <u>Illustrated History of Baker, Grant, Malheur and Harney Counties</u>, Western Historical Publishing Co, 1902

[150] Sacramento Record Union, 13 July 1880, page 2

[151] San Francisco Bulletin, 13 July 1880, page 1

[152] San Francisco Chronicle, 27 July 1880, page 3

[153] Sacramento Record Union, 19 Aug 1880, page 3

[154] San Francisco Chronicle, 23 July 1880, page 1

[155] California Select Marriages 1850-1945, Sonoma

[156] San Francisco Chronicle 6 Nov 1868, page 3

[157] Select California Marriages, 1850-1945, John B Fitch, Sonoma

[158] <u>Lake County California</u>, William W. Elliott, Lithographer and Publisher, Oakland, CA 1885

[159] Petaluma Weekly Argus, 25 March 1881, page 3

[160] Petaluma Weekly Argus, 17 Feb 1882, page 3

[161] Western States Marriage Index, #621497

[162] Arizona Sentinel, 22 Nov 1884, Page 3

[163] Western States Marriage ID #164839

[164] Arizona Sentinel, 14 June 1890, page 3

End Notes

[165] Ukiah Daily Journal, 26 Feb 1892, page 3

[166] Arizona Weekly Citizen, 27 Feb 1892 page 3

[167] Tombstone Weekly Epitaph, 28 Feb 1892, page 6

[168] Wilcox, AR 11 Nov 1893

[169] El Paso Herald, 3 march 1898, page 4

[170] El Paso Herald, 10 April 1901, page 5

[171] Texas Birth Certificate, 1903-1932, Anita Fitch

[172] El Paso Herald, 7 March 1905, page 7

[173] Find A Grave memorial 105113358

[174] San Francisco Chronicle, 20 July 1887, page 3

[175] <u>History of Mendocino County California</u>, Lyman Palmer, 1880

[176] Ukiah Republican Press, 27 Dec 1922, page 2

[177] Watsonville Pajaronian, 2 April 1896, page 3

[178] Santa Cruz Sentinel, 12 Aug 1886, page 3

[179] CA Marriage Records from Select Counties, 1850-1941, Ancestry.com

[180] Los Angeles Herald, Vol 36, #47, 3 June 1891 page 2

[181] Mendocino Index: Marriages 9/49

End Notes

[182] Los Angeles Herald, 8 June 1891, page 1

[183] California Prison and Correctional Records, 1851-1950, SJ Roads

[184] FindAGrave Index – Stonewall Jackson Roads

[185] Mendocino Index: marriage record 3/355

[186] Ukiah Republican Press, 10 June 1892

[187] Ukiah Daily Journal, 13 Jan 1893, page 2

[188] Ukiah Daily Journal, 7 April 1893, page 2

[189] San Francisco Chronicle, 15 June 1902, page 21

[190] Mendocino Index: Cemetery records, Edgar W Scott, died 8/5/1936 in MSH, buried Ukiah Cemetery

[191] San Francisco Area Funeral Home Records 1895-1985, Joseph Rudd

[192] Badge and Buckshot by John Boessenecker, 1988, pg. 91

[193] Mendocino Outlaws, Keller, 1974

[194] History of Mendocino County California, Lyman Palmer, 1880

[195] Ukiah Republican Press, 30 July 1897, Page 1

[196] National Police Gazette, 10 Jan 1880, page 11

[197] Oakland Tribune, 10 Dec 1890, page 5

End Notes

[198] <u>Biennial Message of Governor to the Legislature of State of CA – 1883</u>, page 70

[199] San Francisco Chronicle, 21 Sept 1910, page 4; Ukiah Dispatch Democrat 23 Sept 1910 – page 8

[200] Daily Alta California, Vol 34, # 12613, 25 Oct 1884.

[201] Mendocino Index – marriage records # 3/233

[202] Ukiah Dispatch Democrat, 14 Jan 1910, page 8

[203] Sacramento Record Union, 3 Feb 1886, page 2

[204] Sacramento Record Union, 6 march 1886, page 5

[205] San Francisco Chronicle, 24 March 1891, page 3

[206] Sacramento Record Union, 13 Oct 1890, page 1

[207] Calistogan, Oct 15, 1890

[208] Helen Matilda Sherington, England and Wales, Free BMD Index, 1837-1915

[209] San Francisco Chronicle, 24 Feb 1892, page 5

[210] <u>California White Cap Murders</u>, Helen Rocca Goss

[211] Sacramento Record Union, 24 March 1891, page 1

[212] San Francisco Call, 24 Oct 1890, page 3

[213] California Prison and Correctional Records, 1851-1950, Ancestry.com

End Notes

[214] Washington Death Index, 1883-1960

[215] Ukiah Daily Journal, 3 April 1891, page 3

[216] San Francisco Chronicle, 15 May 1892

[217] Ukiah Republican Press, 20 May 1892

[218] San Francisco Call, 25 July 1892
[219] Hanford Weekly Journal, 26 July 1892

[220] Ukiah Daily Journal, 24 Jan 1896, page 3

[221] San Francisco Call, 30 Sept 1897, Vol 82, #122

[222] Ukiah Republican Press, 1 Oct 1897

[223] Ukiah Dispatch Democrat, 6 march 1903, page 2

[224] Sacramento Record Union, 13 Oct 1897, page 8

[225] Oakland Tribune, 13 Oct 1897, page 2

[226] Los Angeles Herald, 9 Nov 1897, page 5

[227] San Francisco Chronicle, 15 Nov1897, page 10

[228] San Francisco Call, 28 Jan 1898, Page 4

[229] San Francisco Call, 3 Feb 1898, page 5

[230] <u>History of Mendocino County</u>, 1967, page 335

[231] Mendocino Beacon, 9 July 1881

End Notes

[232] Sacramento Record Union, 28 July 1881, page 1

[233] Sacramento Record Union, 24 Nov 1881, Page 4

[234] Ukiah Daily Journal, 26 Dec 1890, page 3

[235] Ukiah Dispatch Democrat, 3 Oct 1902, page 3

[236] Ukiah Republican Press, 4 Nov 1904, page 1
[237] Ukiah Republican Press, 16 June 1905, page 1

[238] Ukiah Republican Press, 15 Sept 1905, page 1

[239] Ukiah Dispatch Democrat, 23 Feb 1912, page 8

[240] Ukiah Dispatch Democrat, 16 Sept 1910, Page 1

[241] Ukiah Dispatch Democrat, 30 Dec 1910, page 5

[242] California Death Index

[243] Ukiah Daily Journal, 26 Feb 1892, page 2

[244] Ukiah Daily Journal, 17 June 1892, page 3

[245] Ukiah Daily Journal, 24 June 1892, page 3

[246] San Diego Union, 30 June 1892, page 8

[247] Ukiah Daily Journal, 11 March 1892, page 3

[248] Ukiah Daily Journal, 22 July 1892, page 2

[249] Ukiah Republican Press, 2 Sept 1904, page 1

End Notes

[250] Nevada State Journal, 6 Sept 1904, page 1

[251] Ukiah Daily Journal, 19 Nov 1915, page 8

[252] Ukiah Dispatch Democrat, 7 Dec 1917, page 1

[253] San Francisco Chronicle, 22 March 1892, page 12

[254] Ukiah Daily Journal, 22 April 1892

[255] Alice Yarish, quoting William Heath Davis, https://www.facebook.com/SouthernCoastMiwok.com1/photos/a.453846784745855.1073741827.453844584746075/974457386018123/?type=1&theater

[256] The Novato Historian, Sept 2002, Vol 25, #3

[257] Find A Grave memorial 75803050

[258] Ukiah Republican Press, 15 Feb 1901

[259] Ukiah Dispatch Democrat, 18 April 1902, page 1

[260] Ukiah Dispatch Democrat, 29 May 1903, page 1

[261] Ukiah Dispatch Democrat, 22 Dec 1905, page 1

[262] Ukiah Republican Press, 29 Dec 1905, page 1

[263] Ukiah Republican Press, 29 Dec 1905

[264] Ukiah Dispatch Democrat, 2 Feb 1906, page 1

[265] Ukiah Dispatch Democrat, 19 April 1907

End Notes

[266] California Prison and Correctional Records, 1851-1950

[267] Ukiah Dispatch Democrat, 23 Feb 1906, page 1

[268] Ukiah Dispatch Democrat, 20 July, 1906

[269] Wikipedia: Camilo Ynitia

[270] Ukiah Daily Journal 14 Jan 1990, page 4

[271] Mendocino Dispatch Democrat, 23 June 1893

[272] Ukiah Daily Journal, 15 Dec 1893, page 3

[273] History of Mendocino County, Alley, Bowen Pub., 1880

[274] San Francisco Bulletin, 30 March 1868.

[275] California Select Marriages 1850-1945

[276] San Francisco CA Funeral Home records, 1850-1931, Alice White

[277] History of Mendocino County California, Lyman Palmer, 1880

[278] San Diego Union, 30 Oct 1899, page 2

[279] California Death Index, 1905-1939, Ancestry.com

[280] Genocide and Vendetta: Round Valley Wars, Carranco + Beard, 1981

[281] History of Mendocino County, 1880, Alley, Bowen Publishers. 1880

End Notes

[282] Mendocino Index: Vital Records – Death, 8/9/1878, Ukiah City Press

[283] Martha J and Hagler McPherson: http://files.usgwarchives.net/nc/cabarrus/bios/hagler07.txt

[284] San Francisco Call, 21 Oct 1895: Interview with Frank Asbill

[285] Bio of Martha Jane Hagler McPherson, 1867 by Anna Hagler Melvin

[286] California Wills and Probates, T W McPherson, Vol A-C, 1954-1884

[287] Los Angeles Times, 8 May 1888 page 3

[288] San Francisco Call, 21 Oct 1895, page 8

[289] The Horrible History of Round Valley, http://chroniclingamerica.loc.gov/lccn/sn85066387/1895-10-21/ed-1/seq-8/ocr.txt

[290] California Death Index: William S Nowlan

[291] San Francisco Call, 21 Oct 1895, page 8

[292] Sacramento Record-Union, 11 Feb 1887

[293] Oakland Tribune, 31 Oct 1887, page 3.

[294] The River Stops here: Saving Round Valley, Ted Simon, 2001

[295] Mendocino Index: Marriage record 2/80, 1872

[296] Mendocino Index: Marriage record 3/225, 1880

End Notes

[297] San Francisco Chronicle 19 Nov 1889, page 8

[298] San Francisco Chronicle, 6 Dec 1890, page 10

[299] San Francisco Call, 29 Aug 1893, page 6

[300] San Francisco Chronicle, 8 Feb 1894, page 4

[301] Mendocino Index: Marriage records 6/251

[302] <u>Genocide and Vendetta: Round Valley Wars</u>, Carranco and Beard 1981, page 272

[303] The Horrible History of Round Valley, San Francisco Call, 21 Oct 1895

[304] Ukiah Daily Journal, 4 Oct 1895, page 7

[305] San Francisco Callm 17 Feb 1898

[306] Mendocino Index, Marriage 7/25, 1894.

www.ingramcontent.com/pod-product-compliance
Lightning Source LLC
Chambersburg PA
CBHW030431010526
44118CB00011B/593